The

Book

of Books

For Eleanor,
daughter,
friend

and for Judy,
colleague,
friend

brilliant teachers
both of them

The Book of Books

of Books

Trevor Dennis

Illustrated by David Dean

LION

Text copyright © 2003 Trevor Dennis
Illustrations copyright © 2003 David Dean
This edition copyright © 2003 Lion Publishing

The moral rights of the author and illustrator
have been asserted

Published by
Lion Publishing plc
Mayfield House, 256 Banbury Road,
Oxford OX2 7DH, England
www.lion-publishing.co.uk
ISBN 0 7459 3625 3

First edition 2003
10 9 8 7 6 5 4 3 2 1 0

A catalogue record for this book is available
from the British Library

Typeset in 13/18 Elegant Garamond BT
Printed and bound in Finland

Contents

Acknowledgments 11

Introduction 13

Chapter 1: In the Beginning 17
God Makes the World 18
God Plants a Garden 22
Things Get Nasty 27
The Great Flood 31
Babel Babble 36

Chapter 2: God's New Family 40
Abraham and the Great Promise 41
Sarah's Cunning Plan 43
Hagar and the God Who Sees 45
Sarah Overhears the Promise 48
Hagar and the God Who Saves 50
Abraham and Isaac 53
A Tricky Twin and a Bowl of Stew 56
Jacob Steals a Blessing 58
The Gate of Heaven 62
Face to Face with God 65
Face to Face with Esau 68
Jacob and His Sons 69
Joseph the Slave 72

Joseph the Prisoner   73
Joseph in the Palace   75
Joseph and the Famine   78
A Strange Discovery   81
Benjamin   82
The Reunion   86

Chapter 3: Moses and the Mountain of God   88
The Brave Midwives and the Pharaoh   89
Moses' Brave Mother and Sister   93
Moses Meets God in the Desert   96
God and the Pharaoh   100
God Splits the Sea   103
The Mountain of God   106
More Teaching from God's Mountain   110
The Golden Calf   111
Making a New Start   115
The Death of Moses   117

Chapter 4: Living in God's Land   118
The Fall of Jericho   119
Eluma, a Woman Despised   123
Hannah, a Woman Without a Child   127
'Samuel! Samuel!'   130
King Saul   133
David the Shepherd Boy   137
David and Goliath   140

David on the Run   145

David and Bathsheba   150

David and Nathan   154

Elijah and the Contest on Carmel   156

Elijah on the Run   163

Elijah, Ahab and the Vineyard   169

Chapter 5: The People of God under Threat   173

'Let Justice Roll Down Like Water'   176

Hosea and the Love of God   183

Jerusalem will Never be Taken!   186

Jeremiah Speaks the Truth   188

Jerusalem Falls   194

Sad Songs of Lament   197

Dreaming of Home   203

A Valley Full of Bones and a New Garden of Eden   209

Rebuilding Jerusalem   214

Daniel: God in the Flames   222

Daniel in the Lions' Den   229

Chapter 6: Fine Stories, Fine Poems   235

Ruth, Naomi and Boaz: Love Wins the Day   236

Jonah, a Big Fish, a Great City and the Forgiveness of God   252

The Book of Job: Shaking a Fist at Heaven   261

Songs of Light   278

Introduction to the New Testament   284

Chapter 7: The New Beginning: Jesus is Born   287
Disgrace Turned Quite All to Grace   288
Gifts Fit for a King   290
Mary Meets an Angel   297
Mary's Song   299
Jesus is Born   301
Jesus' Real Home   304

Chapter 8: Who was Jesus?   307
John Baptizes Jesus   309
A Reading in the Synagogue   311
Peter, James and John   313
Photina: the Woman at the Well   317
Commander of the Dark Forces   321
A Madman Among the Tombs   324
The Hungry are Filled   326
A Man Sees for the First Time   330
A Woman and a Girl are Brought Back to Life   334
Peter Gets it Right; Peter Gets it Wrong   339
The Light of God   342

Chapter 9: Jesus the Storyteller and Poet   345
A Lost Sheep, a Lost Coin and a Lost Son   346
The Good Samaritan   353
The Workers in the Vineyard   357

The Beatitudes   361
Other Sayings and a Prayer   363

Chapter 10: Jesus is Killed: Jesus is Risen   368

Riding into Jerusalem   369
Mayhem in the Temple   373
Jesus is Anointed Messiah   376
Betrayal   379
The Last Supper   380
Arrest   383
The Unfair Trial   386
Peter's Denial   388
Pilate   389
Jesus is Crowned King   393
Crucifixion   394
'Mary'   398
Thomas Gets it Right… in the End   400
Peter Goes Fishing   402

Chapter 11: From Jerusalem to Rome: The Church Begins   405

The Full Truth   406
Wind and Fire   407
Stephen is Killed   410
Paul Meets the Risen Jesus   414
Paul and Ananias   415
Escape in a Basket   417
Peter and a Soldier Called Cornelius   419
Paul and Barnabas Get Mistaken for Gods   424

A Riot in Ephesus   427

A Riot in Jerusalem   432

The Threat of an Ambush   434

Paul Asks to See the Emperor   436

Shipwreck   438

Paul Reaches Rome   441

Chapter 12: Letters to Churches and a Final Vision   444

Quarrelling Christians   445

Paul's Hardships   448

'You are the Body of Christ'   450

Love is the Greatest of All   451

Life After Death   454

A Beautiful Hymn   455

A Final Collection   456

Visions of Heaven   458

Bible References   462

Acknowledgments

About this book and how it came to be written

It all began with other people. Philip Law and Lois Rock, both editors at Lion Publishing, had the idea that I should write a Bible for younger readers. I wasn't sure at first that I would be able to write the kind of book they described, but they persuaded me to have a go and I am very glad they did.

Lois became my editor. She was always encouraging, and the suggestions she made for improvements, both large and small, were always intelligent and perceptive.

I'm also grateful to Olwen Turchetta, who did a great job of copy-editing the book.

There are two other people I have to thank specially. One is my eldest daughter, Eleanor, and the other is Judy Davies, the Education Officer at Chester Cathedral. Eleanor and Judy have much experience of teaching and working with children and young people. They agreed to read everything I wrote, and whenever I came to the end of a chapter, I showed it to them first. They were extremely helpful and encouraging all the way through, and I am so grateful for the trouble they took, that I have dedicated the book to them.

My wife, Caroline, and our other children, Sarah, Jo and Tim, and our son-in-law, John, also took a great interest in the book. Writing it was an exciting but daunting task, and I needed their love and encouragement also to keep me going. I'm glad of this opportunity to say how much I owe them.

There are many other people who helped produce this book and made it possible for you to have a copy. These include: David Dean, who illustrated the book; Jacqueline Crawford, who designed it; and Sarah Toulmin, who advertised it. Without them my work wouldn't have come to anything, and you wouldn't have this book. I hope you enjoy it!

Trevor Dennis

Trevor Dennis, CHESTER CATHEDRAL, JANUARY 2003

INTRODUCTION

*'Who are we? Where did we come from? What makes us different?
Why are we so special? Are we special?' Everyone asks those questions.
Two and a half thousand years ago the people of Israel asked those
questions, and other questions too, such as: 'Why are we having such
a hard time? What's gone wrong? What is God up to?' They lived in
a small country at the eastern end of the Mediterranean Sea, and a
very powerful people called the Babylonians had invaded, destroyed
their towns and cities, killed a lot of them and taken thousands more
into exile in Babylonia, hundreds of miles away to the east. They had
taken their cattle, their goats and sheep as well, and ruined the crops,
so the people left behind also had a terrible time.*

*The Babylonians said they were the best. The Babylonians said
their gods were the best too. The Babylonians said the Israelites ought
to think like Babylonians, live like Babylonians, feel like Babylonians,
worship like Babylonians.*

*Some of the Israelites said, 'We've got to do something, or this will
be the end of us!' 'Let's write a story,' some others replied, 'our story,
the story of our people, our land and our God. Let's collect together the
stories we've been telling our children, and the stories we learned when*

we were children. Let's weave them together, and write some new ones, and tell a tale that our children will tell their children, and their children will tell their children, and so on and so on, for ever and ever!'

And so they did, and we have that story still. It's in the Bible and stretches from the book of Genesis to the second book of Kings.

We don't know the names of any of the people who first told this story. Parts of it are very old, perhaps as old as three thousand years, perhaps older, but often we don't know the century when the individual stories were first composed, let alone the year. Some of them may have been composed by women, but it is clear that most of the storytellers were men. Unfortunately, there are no pieces by children. Most of the storytellers would have lived in the cities. Some of them were priests; some of them were merchants or landowners. A few of the stories may have come originally from the villages. The whole story can't have been finished till some time after the Babylonians invaded and took so many people into exile. We can be quite sure of that, because that is where it all ends.

But the Bible doesn't end there, and nor will this book. The people of Israel, or the Jews as they came to be called, told other stories and recited wonderful poems. Among the poets were prophets – men and women who claimed to be able to see things as God saw them, and to speak with God's voice. The people treasured the finest of their poems and passed them down from one generation to another. Some prophets, as we shall see, saw catastrophe coming and tried to help the people face up to it. During the exile in Babylon other prophets had marvellous visions of how God would rescue them and take them back home. After the exile had ended, the people rebuilt the temple in Jerusalem. A Jew called Nehemiah organized the rebuilding of the walls of the city and left behind his account of it for us to read. Nearly three hundred years after that, another foreign king threatened to wipe out the Jewish religion. In the book of Daniel we find stories told at that time about God coming to the rescue of his friends once again.

There are love stories in the Bible too, such as the tale of the remarkable friendship between two women called Ruth and Naomi, and of how Ruth came to marry a man named Boaz. And funny stories, such as the tale of the hopeless prophet called Jonah, who simply could not accept the truth about God's forgiveness. There is also poetry. An anonymous poet, perhaps the finest poet in the whole Bible, wrote about a man called Job who lost almost everything and suffered a terrible illness, but finally saw God and was transformed by the vision. And in the temple in Jerusalem they sang sacred songs now known as psalms, some very old, some composed afresh after the exile.

You will find these stories and some of the poems and songs in this book.

When we have gone through those, we still won't have reached the end. We will be leaving behind what Christians call the Old Testament, or Jews Tanakh (for all these writings so far belong to the Jews' Bible as well as the Christians' Bible). But then we will come to four more Jewish storytellers, called Matthew, Mark, Luke and John, who wrote about a Jew named Jesus of Nazareth. They claimed that the coming of Jesus marked a new beginning, not just for their fellow Jews, but for the entire world. 'If you want to have the clearest picture of what God is like,' they said, 'then look at Jesus, look at the way he lived, and particularly the way he died, and listen to the stories he told.' Their books are called the Gospels, and for most Christians they are the most important books in the Bible.

Luke added a second volume to his story, and in the book of Acts told how the number of Jesus' followers grew after his death and spread to more and more places. That part of his story is mostly concerned with two men: Peter, who had been one of Jesus' followers during his lifetime, and Paul. Paul was the most important founder of new Christian communities, and the Bible contains some letters of his that he wrote to Christians in places such as Rome in Italy, or Corinth in Greece. These letters were sent before any of the Gospels had been written. The Bible contains other letters from Christians too.

In the very last book of the Bible, called Revelation, we discover some bright visions of heaven, composed by another follower of Jesus called John (probably not the John who wrote the fourth Gospel).

All this is contained in what Christians call the New Testament, and the last six chapters of our book will cover that. Four of the chapters will be devoted to the Gospels and the fifth one to Acts, while the sixth will contain a collection of passages from Paul's letters and the book of Revelation.

The retellings in this book are rather different from what you would read if you turned to an ordinary translation of the Bible. They aim to give a sense of the style of each story in the original languages – sometimes poetic, sometimes funny, sometimes formal and solemn. They try also to give an idea of what lies behind each story or poem, and show things which those who first heard them long ago would have picked up, but which are difficult for us to catch. Some of the names in the original are names with a meaning, and this version tries to bring that out. There are little details which may come as a surprise, for example in the story of David and Goliath, when Goliath is hit on the leg, not on the forehead. This change is because of the details of the original Hebrew and what scholars say about them. Sometimes the story is longer – as the original storytellers might have said them aloud; other times long stories have been shortened, leaving out long lists of kings and so on.

But the best way to find out what is here is to read it, and we must begin at the beginning…

1

IN THE BEGINNING

The Book of Books *begins with a poem, a beautiful poem about the creation of the world. It tells of how the sun, the moon and the stars came to be, and the earth with its seas and rivers full of fish, and its dry land alive with plants and animals. It speaks of us human beings also. It seems to be a poem about the past, the very remote past; but it isn't really that at all. It is meant to give us a picture of the universe, and the earth in particular, as it is meant to be, as God wants it to be, where everything is beautiful, everything is good.*

After the poem comes a story about a garden planted by God. The creation poem begins with God and a heap of water. The story about the garden starts with God and a waterless desert, and tells of a boy and a girl growing up – the very first boy and girl on the earth. They grow up too fast, and suddenly everything is very sad.

In the next story, about two brothers, troubles really begin, and after that we come to the story of the Great Flood, where we find that human beings have completely ruined God's earth and spoiled it with violence, so that God has to wash it clean.

After the Great Flood is everything beautiful again? Is everything good, as it was at the beginning? No. Human beings are just the same.

They go their own way instead of God's way. Once more they threaten to destroy the earth and ruin all God's plans.

All this forms an introduction, or prologue, to the great story about the people of Israel in the book of Genesis. So why did Israel's storytellers start it like this? Why didn't they just begin with their own ancestors? Because they believed their people had a special task to do, one given them by God, the task of working with God to put the world to rights. With the help of the people of Israel, they believed, God would make the world very beautiful again and very good, just as it had been, just as he wanted it to be. God would teach them how to help him. That's what they were trying to say.

God Makes the World

IN THE BEGINNING,
before the world began,
there was nothing:
nothing but God
in the dark
and a heap of water,
and God's Spirit
like a fresh wind blowing,
like a wild bird flying.

Then into the dark
God spoke.
'Let there be light!' he cried.
And there was!

And God looked at the light and said,
'How beautiful you are!
Your name is Day.'
He looked at the darkness and said,
'Your name is Night.'

And there was morning and there was evening,
the world's first day.

And so it went on.
God spoke,
God made,
God split one thing from another.
God gave things their names
and put each in its proper place,
to be what it was meant to be,
to do what it was meant to do.

He made the sky
and placed water above it for the rain.
He made the sun,
the moon and the stars.
He set them in the sky
to mark the days and the nights by their shining,
and by their rise and fall
to be a sign of the seasons of the year.

He made the dry land
and covered it with
brambles and bananas,

grasses and gooseberries,
daisies and dandelions,
peaches and primroses,
plants of every kind.

He made the seas, oceans and rivers
and filled them with
porpoises and pilchards,
triggerfish and turtles,
halibut and harp seals,
sperm whales and sticklebacks,
swimming things of every kind.

He made the currents of the air
and filled them with
kestrels and kingfishers,
hummingbirds and hornbills,
sanderlings and shelduck,
babblers and bulbuls,
birds of every kind.

He made the plains and hills and valleys
and covered them with
polar bears and pumas,
reindeer and rhinoceros,
hedgehogs and horses,
aardvarks and antelopes,
animals of every kind.

The days went by,
and God looked at the creatures he had made.
He blessed them all and cried,
'How beautiful you are!
Reproduce and multiply,
and fill the bright earth.'

On the sixth day,
the day he made the animals,
God said,
'Let me make another creature
to care for the earth with me.
I will make human beings,
men and women, girls and boys.
They will be like me,
my image, my likeness,
kings and queens on this, my fine earth!
They will help me care for the fish, the animals, the birds,
all the creatures that swim in the depths,
or run upon the land,
or ride upon the tall air.'

So God made them,
like himself he made them,
in his very image, his very likeness,
boys and girls, women and men.

Stretching his hands over them,
he blessed them and said,
'Reproduce and multiply,

fill the earth
and have it for your kingdom.
See, I have given you all the food you need.
I have given food for all my creatures,
as many plants as you all want
to fill your stomachs with.'

Then God looked at everything he had made.
Behold! It was very beautiful, so very good!

On the seventh day
God rested from all his work.
He made that day a holiday,
a holy day,
a day of holy rest
for himself and all that he had made.

How beautiful everything was!
How very good!
All was good!
All was good!

God Plants a Garden

IN THE BEGINNING, before the world really began, there was
nothing… only God and a desert. The desert was endless; wherever
you looked was desert. No plants. No animals. No people. Just
desert. And God.

So God got to work. He took some desert dust in his hands and mixed it with some water. He shaped it, moulded it and smoothed it, till it looked like a human being, like a child. The child lay on the ground and did not move. God got down on his hands and knees, bent over the child, put his mouth over the child's nose and puffed the life into him. The child stood up, a living, breathing, laughing human being!

But God couldn't leave the child in the desert all on his own. He would be sure to die of hunger and thirst. So God planted a garden in Eden, far away in the east, in a place beyond all telling, and he put the child there. It was a wonderful place, full of trees, beautiful to look at, with fruit that was perfectly delicious to eat. There was a spring gushing with water, and the spring became a stream, and the stream became a torrent, and the torrent turned into four mighty rivers, enough to bring water to the whole earth. Whenever the child felt hungry, all he had to do was pick another banana, or orange, or mango, or apple, or anything else he liked. Whenever he felt thirsty, all he had to do was go down to the spring and scoop handfuls of water into his mouth.

In the middle of the garden were two special trees – the Tree of Life and the Tree of Knowledge of Good and Bad. God said to the child, 'Look after the garden for me and keep it nice and wild. You can eat any of the fruit, except the fruit of the Tree of Knowledge of Good and Bad. You mustn't eat that, or you will die.'

The garden was a wonderful place! It didn't take much work to keep it nice and wild, and the child had plenty of time to play. He built islands in the stream and climbed the trees. He even made himself a tree house. The garden was filled with his laughter.

Then one day God listened and couldn't hear anything. He looked for the child and saw him trying to play hide-and-seek; but hide-and-seek on your own doesn't work. God looked again, and this time the child was pulling on a large branch that had fallen into the stream. He was tugging and tugging, but it was no good – the log was too heavy for him. This won't do, said God to himself. The child needs a helper and someone to play with.

So God took some more dust and water and made the animals and birds, and he brought them to the child to see if they would do. The child gave them all names. 'Kangaroo,' he said, but before he could ask, 'Could you help me with this log?' the kangaroo hopped away. 'Tiger,' he said, but before he could ask, 'Would you like a game of hide-and-seek?' the tiger slid behind the trees and was gone. God brought him a huge bird, but he only had time to say 'Golden eagle' before it flew off.

At the end the child stood there on his own. He had given names to all the animals and all the birds, but they were all gone. He was still on his own.

This still won't do, said God to himself.

Then he had a bright idea, a mysterious idea, a brilliant idea. First he put the child into a deep, deep sleep. Then he bent over him and took one of his sides. It didn't hurt at all. He sewed him up so well you couldn't see any stitches. Next he shaped the side he had taken into a new creature. God looked at her. He clapped his hands. 'You'll do!' he cried. He woke the boy up.

'Goodness me!' cried the boy. 'A GIRL! Look, side by side, we fit together. Brilliant! How did you do that, God?'

God smiled and said nothing.

And all was well, and all was well… till the day the snake turned up.

One sunny day, the girl and the boy were playing beside the two trees in the middle of the garden, the Tree of Life and the Tree of

Knowledge of Good and Bad, when the snake walked in. The snake was *very* clever. The snake knew everything. Or it thought it did anyway. It sidled up to the girl. 'Ssssssay girl,' it hissed. 'Did God say you mustn't eat any of the fruit on the trees, like these delicious apples, for instance?'

'Well,' the girl said, 'God said we could eat any of the fruit, except from the tree here in the middle of the garden. "If you eat the fruit of that tree, or touch it, you'll die," that's what God said. It's a holy tree, that's why. It's special.'

'Die!' cried the snake. 'You won't die! Eat the fruit of the Tree of Knowledge of Good and Bad, and you'll be just like God. You'll know everything. Both of you. Look at the tree! It's beautiful, with *deliciouss* fruit to eat, the best in the garden. Scrumptiousss.'

The girl looked at the tree again. Perhaps it wasn't so different from the others after all. In fact, it didn't look any different really. It didn't *look* holy. Perhaps there was nothing special about it.

She reached up her hand, picked some of the fruit and took a bite. The snake was right. It was delicious. She picked some more and gave it to the boy, and he took a bite. Then he took another bite, and she took another one, and another, and another.

They began to feel a bit odd. They looked at one another. They didn't have any clothes on! They were growing up, and that was alright, only they were growing up much too fast. All of a sudden, before they could think it out properly, they knew far too much, and it frightened them. They didn't say anything to each another, but they found a fig tree that had great big leaves. They tied some of the leaves together and turned them into skirts – well, sort of skirts. They put them on. They looked ridiculous. But they didn't laugh; they were too frightened.

Then they heard God coming. Now, all of a sudden, they were frightened of him too. They hid behind some bushes. They heard God's footsteps coming closer and closer.

'Where are you?' God called.

'Behind this bush,' the boy replied. 'I heard you coming, and I was afraid because I didn't have any proper clothes on, and I hid.'

'Who told you about clothes?' asked God. 'Have you eaten some of that fruit I told you not to eat?'

'It's not my fault!' cried the boy. 'That girl you gave me, she picked some of the fruit and gave it to me. It's all *your* fault God,' he added under his breath.

God turned to the girl. 'Did you do that?' he asked.

'It's not my fault!' she cried. 'The snake tricked me into it.'

The snake said nothing, but slid itself down to the ground and went to hide behind a pile of leaves.

'That's right, snake,' said God. 'That's how life will be for you from now on. Sliding around on the ground and hiding and biting too and being hit with sticks.'

Then God turned to the boy and girl. There was a deep sadness in his voice. 'When you really are grown up,' he said, 'This is what life will be like for you. There'll be no more playing in this beautiful garden. You'll be working all the hours I've made, both of you. You,' he said to the girl, 'will have children round your feet all day long, and babies waking you up every night, and you'll be tired out. And you,' he said to the boy, 'will be sweating in the fields under the hot sun, until your back feels like breaking. And what will you get for it? Thorns and thistles! And one day you'll be worn out, and you'll die.'

The boy and girl hung their heads. They would have to leave the garden now. And so they did. There was no going back. They were very sad. God was too.

I wonder what would have happened if we'd eaten some fruit from the Tree of Life instead, the girl said to herself. After all, God never said we mustn't eat *that*.

But it was too late. They were outside the garden now. There was no going back.

Things Get Nasty

THE BOY AND THE GIRL left the Garden of Eden and became a man and a woman. They were called Adam and Eve. They settled down to the toil of their daily lives.

One day Eve noticed her tummy was getting larger. It grew bigger and bigger until, a few months later, a baby arrived. It was a boy. She looked at him lying so small beside her and cried with astonishment and joy. 'Our pride and joy,' she said to Adam.

So they called him Cain, which means Pride-and-joy.

It was wonderful having Pride-and-joy! But then another baby arrived, another boy. Eve remembered what God had told her before they left the garden, about children being round her feet all the time, and babies waking her up every night. She and Adam hadn't wanted another baby – not that soon, at any rate.

They called him Abel, which means Nobody.

Pride-and-joy remained their favourite. They didn't take any notice of Nobody.

Pride-and-joy and Nobody grew up. Pride-and-joy became a farmer, ploughing the ground and growing crops. Nobody became a shepherd.

At the end of the season they both brought some presents to give to God. Pride-and-joy brought some of his best corn and vegetables. Nobody brought some meat from his best animals, the bits he hoped God would like the most.

God was delighted with Nobody and his present, but he seemed to take no notice of the present Pride-and-joy was giving him, or of Pride-and-joy himself.

Nobody suddenly felt tall, as tall as a giraffe. No one had taken any notice of him before, but now God himself had noticed him, and liked him too, and his present! He was overcome with joy.

Pride-and-joy, however, was furious. 'What's wrong with my present?' he muttered to himself. 'What's wrong with *me*? And

what's so special about my kid brother's present? What's so good about *him*? He's Nobody, *nobody*! I'm older than him. I'm better than him at everything. *It's not fair!*'

But he didn't say this to God. He didn't say it to anyone. He kept it to himself, and the hurt and the dark anger grew and grew inside him until he was fit to burst.

God looked at him and saw the expression on his face. 'Why are you so angry?' he asked.

What a stupid question! thought Pride-and-joy. You know very well, God, why I'm angry. It's all your fault! But he still didn't say it out loud. He bit his lip and looked down at the ground.

'Be careful!' God warned him. 'Be careful, or your anger will get you. Then you will do what your anger wants, and that will be something terrible. Don't let your anger order you about. *You* give the orders and tell your anger to behave itself.'

Pride-and-joy turned on his heel and went away. He didn't listen. He still didn't say anything. He just planned a dreadful plan.

One day he called out to his brother. 'Nobody!' he said.

'What do you want?' asked Nobody.

Pride-and-joy didn't reply but started walking out into the fields.

Nobody was puzzled. Oh well, he said to himself, I'd better follow him and find out.

They kept walking until their home was a small speck in the distance. Pride-and-joy worked out they were too far away for Adam and Eve to see or hear anything. He was walking a few paces in front, when suddenly he whisked round and leaped on Nobody like a lion attacking an antelope. His brother was not expecting it. He threw up his hands to defend himself, but he was too late. Pride-and-joy killed him. Nobody was dead, and his blood trickled from his body onto the dry, dusty ground.

Pride-and-joy turned his back on him and began to walk away. God stopped him in his tracks. 'Where is your brother, the one you all call Nobody?' he asked.

Pride-and-joy looked at God out of the corner of his eye. 'I don't know,' he answered. 'It's not *my* job to look after him. No', he added under his breath, 'it's *your* job, God, and you haven't done it very well, have you?' He laughed quietly to himself.

'What have you done?' God cried. 'What have you done? Your brother's blood is howling to me from the ground. I wanted to bless you both, but now your brother is dead, and you are cursed. From now on, when you plough the soil, it will give you nothing. A vagabond and a vagrant you will be.'

The tears ran down Pride-and-joy's face. For the first time he looked straight at God. 'That's too much to bear!' he shouted. 'You've driven me away from the soil. And I'll never be able to meet you any more. I'll be a vagabond and a vagrant, just wandering about, without a home or any place to call my own. When there are more people on the earth, everyone will want to kill me.'

God didn't want any more killing. He didn't want another body lying crumpled and lifeless, with its blood soaking into the soil. 'I'll put a mark on you,' he said, 'so no one lays a hand on you.'

So the one whom Adam and Eve had named Pride-and-joy went on his way. He left God behind. He had a strange mark on his forehead. He lived a long time, and soon there were lots of other people around. Those who met him knew at once what the mark meant: Murderer. Brother-killer. They left him well alone.

He lived in the Land of the Lost, far from Eden. No one knows where it is.

The Great Flood

WHEN CAIN KILLED ABEL, it was the first killing in the world. God didn't want any more killing. But as time went on, and more and more people inhabited the earth, so the killings increased too, till the earth shook with violence.

God looked at the beautiful earth he had made. It was ruined, all ruined! He looked at the human beings. He had made them to care for the earth for him, to keep it in good order and guard its beauty. They had ruined everything. He looked and looked, but still he saw nothing but dark thoughts and dark, evil deeds.

He was overcome with grief and anger. I'm sorry I made those human beings, he said to himself bitterly. I will have to wipe them off the face of the earth, and all the other creatures with them, and start all over again.

He looked at the earth once more. This time he noticed a good man, just one, called Noah.

Noah was married, and he and his wife had three sons, Shem, Ham and Japheth.

One day God spoke to Noah. 'The earth is ruined and full of violence,' he told him. 'I've seen everything. I've decided to destroy it all. But I'll keep you safe, and your family, and a few of the animals and birds and snakes.

'You must build an ark, a huge boat, with enough room in it for you and your family and the creatures you're going to take with you, and space for a lot of food. I'm going to send a Great Flood upon the earth, and it will wash away everything except you, your family and the creatures with you inside the ark.'

Noah was stunned. He didn't know what to say. He was so

frightened he couldn't speak. God was right, of course. The earth certainly had become a very wicked place, but to drown it all in a Great Flood… that was terrible! He wanted to argue with God, but the words wouldn't come out. He heard God giving him instructions about the ark, what wood he should use, how long and wide and high it should be, how many decks it should have, and so on. He still couldn't get the words out. 'The animals will come to you in pairs,' God was saying, 'a male and female of each. When the Great Flood is over, they will be able to have young ones and start all over again.'

Noah's heart was beating like a drum, and his knees were knocking so loudly he could hardly hear what God was saying. He still couldn't find any words to say. Finally, God finished speaking. Noah gave a huge sigh and set about building the ark.

He made it just as God had told him. When it was finished, he went inside with his family, and all the animals came in their pairs, just as God said they would. God shut the door so no water could get in.

In the beginning, when God made the world, he started with a huge heap of water. When God first made the sky, he put some of the water above it for the rain. So far he'd made sure the rain fell gently. But now he drew up all the sluices in the sky together. The rain fell in torrents, in bucketfuls. And it kept raining… day after day after day after day.

When God first made the world, he hid some of the water deep down, in underground springs and rivers and lakes. Till then the water had come gently bubbling up to the surface. But now God made it shoot up in huge fountains and geysers. And they kept gushing out… day after day after day after day.

For one hundred and fifty days the waters on the earth continued to rise. In the end even the highest mountains were under water. Everything was drowned by the Great Flood, except for Noah and his family, and the creatures with them in the ark.

Where were they going? They didn't know. The ark didn't have a rudder, and anyway, where could they go? There was nothing but water everywhere.

When would it end? They didn't know. God had said that one day they would be able to start all over again. But when would that be?

All they could hear was the sound of the raindrops hammering on the ark's covering above their heads, and the water splashing against the side. The terrible sound of water never stopped, but went on day after day after day after day.

Otherwise it was very quiet. Noah and his family didn't say anything to one another. The animals and the birds and the snakes were silent too. The sheep didn't bleat, the nightingales didn't sing, the rattlesnakes didn't rattle. They all huddled together and waited, while the ark floated on the huge heap of water. It was just like the beginning, before the world was made. They never saw the sun, or the moon or the stars. They looked out of the window, but all they could see was water: water pouring down from the sky, water gushing up from below, water all around them.

It was terrible!

Then God looked at the ark and at Noah and his family and all the creatures inside. They looked so tiny on that great mass of water. He shut the sluices in the sky; it stopped raining. He closed the fountains and the geysers; the gushings ceased.

When God first made the world, his Spirit blew like a wind and flew like a bird over the heap of water. Now God sent another wind, to blow over the face of the waters and blow them away. Day after day after day after day the waters went down.

One day Noah felt a slight bump under the ark, and it stopped. They must be on land! But how much land was there? Was it safe to leave the ark? Noah didn't know; he couldn't see. So he sent out one of the ravens. The raven didn't come back. There was still nowhere for it to land, and it had to keep flying till the Great Flood was all over and it could join its mate. Noah didn't see it again. Next time he sent a dove to see if that could find land, but it couldn't and flew back to the ark. Noah saw it coming and stretched his arm out of the window. It landed on his hand, and gently he took it back inside. He waited another seven days and sent out the dove a second

time. Again it came back, but this time it had a freshly plucked leaf from an olive tree in its beak. Noah danced up and down with delight and then went running off to show the leaf to his wife and the others. Seven days later he let the dove go a third time. This time it didn't return; it had found a place to live.

'The waters must be nearly gone,' said Noah. He rolled back the covering they'd put over the ark and looked around. The waters had disappeared, and the earth was drying out.

'Come on!' cried Noah. 'Let's have a party!' And so they did. How the sheep bleated! How the nightingales sang! How the rattlesnakes rattled! Noah and his family and all the creatures on the ark danced together the whole of that day, and right through the following night.

Then God said to Noah, 'Leave the ark now, all of you. The Great Flood is over. The earth is dry. You can start all over again.'

It felt so funny being back on dry land, but also quite wonderful. Noah said to his wife, 'Let's give God a party too.' So he built an altar, lit a fire upon it and offered sacrifices to God. God smelled the rich, soothing smell of the fire.

But God knew what human beings would be like. They haven't changed, he said to himself. The Great Flood hasn't washed them clean inside. They'll still be wicked, still be dangerous, still be violent. But I will never destroy the earth again. Whatever human beings do, I will never again take control. Never again will I take away the power I gave them at the beginning. I will live with them as they are, whatever the price I have to pay.

God blessed Noah and his family. 'Reproduce and multiply,' he said, 'and fill the earth! All the other creatures of the earth will go in fear of you now,' he added more quietly. 'For I can see you will hunt them, kill them and eat them.'

God was sad when he spoke those words. In the beginning it had been different. He had given human beings plants to eat then, like the animals. There had been no killing for food. There was not meant to be any killing at all. Human beings had changed all that. God would have to live with them as they were and not punish them as they deserved.

God spoke to Noah and his family and to the creatures that had come out of the ark. 'I promise solemnly never to bring another

Great Flood,' he said. 'I will put a mark of that promise in the sky to remind me: the rainbow. You cannot have a rainbow without the sun. The rainbow will remind me never to let the rain go on and on and blot out the sun day after day after day after day. Never again will I answer ruin with ruin. You are safe now. You have my word.'

Babel Babble

The Bible begins with a poem and a few stories about the beginning of time. Those stories are about mysterious things: a garden where God makes human beings out of dust and puffs the life into them; a patch of ground stained with the blood of a murdered man that howls its grief to God; and a Great Flood that overwhelms not just a single river valley, not even just a single country, but the whole earth. Strange things happen in this next story too, yet suddenly we find in it something straight from history, and not particularly early history at that.

Two and a half thousand years ago the Babylonians, who came from the country now called Iraq, invaded the land at the eastern end of the Mediterranean Sea, where the people of Israel lived. They captured the capital, Jerusalem, and destroyed it. They knocked everything down, or burned it, and smashed God's temple to pieces. They boasted that their god Marduk had beaten the God of Israel. The Israelites said their God had created the world and had looked after them through all the years. But the Babylonian soldiers laughed and said, 'Well, he's not looking after you now, is he!' They forced many of the people to walk hundreds of miles to Babylon, beside the river Euphrates.

Perhaps the person who composed this next story was one of those people. It was certainly an Israelite who had seen Babylon. In the middle of that great city was a huge temple, like a small mountain. It went up in six vast steps, and on the top was a house for Marduk. The Babylonians were very proud of it. They told stories about it and sang songs about it. They said its roots went down deeper than the earth, and that its top was as high as heaven.

Our anonymous storyteller from Israel was not proud of it at all. To him it was a symbol of tyranny and the brutality of war. He decided he would tell his own story about it. Parts of his story were quite funny, but it summed up so much that was wrong with human beings, and so it was a fitting story to put after the story of the Great Flood.

And that's how Babylon, or Babel, as the Israelites called it, got into the series of stories about the beginnings of the world.

This is the story the great storyteller told.

AGES AND AGES AGO, near the beginning of time, all human beings on the earth spoke one language. God had told them to go and live in every part of the earth. But some didn't listen. Instead they decided to settle in one place, beside the river Euphrates. There they learned how to make bricks. The bricks gave them ideas. They dreamed of building a great city, with thick walls, and a huge temple inside the walls, with its roots down deeper than the earth, and its top as high as heaven. So they started to build. As the walls grew thicker, and the temple grew higher, they became more and more proud of themselves. We can do anything, they thought. We're as great as God himself, if not greater. His plan for us to scatter all over the earth is stupid. We'll stay here and become famous.

God looked at their fine city and their tall temple. To him they looked tiny, but he knew what the builders were thinking. Before long the whole earth would be ruined again. He could see that. He had to put a stop to them.

God smiled to himself as he put his plan into action.

'Pass me another brick,' one of the builders said one day, and his workmate replied, 'Yes, isn't it a lovely day!'

'The view is fantastic from up here!' another one exclaimed, and his friend scowled at him and said, 'Stop saying rude things about my nose!'

'We must be near heaven by now,' a third one said, and the woman next to him cried, 'What do you mean, my husband looks like a toad?'

God was making them speak different languages. They couldn't understand one another!

Fights broke out, and things got so serious they had to stop building. In the end they had to give up living in the city altogether. They went off in groups to different parts of the world, according to the different languages they spoke.

They left the city and the great temple behind. The deserted buildings fell into ruin and became no more than piles of rubble. People called the place Babel, because that was where God mixed up the languages and turned them into babble, Babel-babble!

God's plan had worked. Human beings were scattered over the whole earth now, as he had wished.

But how could the world become what he really wanted it to be? How could the earth and everything in it become beautiful again, and very good, as it was at the beginning? God needed another plan.

2

GOD'S NEW FAMILY

'Then God looked at everything he had made. Behold! It was very beautiful, so very good!' That's how it all begins. But then everything goes wrong. The first boy and girl on the earth have to leave God's beautiful garden. They grow up and have two boys, but when the boys become men, one kills the other. Eventually the earth becomes such a violent place that God decides to wash it clean with a Great Flood and start all over again. But that doesn't work either. Human beings are just the same, still going their own way. God wants them to walk with him and keep him company, but they don't want to do that. They are happier building their grand temples and filling themselves with pride. They start thinking they are as great as God, if not greater still.

What can God do now? He can't bring another Flood upon the earth. He has promised never to do that again. He can't just take over.

He will need a whole people to help him. Noah and his family helped him save the animals, the birds and the snakes from the Great Flood. But he needs more than that if the world is to become very beautiful and very good once again. There must be a special people of God, a people who understand God's mind and share his dreams, who will keep close to him and work with him as the years and the centuries go by. This people must have their own land and their freedom too. It will not work if they are taking orders from another nation which does not know God.

This chapter tells the story of the ancestors of that people. It tells of a single family and starts with just two people: Abraham and his wife, Sarah.

Some peoples turn their ancestors into great heroes. But when the people of God, the people of Israel, composed their stories about the family of Abraham and Sarah, they didn't do that. They didn't have the members of the family performing lots of fantastic feats. They didn't even make them especially good. They described them as quite rich, but in many ways they made them remarkably ordinary, with lots of problems, including ones that are still common in families today. This is one of the things that makes their stories so fascinating and so alive.

Abraham and the Great Promise

WHEN GOD DECIDED to bring the Great Flood upon the earth, he looked hard to see if he could find someone who would help him save one human family and enough animals, birds and snakes to start all over again once the Flood had gone. He found Noah.

When God decided to have a people of his own, he found Abraham. Now Abraham was not a particularly good man, not like Noah. But he was someone God could talk to, and, what's more, sometimes Abraham listened.

Abraham lived with his wife, Sarah, his father, Terah, and his nephew, Lot, in a place called Haran. They had all moved from Ur, a city on the river Euphrates. It had been a long, long journey, but they liked Haran and felt settled there.

Abraham believed he was going to stay in Haran for the rest of his life. But one day God said to him, 'I want you to leave Haran. I want you to leave your father behind. I want *you* to be head of the family now. I want you to start a new family, not just your family, but *my* family. I will give you a country to live in, a Special Land, and I will turn you into a great nation and make you famous. I will bless you, and you must be a blessing to all you meet. That way I can make sure the world becomes as good and beautiful as it was in the beginning.'

All that came as something of a surprise, several surprises in fact. Yet Abraham did what God wanted him to do. He left Haran. He left behind everything he knew. He didn't understand where he was going or what would happen. Sarah, his wife, came with him, of course, and Lot too, and their servants and all their animals. They travelled west and then turned south. They went a long, long way. In the end they came to a country called Canaan.

'This is it,' said God. 'This is the Special Land I promised you. This is where you must settle. This is where you must be my family, and, when there are enough of you, my people. I will bless you here. And remember Abraham, be a blessing to all you meet!'

There were just two problems about these promises from God. First, the Special Land was full of people who already lived there. What about them? Well, Abraham didn't have to worry about that one yet. But the other problem was very much on his mind, and would have been on Sarah's too if he'd told her anything about what God was planning for them. How was he going to become a great nation when he and Sarah didn't have any children? In fact, it seemed Sarah *couldn't* have any children. They'd been married quite a long time. They'd tried to have children, but nothing had happened. Everyone said children were a blessing from God. How was God going to bless him if Sarah couldn't have a child? And what about this Special Land of Canaan? It wouldn't be very special, if there was no one left in their family after he and Sarah died. That would be the end of that. It would be the end of everything – no being famous, no becoming a great nation, no people of God. Nothing.

Sarah's Cunning Plan

ABRAHAM'S WIFE, SARAH, knew nothing of what God had said to him. Abraham hadn't told her about a Special Land and a great nation and becoming famous and blessings and all that. She just wanted a baby. For years she'd wanted a baby. All the other married women she knew had children. She blamed herself and felt like a terrible failure. As the years went by she got more and more desperate.

Perhaps Abraham would have to have a second wife. The custom of those days allowed that. When they'd been in Canaan ten years and still didn't have any children, Sarah had an idea of who the second wife might be. Abraham thought it was a very good plan. After all, God had told him he would have a son, but God hadn't said anything about Sarah being the mother.

Sarah had a slave girl called Hagar. She was Egyptian. Perhaps, thought Sarah, if I give Hagar to Abraham as a second wife, she will have a child for me, and the years of failure will be over. Let's face it, Hagar's only a slave and slaves don't count. Hagar's a nobody. If she has a baby, the child will count as mine, not hers. I'll be able to bring him up as mine. Abraham wants a boy, I know, and I bet the woman will have a boy. Everyone will say, 'What a fine boy you've got, Sarah!', and I'll be able to hold my head up high at last. They won't be able to look down on me any more, or make rude remarks about me. I'll be a mother!

That was Sarah's cunning plan.

So she gave Hagar to Abraham as another wife, and Hagar got pregnant straight away. But then Hagar's tummy started to swell with the child growing inside her. Sarah looked at her and suddenly realized what would happen. She saw she would never really be the child's mother. Hagar would be the mother, not her. Just look at her, Sarah thought, with that round, bulging tummy! She's so proud of herself!

'Put your hand on my tummy,' Hagar would say to Sarah. 'He's kicking really hard today!' Sarah couldn't bear to touch her. Hagar was a *slave*, a *nobody*! But now she made Sarah feel like a nobody. Sarah couldn't take it any longer.

'Look what you've done now!' she screamed at Abraham. 'You've made that woman pregnant! She looks down on me, I know she does! She's a *slave*, and a foreigner too, and she looks down on *me*, her mistress. It's all wrong!'

'Do with her what you like,' said Abraham coldly. 'She's still your slave-woman.' He walked away, leaving Sarah feeling even more alone and hurt.

Poor Sarah! She wanted Abraham to take her in his arms and comfort her and tell her he loved her. But all he'd said was, 'Do with her what you like.' Right, then, she would! She would make Hagar's life a misery, and worse.

She shouted at her when the slightest thing went wrong, and even when it didn't. Then she started hitting her. Hagar got very frightened, and not just for herself. One day, perhaps, Sarah would hit her so hard she would lose her baby. She decided to run away. She decided to go back to Egypt, to her own land. They would be kind to her there. And her child would be safe as well. She would have her baby in her own country, among her own people, as a free woman and no longer a slave.

Hagar and the God Who Sees

HAGAR WAS ON THE RUN from her cruel mistress, Sarah. She had a long way to go, and she was going to get tired quickly, with her tummy getting bigger as the baby grew inside her. It was miles back to her own country, Egypt, and desert almost the whole way too.

But she wasn't frightened. She knew the tracks; she remembered where the oases were and the wells where she could get water. The desert people would give her food and shelter. They always looked after strangers. They would be kind to her – not like Sarah and her husband, Abraham.

One morning, when she'd been walking for several days, Hagar came to a spring of water. She bent down and scooped handfuls of water into her mouth and splashed it onto her face. It was wonderfully cold.

'Where are you going, Hagar?' a voice said. 'You are Sarah's slave-woman.'

Hagar froze, with her hands in front of her face and the water running down the sleeves of her dress. Who was this, who'd suddenly appeared in the middle of the desert? The voice was strange, as if coming from far away, but at the same time it seemed very close, as close as the water cooling her throat. And how did this stranger know her name, and know about her being Sarah's slave?

'I'm running away from my mistress, Sarah,' she said softly, still not daring to look up.

'You must go back to her and return to her cruelty,' the voice said.

Hagar trembled. Whose side was this stranger on? Not hers, it seemed. I can't go back, she thought, I *can't*. But she was used to doing what she was told. All her life she'd obeyed other people's orders. She kept quiet and wondered if the stranger had anything more to say. She kept staring down into the water.

A deep silence fell on the desert. Then the stranger spoke once more:

'I have seen your misery, Hagar,
and Sarah's cruelty.
I have counted all your tears,
every one.
I have kept them all.

You, Hagar, will have a son!
He will roam the desert,
as free as a wild ass,
at no one's beck and call.
He will be no one's slave,
and nor will you.
You will be the ancestress of a great people,
a people too many to count!
I promise you.
I promise.'

Hagar let her hands drop from in front of her eyes. She recognized the voice now. She looked up, and found herself looking straight into the face of God!

'I have seen God!' she whispered. 'And God has seen me. I will give you a name, God, a new name for you to take away with you from here. I will call you God-Who-Sees!'

To this very day they call the spring of water at that place, 'The Spring of the Living One who Sees.' People used to go there to find God, to hear his voice and see his face. Perhaps they still do.

Sarah Overhears the Promise

SARAH WAS A WOMAN whose hope had died. She still had no child. Her world seemed empty, without meaning. Her husband, Abraham, didn't seem to see her misery, nor care about it. And God, for Sarah, seemed silent also. She prayed, but her words disappeared into the air and remained, as far as she knew, unheard. God had told Abraham again that he would have a son, and this time he had told him the mother would be Sarah. But Sarah knew nothing of that. Abraham hadn't told her a thing.

One day Abraham was snoozing in front of his tent. It was midday and very hot. A shadow fell across his face and woke him up. He opened his eyes and saw three strangers standing in front of him. He jumped up at once.

'I'm so sorry,' he said. 'I was having a nap. Please, come over here and sit in the shade of the trees. I'll bring some water and wash your feet. They must be tired and sore. I'll get you something to eat and drink. Just wait in the shade, I won't be long.'

What Abraham didn't know was that the strangers were God and two companions from heaven.

He hurried off to the tent and told Sarah to start cooking. Huge mounds of cakes she made, while Abraham and his slave roasted a calf and fetched buckets of milk. He staggered back to his guests and put the meal in front of them. God smiled at the huge heap of food. Abraham didn't eat anything himself. It was for them, not for him. As for Sarah, she had to stay in the tent. She always had to stay out of sight when visitors came. Abraham watched his three guests as they tucked into the roast beef. He still didn't realize who they were.

'Where is Sarah, your wife?' God asked.

Strangely, Abraham didn't recognize the voice he knew so well. 'In the tent,' he replied.

'I'll come back soon, and Sarah will have a son,' God said.

Now, if he'd had his wits about him, Abraham would have said to himself, 'How does this stranger know my wife's name? And what's this about us having a baby? Only God and I know about that! Can this stranger be God? He must be. Good heavens! I'm entertaining God, and I didn't know it!'

But Abraham didn't think any of that. He just kept watching them eat.

Sarah overheard everything. She was listening just inside the entrance to the tent. She couldn't believe her ears. A baby? At her age? With a husband as old as Abraham? She still wanted a baby, of course. With all her being she wanted one. But she couldn't have one, and that was that. The idea was ridiculous! It must be a joke, a cruel joke. She let out a bitter laugh.

God said to Abraham, 'Why did Sarah laugh? Is giving her a child something too wonderful for God to do?'

Suddenly Sarah was frightened. This stranger knew all about her! She crept out of the tent. 'I didn't laugh,' she whispered.

'Oh yes, you did,' said God.

After that God and his two companions went on their way. Abraham never realized who they were, but they left Sarah thinking and wondering and, for the first time in years, beginning to hope.

God did come back, as he said he would. And Sarah did have a child, the child she had longed for for so long. They called him Laughter. Well, Isaac really, but that's what the name Isaac means, laughter – Sarah's laughter, Abraham's laughter, God's laughter.

Hagar and the God Who Saves

SARAH WAS FULL OF JOY at having a child. All her adult life she had wanted a child. And now, when she had thought she was far too old to have one, she had conceived Isaac and brought him safely to birth.

However, her joy was not to last. Her Egyptian slave, Hagar, had returned after running away into the desert. Hagar had a son as well. He was Abraham's son too and was called Ishmael. He was a few years older than Isaac.

Lots of babies died in those days. If they survived till they were over two and their mothers could stop breast-feeding them, then there would be a great party to celebrate. So when Sarah stopped breast-feeding Isaac, Abraham held a feast and invited everyone along. There was music and dancing, and lots to eat and drink.

They were all having a fine time… till Sarah saw Ishmael. It was Isaac's great day, but Ishmael was showing off as if it was *his* party. Just because he's the older one, thought Sarah, he thinks he's more important. I'm not putting up with this. Then she thought some more. Because he's the older one, he'll get everything when Abraham dies. That's the way it is. The older son always gets everything, and the younger one gets nothing. Show-off Ishmael, the son of that Egyptian Hagar, that good-for-nothing slave, will inherit all Abraham's best camels and sheep and donkeys – everything. He'll be head of the family. He'll be able to order my Isaac about. I haven't waited all these years for a child, just to have him bossed around by a slave-woman's son!

She marched across to where Abraham was sitting. 'Throw that slave-woman out,' she shouted, 'and her son with her. I'm not going to let a slave-woman's son inherit all your fine things instead of my Isaac. Throw them out!'

Abraham was angry and sad. He told Hagar she had to go, and Ishmael with her. He got up early the next morning, gave her some bread and a leather bottle full of water, put Ishmael on her shoulder and sent them away into the desert.

Hagar's eyes were full of tears, and she couldn't see where she was going. She was full of fear and grief, and she couldn't think straight. Last time, when she'd run away, she'd followed the tracks towards Egypt with her head held high. This time she stumbled about, her shoulders bent beneath the weight of her son.

She gave the bread to Ishmael, but soon there was no more left. She gave him most of the water too, but then that ran out. She looked around her. Dry, broken hills and sharp rock everywhere. They were lost, and there was nothing to eat, nothing to drink. They wandered about for three more days. Her son would die, she thought. He was already very weak. Once God had made fine promises about him. He had told her that Ishmael would roam the desert as free as a wild ass; that she, Hagar, would be the ancestress of a great people. Where were those promises now? It seemed they had come to nothing. It seemed she and her son had come to nothing also, nothing but death in an empty desert.

She couldn't bear to watch Ishmael die. She couldn't bear to listen to him crying either, so she laid him gently in the shade of a tamarisk tree. She walked away till she couldn't hear him any more and he was just a small shape on the ground. Then she sat down and buried her face in her hands. She would die too, of course. But that didn't matter.

Suddenly, she heard that voice again, the same one she'd heard in the desert before. It was God's voice! This time she recognized it at once.

'Don't be afraid, Hagar,' God said. 'I can hear your son crying. I haven't forgotten what I promised. I keep my promises. Ishmael will become a great people, in this desert here. I will make quite sure of that. Go to him. Pick him up and hold him tight. Look!'

Hagar looked and was astonished. She saw a well. It had been there all the time, only she hadn't been able to see it through her tears. She rushed over to it, filled the bottle with water, ran to Ishmael and gave him a drink. They were saved! They would find food too. With the cool water down their throats, her old knowledge of the desert came flooding back. They could live in the desert. They could flourish there. They would enjoy its freedom. She would be no one's slave, nor would Ishmael. Her son would grow up to be a great hunter with a bow and arrow. He would have lots of children, and his children would have lots of children too, until they became a great people, a people too many to count. She would have to find him a wife first, of course, when he was ready. She would go back home for one, to the land where she had been born and where she had spent her childhood, the land where she had lived before Sarah had taken her away. She would go to Egypt.

God had saved them. They would be safe now.

Abraham and Isaac

ABRAHAM LOVED ISAAC, the son that Sarah had borne in their old age. His other son, Ishmael, the son of Sarah's slave-woman, was gone, and his mother, Hagar, with him. He would never see them again. There was just him and Isaac now.

Isaac grew up healthy and strong. Then one night, one terrible night, Abraham heard God's voice. This time he recognized it immediately.

'Abraham!' God called softly.

'Here I am,' replied Abraham.

'Take your son, your only son, the one you love, Isaac. Go to the Land of Seeing, to a holy mountain I will show you, and offer him up there as a sacrifice.'

That was all. The silence of the night fell back on Abraham and Sarah's tent. Abraham lay rigid on his bed, his eyes wide open. He wanted to ask God what he was playing at. He wanted to give a cry of anguish sharp enough to split the heavens, and a howl of protest that would shrink God's heart. He opened his mouth. Nothing came out. Sacrifice his son? Kill Isaac? How could he do that?

Dawn came. With a heavy heart Abraham rose from his bed. He got everything ready. He cut the wood for the sacrifice and loaded it onto his donkey. Then he set out with two of his servant boys, taking Isaac with him. He didn't say where they were going, or what he was going to do. He said nothing at all. He walked on in front of the donkey, his eyes fixed on the stony ground.

For two days they travelled on, and still Abraham was silent, as if in a world of his own. On the third day he looked up and saw the mountain they were aiming for. He knew it was the one. He stopped. 'Stay here with the donkey,' he said to the servant boys. 'There's a holy place on this mountain. The boy and I will go and worship there and then come back.' He didn't look at them as he said it, and his voice was so quiet they hardly understood him. He knew very well Isaac wouldn't be coming back.

He took the wood off the donkey and piled it on Isaac's back. Then he took the special knife he used for sacrifices, and a small fire in an earthenware jar to start the wood burning.

They started to climb the mountain together. Isaac was carrying the wood for his own sacrifice, though he didn't know it. But Abraham had more to carry than his son did. Apart from the fire and the knife, he had to carry the terrible command of God. His heart was nearly breaking with the strain.

'Father,' Isaac said.

'Yes, my son?' Abraham answered.

'We've got the fire and the wood, but where's the lamb for the sacrifice?'

'God will provide the lamb for the sacrifice, my son.'

Abraham nearly choked as he said the words. He knew what the 'lamb' would be – his son, the one he loved so much, Isaac.

They climbed on up till they reached the holy place. There was no altar for the sacrifice, so Abraham had to build one. As he carried the stones and put them in place, each one felt like the body of his son.

The altar was finished. It was time. This was what he had come for. This was what God wanted. There was no lamb. He put the wood on the altar, and then he tied up his son and put him on top of the wood. He took the knife, the special knife for sacrifices, and raised his hand to kill his son.

'Abraham! Abraham!' a voice called urgently. It was the voice of God.

Abraham paused. 'Here I am,' he whispered.

'Do not harm the boy!' the voice said. 'I've been testing you – to see whether you would realize that Isaac is not just your son, but mine too; to see whether you would keep him to yourself, or be prepared to give him back to me. I have seen. I have seen enough! The old promises I gave you still hold. Your descendants will be as many as the stars in the sky and the grains of sand on the sea shore, and I will give them a land of their own, my Special Land. I will indeed bless you, and through your descendants all the nations of the earth shall find blessing too.'

Abraham raised his eyes and saw the sacrifice he hadn't dared hope for. A ram was caught in a thicket by its horns. He offered that upon the altar instead of his son. Then he gave the holy place a new name, 'God Sees'.

God had saved his son. They would be safe now.

A Tricky Twin and a Bowl of Stew

ABRAHAM HAD BEEN the Blessing-bearer. God had given him the blessing, and he had to hand it on to the next generation. Now he was dead, and his son Isaac was the Blessing-bearer in his place. He had to hand it on also.

Isaac had grown up and married a woman called Rebekah. The years went by, and still they had no children. It seemed Rebekah was unable to conceive. That's what everyone thought, at least. Twenty years went by: still no children.

Then Isaac prayed to God, and, at long last, Rebekah conceived: not just one child, but two. She was pregnant with twins!

The pregnancy was a terrible time for her. It felt as if the babies were fighting with each other all the time inside her. It went on day after day, pushing and shoving and kicking. They were wearing her out. They would surely be the death of her. She'd yearned for a child for so long, but she never knew it would be like this. She spread out her pain and despair before God. 'What shall I do?' she cried.

> God answered:
> 'Two nations are in your womb,
> two divided tribes shall spring from you;
> one tribe shall be stronger than the other tribe:
> the older one will serve the younger.'

That's all topsy-turvy, thought Rebekah, the wrong way round. Among our people younger sons take second place, not first.

When they were born, the first baby came out with a fine reddish down all over his body. They called him Esau. The second twin came out holding his brother's heel, so they called him Jacob, which means Heel-catcher.

Esau grew up to become a hunter, a man of the wild open spaces. Jacob stayed close to the family tents, looking after the goats. Esau was Isaac's favourite. Jacob was Rebekah's.

One day Jacob was boiling some lentils over a fire by one of the tents. The stew was red, just like the red hair all over Esau's body. It looks just like Esau, said Jacob to himself and laughed.

Just then Esau returned from the hunt. He'd been gone a long time and had caught nothing. He was famished. The smell of cooking drove him mad. 'I'm half dead!' he said to his brother. 'Let me have some of your stew.'

Jacob saw his chance. He was Esau's twin, but he'd been born second. When their father Isaac died, Esau would get much more than him, unless he took things into his own hands. He'd been looking out for an opportunity for a long time. Now the moment had arrived.

'I'll give you some bread and some of these lentils,' Jacob said, 'if you give me your birthright. You give me the privileges of the older son, and I will give you as much as you like of this delicious lentil stew and some fresh, hot bread to go with it. How's that for a bargain?'

'If you don't give me something to eat,' Esau replied, 'I'll die, and then what good will my birthright be to me?'

'Swear an oath,' said Jacob, waving an empty bowl under Esau's nose. 'Swear that I can be first.'

'I swear,' said Esau. 'Just fill that bowl up and give it to me.'

'Certainly,' Jacob cried. 'Here you are. Lovely food! Have seconds if you want. But you'll have to serve yourself, because, don't forget, I'm in first place now. You have to do whatever I say, and I'll have the pick of everything.'

Esau didn't care. He was too hungry. He ate the meal, had seconds, and thirds, and then returned to the wild, empty hills.

Jacob Steals a Blessing

JACOB WANTED TO MAKE quite sure he got the pick of everything when his father, Isaac, died. His twin brother, Esau, was older than he was. Only by a few minutes, it was true, but it could still make all the difference.

Isaac was very old. He had lost his sight, and death wasn't far away. The last thing he would do before he died would be to bless his son, his older son, Esau. Jacob had already tricked his brother into promising him the privileges of the older son, but Isaac didn't know that, and anyway, Esau was his favourite. If he blessed Esau, then Esau would get the pick of everything after all, and Jacob would end up second best.

Jacob had no idea what to do.

Not until the day that his mother, Rebekah, overheard something very important.

Isaac was very tired and lying down inside his tent. He was speaking to Esau. Rebekah was on her way to bring Isaac something to drink. She was about to enter the tent when she heard Isaac's voice. She stopped to listen.

'I am very weak, my son,' Isaac was saying. 'I could die any day. Give me some pleasure before I die. Go out hunting. Go and find me something tender and juicy. Carry it back here and cook it for me, the way I like it. Then bring it to me in my tent and I'll eat it, and it will give me the strength to bless you before I die.'

Rebekah watched as Esau fetched his bow and arrows and strode out towards the hills. As soon as he had gone, she ran to Jacob.

'Quick!' she whispered. 'Your father has sent Esau out to hunt some game for him. He's told him to cook it and bring the meal to his tent. Then, when he's eaten it, he's going to give him his death-bed blessing. You know what that means! But listen, I've got an idea. Go and fetch two of the kid goats from the flock, the best ones. I'll make your father a meal out of them, just the way he likes it. Then you can take it to him, and he will bless you instead. But hurry! We don't know when Esau will get back.'

'But Esau's like a goat! He's hairy all over,' Jacob cried. 'My skin's as smooth as a baby's. If my father touches me, he's bound to know it's me. He'll think I'm nothing but a low-down trickster, and I'll leave with his curse instead!'

'Don't worry,' Rebekah replied. 'I've already thought of that. Anyway, if he does curse you, may the curse rest on me, not you. Just go and fetch the goats, and be quick about it!'

Jacob did as he was told. Rebekah made a delicious stew, just the way Isaac liked it. Then she took strips of the goatskins and wound them round Jacob's smooth hands and neck. She gave him a bowl of the stew and some bread, and told him to take them to his father. She followed behind and waited outside Isaac's tent to see what would happen.

Jacob slipped in to see his father.

'Hello, Father!' he said cheerfully.

Isaac was expecting Esau, but it sounded like Jacob.

'Which one are you, my son?' he asked.

'I'm Esau, your firstborn,' said Jacob. 'I've done as you asked. I've been hunting and I've made a lovely stew with what I killed. Eat it up and then you'll have the strength to give me your blessing.'

'You've been very quick, my son,' said Isaac. 'I wasn't expecting you for at least another hour.'

Jacob coughed. 'God helped me,' he said. 'I've never had hunting so easy. Eat up, Father. You don't want it to get cold.'

But still Isaac wouldn't take the food. Rebekah, waiting outside, hopped from one foot to another. Every so often she looked across to the hills, to see if Esau was coming back.

'Come close to me, my son,' Isaac said to Jacob. 'I want to make sure you really are Esau.'

Jacob stepped forward. Isaac couldn't see him at all; he was completely blind. He ran his trembling fingers over the goatskins covering Jacob's hands. Jacob held his breath. His heart thumped. So did Rebekah's outside. She could see Esau in the distance!

'Your voice is Jacob's voice,' said Isaac, 'but your hands are all hairy like Esau's. Are you really my son Esau?'

'Yes, Father.'

'Alright, give me the stew. I'll eat some of it and then I'll be able to give you my blessing.'

Jacob put the food beside his father, and some wine for him to drink. Isaac's taste buds were not very sharp any more. He couldn't tell goat from venison. But he still wasn't quite sure it was Esau. When he'd finished eating, he said, 'Give me a hug.' Jacob hugged him, and Isaac sniffed his hands and neck. The goatskins were very smelly. They reminded him of how Esau smelled when he came back from the hunt with an animal across his shoulders. It must be Esau, he said to himself. Now he could bless him.

> 'See, the smell of my son
> is like the smell of a hunt

that God has blessed!
May God give you the dew of the heavens
and the richness of the earth,
abundance of corn and new wine.
May nations serve you,
and tribes bow before you.
Be lord over your brother,
and may he bow down to you.'

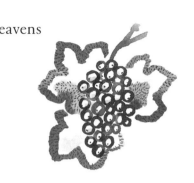

It was a fine blessing! Jacob breathed a sigh of relief, bowed to his father and left. Outside the tent he and Rebekah danced with delight. Then they ran and hid. For just then Esau came back from the hunt, with a gazelle over his shoulders.

He cooked it and carried the meal to Isaac's tent. 'Here you are, Father,' he said. 'I've hunted it for you, just as you asked. Eat it up. It will give you the strength to bless me.'

'Which one are you?' Isaac asked.

'Your son, your firstborn, Esau, of course.'

Isaac started shaking all over. 'Who was it then, who brought me a stew just now? I ate it not long before you came and gave him my blessing.'

Esau gave a loud and bitter cry.

'It was Jacob all the time!' his father exclaimed. 'He tricked me and took away your blessing.'

'That's why he's called Jacob, Heel-catcher,' Esau said bitterly. 'He trips people up and makes them fall flat on their faces. He's done it to me twice now. He paid me a bowl of lentil stew for my birthright, and now he's stolen my blessing. Haven't you still got a blessing kept by for me, Father? Bless me also, Father!'

Isaac shook his head. 'I've given all the best things to your brother,' he said. 'I can't take my blessing back, or make it unsaid. I've made him lord over you. What is there left for you, my son?'

'Do you only have one blessing to give, Father? Surely you have another. Bless me also, Father.' He broke down in tears.

His father spoke, his voice still shaking:

> 'Behold, away from the richness of the earth
> you must dwell,
> and away from the dew of the heavens.
> You will have to live by your sword,
> and you will serve your brother.
> But one day, one day
> you will shake him off.'

That was the best Isaac could do. Esau left his father's tent, tears of anger and grief still streaming down his face. He would get his own back on Jacob.

The Gate of Heaven

ESAU WAS WALKING among the tents where they lived. He couldn't forget the trick his brother, Jacob, had played on him, the way he had stolen their father's blessing from him. 'My father will die very soon,' he said out loud to himself. 'Then when the days of mourning for him are over, I will get even with Jacob. I will kill him.'

Someone overheard Esau and told Rebekah. She went running

to Jacob. 'Quick! Get out of here!' she said. 'Esau's out to kill you as soon as he can. Get right away, out of the country, to my brother Laban in Haran. That's hundreds of miles away. You should be safe enough there. Stay with him a while. I'll send a messenger to tell you when it's all right to come back. If you stay here and Esau kills you, people will punish him immediately by taking his life. I don't want to lose both of you on a single day.'

So Jacob left for Haran, back to where his grandfather Abraham had come from many years before.

He had a long journey ahead of him, and he didn't know whether he would make it. Did he have enough food and clothing for the journey? He wasn't sure. If he did get to Haran, how would his uncle Laban treat him? And would Esau ever forgive him? Would he ever be able to come home? He'd tricked his brother and his father, but the birthright and the blessing he'd stolen from them didn't seem to count for anything any longer. It had all gone wrong.

He hadn't gone very far, when he came to a town called Luz. He was a trickster, a thief. No one would want to give him lodging. So he found a place where he could be on his own for the night, out in the open. He lay down to sleep. Night fell. Thick clouds hid the moon and the stars. The blackness was complete.

Then he had an extraordinary dream. A strange light shone around him, and he could see a stairway. Its foot was close beside him, and its top reached as far as heaven. God's messengers were going up and down on it, to speak the truth of heaven and take back to God the hopes and fears of the world. But wait – God himself was standing beside him! God was speaking, and the words were as clear to Jacob's ears as a nightingale's song:

'I am God,

the God of Abraham and Isaac.

The land on which you lie sleeping,

I will give to your descendants.

They will be as many as the grains of sand on the seashore.

All the families of the earth will find blessing

in you and your descendants.

And see, I am with you.

I will watch over you

wherever you go,

and I will bring you back to this land.

I will not leave you.'

Jacob woke up with a start. 'God's in this place,' he cried, 'and I didn't know it. This is the House of God and the Gate of Heaven too! It shall not be called Luz any more. I will rename it Beth-El, which means the House of God.'

God was still standing at the foot of the stairway. Jacob turned towards him and said. 'If you really look after me, God, and bring me safely to Haran, so that afterwards I can come back home in peace, then I will turn this spot into a holy shrine and call it your house, and people will come here for centuries, just to find you. How's that for a bargain?'

'Still out for a bargain, are you, Jacob?' God said softly to himself. 'But a promise is a promise, and I never break my promises.'

Face to Face with God

JACOB REMEMBERED his mother's parting words. 'Stay with Laban a little while,' Rebekah had said. Jacob had been with him for *twenty years*! He was Laban's nephew, but Laban treated him no better than a hired hand. He had married Laban's two daughters, Leah and Rachel, and their women-servants, Bilhah and Zilpah, but his uncle still made his life a misery, and he couldn't wait to get back home.

Rebekah had promised to send word when it was safe to return. No messenger had arrived. But the time came when it wasn't safe to stay either. Laban and his sons had had enough of Jacob. They looked as though they were out for his blood. They reminded him of Esau. God spoke to him again, telling him to go back to Canaan. 'I will be with you,' he said.

Jacob upped and went as fast as he could. His wives came with him, and their children and his servants. He had large flocks and herds, and lots of camels. They were his wages for all the years of hard work he'd given his uncle. He'd come to Haran with nothing. He was going back to Canaan a rich man. Perhaps he hadn't done so badly after all. But what would it be like back home? Had Esau forgiven him? There was still no news from Rebekah.

Slowly the miles went by, and Jacob grew more and more nervous. When he got near the border, he sent some of his men ahead to find Esau. 'Tell him I'm returning home a rich man, and that I hope he will receive me in peace,' he said.

The messengers came back sooner than he'd expected. 'Esau's on his way to meet you,' they reported, 'and he's got four hundred men with him.'

Four hundred men! That was nearly an army. Esau was out to get him, for sure. What could he do? Split into two separate camps. Yes. If Esau found one, perhaps he wouldn't find the other. Pray to God. Yes. God had promised to protect him. 'Well, now I need your protection, God, and I need it badly!' he prayed. Try to bribe Esau. Yes. Three times. Send three lots of goats and sheep and camels and cattle and asses ahead with some servants, and tell the servants to say each time, 'The animals are a present from your servant Jacob, my lord.' Yes, that should do it. But would it work? Four hundred men. Nearly an army!

Jacob reached a water course called the Jabbok. It was night. The rains had come and the river bed was full of rushing, tumbling water. The servants and the livestock were well ahead. Jacob got his wives and children and women-servants across the river safely and up the other side of the valley. Then he hesitated. He went back down towards the water. Which way should he go? Should he make a run for it? Once across the Jabbok there would be no turning back. Esau and his men must be quite close by now. The darkness of the valley wrapped Jacob round in its black shroud. He felt small and alone, and very frightened.

Suddenly, he felt someone's hands on him. A mysterious stranger started wrestling with him, and he found himself using all his strength to keep his feet on the ground. It must be Esau! Jacob thought. He must have come on ahead to attack me.

The struggle went on for hours, right through the night. Yet the longer it went on, the more it seemed like a dream. Jacob's assailant touched his hip and dislocated it. A mere touch, and his hip was out of joint. Yet Jacob felt no pain and wrestled on as if nothing had happened.

The first light of dawn began to creep down the sides of the valley. 'Let me go!' the other said.

'Not unless you bless me,' Jacob replied. His father had blessed him. Now he needed Esau's blessing too.

The other said, 'What is your name?'

'Jacob.'

'I will give you a new name. You won't be Jacob, the Heel-catcher, the one who trips people up, any more. Your name will be Israel, God-fighter, for you have fought with God and with human beings, and you have won.'

This doesn't sound like Esau at all, thought Jacob. 'What is *your* name?' he asked.

'Why do you ask my name?' the other replied. And then, just when Jacob was not expecting it, he blessed him.

The rising sun flooded the valley with light and warmth, and Jacob was on his own once more. He realized who the stranger had been. 'It was God!' he cried. 'I've seen God face to face! I've struggled with God all night, and now I have a new name and his blessing too. I'm safe at last!'

He climbed out of the valley and joined his wives and children. As he came towards them, they noticed he walked with a limp, as if his hip was out of joint.

Face to Face with Esau

JACOB HAD SPENT the night wrestling with God. In the light of the new morning he looked to the south. Esau was coming with four hundred men. Jacob's heart started thumping again. When God had left him, he had felt safe. But he didn't feel safe any more. As he approached his brother he bowed himself to the ground seven times, as if he was greeting a great king and begging for his pardon.

In truth, Jacob had nothing to fear. Esau's anger and jealousy had gone. He had forgiven his brother long ago. He was glad, very glad that Jacob had come back safely. So when he saw him, he ran to meet him, hugged him, flung his arms around his neck and kissed him. For a long time the two brothers wept on each other's shoulders.

'Who are these women and children?' Esau asked.

'The family God has blessed me with,' said Jacob.

'And what about all these animals and servants? They met me on the way here, first one lot, then a second, then a third.'

'Presents for you, my lord.' Jacob still couldn't quite believe Esau had forgiven him.

Esau laughed. 'I have plenty of my own, Brother.'

Brother! He had called him brother! Jacob had been blessed by

God at the river Jabbok, just when he wasn't expecting it. Now he had another blessing beyond his wildest dreams, Esau's love and forgiveness. 'Seeing your face,' he said to Esau, 'is like seeing the face of God.' He paused, while more tears ran down his cheeks. 'But please,' he continued, 'please accept my gifts. Have them as a blessing. It's time you had a blessing from me after all.'

'Then I accept them,' Esau said. 'Thank you. We can travel on together now.'

Esau wanted Jacob to go back with him to his own home. But Esau had settled in a country called Edom, to the south of the Dead Sea. Jacob could not settle in Edom. He had to live in Canaan, the Land promised by God to his father and grandfather and their descendants. 'You go on ahead,' he said to his brother. 'I'll catch you up later.'

He watched Esau turn back towards Edom, waited till he was over the horizon and then led his family west, towards Canaan.

Jacob and His Sons

JACOB HAD FOUR WIVES and lots of children: one daughter and twelve sons. His favourite wife was Rachel. For a long time she wasn't able to have children, but in the end she had two sons, Joseph and Benjamin. When she went into labour with Benjamin, the pain seemed to go on for ever. In the end Benjamin was born safely, but by then Rachel was so weak, she could only just whisper his name before she died.

Joseph and Benjamin were Jacob's youngest children and his favourites. He was an old man by the time they were born, and he hadn't expected to be a father again at that age. They were the only children of his beloved Rachel too. Joseph was the most special of all. He reminded Jacob so much of Rachel. Whenever he looked at Joseph, he remembered her. So he gave Joseph a special coat that made him look like a prince. Joseph felt very important in that coat, much more important than his older brothers. None of them had a coat half as good, a quarter as good as his.

Joseph's brothers hated him. He used to tell on them to Jacob, for a start. Then he began saying he was having dreams about them. In the first dream they were like sheaves of corn, he said, and his sheaf was standing upright, while all their sheaves were waddling in circles round and round him, bowing to him, as if he were a prince. In the second dream he said his father and mother were like the sun and the moon, and his brothers like eleven stars. They were all bowing down to him, as if he were a king. Joseph thought the dreams were marvellous. His brothers thought they were dreadful. Even Jacob thought the second one went too far.

One time Joseph's brothers went off to the north to find pasture for the sheep. They were gone a long time, much longer than usual. Jacob became anxious. 'Go and find them and make sure they're all right,' he said to Joseph.

Joseph walked for several days. There was still no sign of his brothers. But then a man told him he'd met them and overheard them saying they were moving on a few miles further, to a place called Dothan.

His brothers spotted him coming. 'Hey look!' they said. 'Here comes the dreamer. Now's our chance. Let's kill him and tell Dad he was killed by an angry lion. That'll put an end to his dreams!'

'Let's not kill him,' said Reuben, the oldest. 'Let's just throw him in this pit here and leave him there.'

When it gets dark, Reuben thought to himself, I'll pull him out and take him back home.

When Joseph arrived at their camp, all dressed up in his prince's coat, they set upon him, tore the coat off him and threw him into the pit. It was far too deep for Joseph to climb out, and he had neither food nor water. The other brothers sat down to eat their evening meal, while Reuben went off to his tent and waited for nightfall.

Suddenly, the brothers looked up and saw a camel caravan coming towards them. Another of them, Judah, had an idea. He didn't want to see Joseph left to die either. 'Joseph *is* our brother,' he said to the others. 'We can't kill him. Let's see what we can get for him from these merchants. Let's sell him to them as a slave.'

The merchants thought Joseph would fetch a good price in Egypt. They handed over the money, tied Joseph on a long rope to one of their camels and went on their way towards the Egyptian border.

Night fell. Reuben knew nothing about the merchants and the deal his brothers had made. He crept out of his tent and went up to the lip of the pit. Joseph wasn't there! He rushed back to his brothers' tents. 'He's gone!' he shouted. 'The boy's gone! What shall I do?'

'I know,' said one of them. He fetched one of the goats, killed it and dipped Joseph's precious coat in the blood. Then he tore the coat into shreds. He smiled. 'In the morning,' he said, 'we'll go back to Dad and show him this.'

When they got back, they went at once to see Jacob. They held up the coat, all torn and covered in blood. 'We found this,' they said. 'Do you recognize it?'

'It's Joseph's!' Jacob cried. 'A lion must have attacked him and eaten him. He must have been torn to pieces!'

His sons and daughter tried to comfort him, but he wouldn't be comforted. 'I'll die before I finish mourning for my son,' he said.

A long time ago Jacob had tricked his own father, Isaac. Isaac had been a very old man then. Now Jacob was old himself, and his sons were playing a cruel trick on him. He didn't suspect anything. He believed his favourite son, Joseph, was dead.

Joseph the Slave

JOSEPH'S BROTHERS had sold him as a slave to merchants on their way to Egypt. When the merchants reached Egypt, they took Joseph along to one of the slave markets and sold him to a rich

Egyptian called Potiphar, one of Pharaoh's courtiers. At that time Egypt was the richest and most powerful country in the world.

God didn't abandon Joseph. He stayed with him and helped him. Potiphar was very pleased with Joseph and the work he did. It seemed that Joseph had the golden touch, for everything he did succeeded. Potiphar put him in charge of all his affairs.

All went well, until Potiphar's wife fell in love with Joseph. 'Come to bed with me!' she kept saying to him.

'How can I?' Joseph replied. 'You're my master's wife. He trusts me. How could I do that to him? How could I so dishonour God?'

She kept on pestering him. Every time, he refused. Then, one day, when they were alone in the house together, she made a grab for him. 'Come to bed now!' she cried, and snatched at his cloak. Joseph wriggled free and ran out of the house. She shouted for the other servants to come indoors. 'That foreign slave tried to rape me!' she cried. 'I screamed, and he ran off, leaving his cloak behind. Look!' She held up the cloak for them to see.

As soon as Potiphar returned from the palace, she ran to him and told him the same story, sobbing on his shoulder. He was furious. Without more ado he had Joseph caught and thrown into prison. Joseph wasn't given the chance to put his side of the story.

Joseph the Prisoner

JOSEPH FOUND HIMSELF in the stench and the darkness of an Egyptian prison. Yet still God didn't abandon him, but stood by him and helped him. As a result, he so impressed the governor of the prison that the governor let him look after all the other prisoners for him.

Now two of the prisoners were the pharaoh's chief cupbearer and chief baker. They had got into serious trouble with the pharaoh, and he'd thrown them into prison, to stay there while he decided what to do with them. Would the pharaoh release them or have them killed? They didn't know.

One night each of them had a dream. The Egyptians believed you needed an expert to interpret dreams, and there weren't any experts around inside the prison. Having dreams and then not being able to understand them only made the two men more frightened.

The next morning Joseph noticed they were both looking especially miserable. They explained about the dreams. 'You don't need experts to understand these things,' said Joseph. 'It's God who interprets dreams. Anyone can interpret them with God's help. Tell me what you dreamed.'

So they did. First the cupbearer told his dream. 'I saw a vine,' he said, 'with three branches. There were wonderful grapes on it. I had the pharaoh's wine cup in my hand, so I picked the grapes, pressed them, filled the cup and handed it to the pharaoh.'

Joseph told him that in three days the pharaoh would set him free and give him his old job back. 'When you get out of this prison,' he said, 'tell the pharaoh about me. I've done nothing wrong. I don't deserve to be in here.'

When he heard the good news Joseph had for the cupbearer, the baker quickly told Joseph his dream. 'I was carrying three cake baskets on my head,' he explained. 'The top basket was full of all sorts of wonderful cakes for the pharaoh, but there were birds all over them, gobbling them up as fast as they could go.'

He looked at Joseph eagerly, waiting for his answer. He noticed Joseph had a very gloomy expression on his face. 'In three days,' he told the baker, 'the pharaoh will hang you, and the birds will come and gobble you up.'

And that is exactly what happened. Three days later the baker was hanged, and the cupbearer was pardoned and back at his job, serving wine to the pharaoh.

But the cupbearer forgot to say anything to the pharaoh about Joseph.

Joseph in the Palace

JOSEPH WAS SHUT UP in prison for something he hadn't done. The pharaoh's cupbearer had been in prison with him, and when he was released he promised Joseph that he would put in a good word for him with the pharaoh. But he was so glad to be out of the prison and back at his old job that he forgot all about it.

Two more long years went by. Then the pharaoh dreamed some puzzling dreams. The dreams worried him, and he called in all the Egyptian experts to interpret them for him. None of them knew what they meant.

The news about the pharaoh's dreams went round the palace. Everyone was talking about them. The cupbearer got to hear of

them, and suddenly he remembered his old friend. He hurried off
to the pharaoh and told him all about Joseph; how he'd met him in
prison; how he and the chief baker had both had dreams; how
Joseph had told them what they meant; how it had all come true;
how Joseph had asked him to tell the pharaoh that he was innocent;
how he'd forgotten all about it; and how he was very sorry.

'Hurry!' cried the pharaoh to two of his slaves. 'Go to the prison,
fetch this Joseph and bring him here at once!'

Joseph couldn't come to see the pharaoh straight away. He hadn't
shaved all the time he was in prison. His beard was long and
straggly, and he smelt awful too. He needed a good wash and some
smart clothes.

The slaves in the pharaoh's palace got him ready as quickly as
they could and brought him into the pharaoh's throne room. Joseph
had never seen the pharaoh before. There he was, the most powerful
man in the whole world, sitting on his throne in all his finery, and
all his experts and wise men around him.

'I've had two dreams,' Pharaoh said to him. 'I hear you're an
expert at interpreting dreams.'

'Not me, Your Majesty. God is the expert,' replied Joseph. 'God
and I are good friends.'

The pharaoh smiled at him. 'Are you, indeed?' he said. 'Well, let's
see what you and your God can make of this.' And he told Joseph
both his dreams.

'I was standing on the edge of the Nile river,' he said, 'when seven
cows came up out of the water and started to feed. They were
beautiful, fat beasts, with shining coats. Then seven more cows
came out of the river. They were the thinnest, ugliest cows I've ever
seen. The thin cows ate up the fat ones, but they stayed as thin and
ugly as before. Then I woke up.'

Joseph listened carefully. He waited for the pharaoh to tell the second dream.

'I fell asleep again, and this time I saw a stalk with seven ears of grain, fat and full, shining in the sun. Then another stalk grew up beside the first one. This too carried seven ears of grain, but those were thin and hollow, dried up by the scorching wind. The thin ears swallowed up the fat ones.'

'None of my experts can tell me what the dreams mean,' he concluded. 'Can you do any better?'

'I certainly can,' replied Joseph. 'It's as clear as day, as obvious as the pimple on the end of that wise man's nose over there!'

The wise man blushed and looked down at the floor.

'God is using these dreams to show you what's going to happen,' continued Joseph. 'The cows and the ears of grain stand for seven years. There'll be seven years of good harvests, and then seven years of terrible ones. The years of famine will swallow up the good years. It will be a worldwide disaster.

'Now this is what you have to do. You must collect all the spare grain in the seven good years and store it in huge storehouses. Then when the famine comes, there'll be something for the people to eat. You'll need to choose someone very wise and capable to organize it all.'

'How about you?' the pharaoh said. He turned to his experts and wise men. 'This shepherd from Canaan seems just the wise and capable man we want, don't you think?'

The experts and wise men all blushed, and nodded furiously.

'That's settled then.' He smiled again at Joseph, a broader smile this time. 'Since you and your God are such good friends, and some of God's wisdom has obviously rubbed off on you, and since my own wise men are such idiots, I appoint you my viceroy! You shall be the second most powerful person in Egypt. I'm the first, of course. You will be the second most powerful person in the world. Here, let me place this ring on your finger. And put these fine robes on, and let me hang this gold chain round your neck. You shall have your very own chariot, and when you drive through the streets slaves will run ahead telling everyone to kneel as you go by. People will not be able to lift a finger in Egypt unless you say they can.'

That sounds a lot better than being in a smelly prison! thought Joseph.

What Joseph had predicted came true. Seven excellent harvests were followed by seven years when the harvests all failed. A terrible famine set in throughout the world. But Joseph had organized everything, and by the time the famine came, there were vast heaps of grain in the storehouses in Egypt, enough to feed not just the Egyptians, but all the people in the entire world.

Joseph and the Famine

ALL THE WORLD was in the grip of a terrible famine. The shortage of food was as bad in Canaan as everywhere else. Joseph's father, Jacob, and his family had virtually nothing left to eat.

Jacob believed Joseph had been killed by a lion years before. Joseph's brothers knew that wasn't true, because they'd thrown him into a pit in the desert and then sold him to some merchants travelling to Egypt and lied about it all to their father. But they hadn't seen Joseph, or heard anything more about him, not since the merchants had led him off tied to one of their camels.

The family's storehouse was almost completely empty. One day Jacob heard there were heaps of grain in Egypt. 'What are you waiting for?' he said to his sons. 'Go down to Egypt and buy some grain. If you don't, we'll all die. Benjamin must stay here though. It's a dangerous journey and I've already lost Joseph. Rachel was my favourite wife, the one I loved the most. I don't want to lose her second son as well.'

So the other ten sons travelled down to Egypt. It so happened that Joseph was looking after the sale of grain from one of the Egyptian storehouses. He saw his brothers in the queue and recognized them at once. But they didn't recognize him. They weren't expecting to see him after all. The merchants had taken him to sell as a slave. Slaves usually didn't live very long, and they thought Joseph would only have lasted a few years. In any case, if they had been looking out for him, they certainly wouldn't have expected to meet him dressed in the robes of the viceroy, the second most powerful man in the land.

As they came close to him, they bowed low to the ground, and Joseph remembered some dreams he'd had when he was a boy. Here they are, he thought to himself, bowing down to me! After all these years my dreams have come true.

He pretended not to know them. 'Where do you come from?' he asked.

'From Canaan,' they replied, 'to buy food.'

'You're not here to buy food at all!' shouted Joseph. 'You're spies!'

'No, my lord, we're not spies,' they replied.

'I only have your word for that,' said Joseph. 'Where have you come from?'

'Your servants, my lord, are twelve sons,' they said. 'The youngest of us is back home with our father. And one is no more.'

'You're spies!' repeated Joseph. 'We'll soon see anyway. One of you must go and fetch your youngest brother and bring him here. Meantime, the rest of you will be my prisoners.'

Joseph put them in prison for three days. Then he thought of Jacob and the others starving in Canaan. 'I'll tell you what I'll do,' he said to his brothers. 'Let one of you stay here in prison, and the rest can go home and take your ration of grain with you.'

'What we did to Joseph has finally caught up with us,' the brothers said to one another. 'When we put him in the pit, we heard his cries of distress, but we didn't listen. That's why this distress has come upon us now.'

They didn't realize Joseph could understand them. He'd been speaking through an interpreter, pretending not to speak their language. When he heard what they said, he couldn't control his tears any more. He turned away from them and wept. He knew now that his brothers realized what they'd done to him and were sorry about it. Perhaps he could be reconciled with them after all. But not just yet. He would have some fun with them first. And he wanted to see his brother Benjamin.

He picked out his brother Simeon, put him in prison and sent the others on their way home. He packed their sacks with grain, tucked some silver into the top of the sacks and gave them food to eat on the way.

And so they set out for the long journey home.

A Strange Discovery

JOSEPH'S BROTHERS started out from Egypt to go back to their father, Jacob, in Canaan. Great round sacks of grain swung heavily against the sides of their donkeys. The journey was going to take them several days.

The first evening they arrived at a lodging place, and one of them opened his sack to give some grain to his donkey. 'Come and look at this!' he shouted to the others. 'My share of the money we paid is in the top of my sack. What's going on? What will become of us? When we have to go back to Egypt, they'll accuse us of being thieves as well as spies!'

When they arrived home, they told Jacob almost everything. They told him that the man in charge of the grain supplies had accused them of being spies. They told him he had demanded to see their younger brother, Benjamin, and had put Simeon in prison. They didn't tell him about the money in the top of the sack. But then, when the rest of them opened their sacks, they all found their bundles of money in the top of them.

Something very strange was going on. They were really frightened. Jacob was frightened too. 'They think you're spies and thieves!' he cried. 'Joseph is no more; Simeon is no more; and now you want to take Benjamin away from me!'

Yet still the famine did not come to an end. Eventually Jacob realized that if his sons did not return to Egypt, they would all die. They were near the end of the supplies they'd brought up from Egypt, and their own fields were dried up and cracked, still yielding nothing.

'You will have to go back and buy some more grain,' he told them.

'But we can't go back without Benjamin,' said Judah, one of the oldest of the brothers.

'Why did you have to tell the man in Egypt you had another brother?' Jacob asked angrily.

'He asked all about our family,' the brothers replied. '"Is your father still alive? Do you have another brother?" All that sort of thing. He asked us and we told him. We had to tell him the truth. We didn't know he would order us to fetch Benjamin.'

'Let Benjamin come with me,' said Judah. 'I'll take responsibility for him. I'll look after him. He'll be all right with me.'

Jacob sighed. 'Go,' he said. 'Take the man a present and two lots of silver – one to buy more grain and one to pay back what was in your sacks. As for your brother Benjamin, go on, take him with you.'

Benjamin

THE BROTHERS HAD TO GO all the way back to Egypt to buy more grain and to find Simeon. They took two bundles of silver, as their father Jacob had said, and a present for the man in charge of the grain stores. This time Benjamin went with them. They didn't quite know what to expect, but they thought they were in for trouble. They wondered if any of them would ever come back home again.

When they arrived in Egypt, they met their brother Joseph again. They still didn't recognize him. Joseph noticed at once that Benjamin was with them and said to his steward, 'Take them to my house. We will have a great feast together at noon.'

The brothers couldn't understand it. Last time the man had accused them of being spies; now he was inviting them to eat with him. It must be a trick. Something to do with the silver in their sacks, no doubt. His men would probably arrest them all and turn them into slaves. And where was Simeon?

Terrified, they approached Joseph's steward and told him all about the silver they'd found. 'We can't think how it got there, sir,' they said. 'It's a complete mystery to us.'

'Don't worry,' the steward replied. 'Your God must have put it there. He seems to be looking after you very well. I got your money last time. There was no problem. I'll fetch Simeon now. He's quite safe.'

Relieved, but still bewildered, the brothers were reunited with Simeon. Then they went all together into Joseph's house, bowed low in front of him and offered him the present they had brought from Canaan.

'Is your father well?' Joseph asked quietly.

'Your servant, our father, is well, thank you, sir.' And they bowed low once again.

Joseph looked across to Benjamin. Clearly Benjamin hadn't recognized him either. 'And is this your youngest brother?' he asked. 'May God bless you!' he said to Benjamin. A lump came into his throat, and he rushed out of the room and burst into tears.

Eventually he stopped crying, washed his face and came back into the room. 'Let us eat together,' he said.

What on earth was going on? The brothers couldn't make it out. They'd never had such a feast in all their lives, and Benjamin was served five times as much as any of the rest of them.

Joseph still couldn't bring himself to tell them who he was. He hadn't forgotten that pit at Dothan, the pit his brothers had thrown him into all those years before, when he had gone looking for them. He had one more test to give them, to see whether they were truly sorry for what they had done, to see if they had really changed or not.

Before his brothers departed once again for Canaan with their new supplies, Joseph ordered his steward to put a precious goblet, one of his most valuable possessions, in the top of Benjamin's sack of grain.

This time the brothers were scarcely outside the city, when the steward came riding up with a band of Joseph's men.

'Is this how you repay my master?' the steward shouted. 'He gave you that great feast, and one of you has stolen his precious goblet.'

'We would never do such a thing!' they exclaimed. 'Search our sacks and see. If you find it in anyone's sack, then take him and kill him, and the rest of us will be your master's slaves.'

The steward started with Reuben's sack, since he was the oldest. It was clear. So was the next one, and the next. They were all clear. There was only one left, now, Benjamin's. The steward untied it. He drew out the goblet and held it up for them to see. 'Never do such a thing, eh?' he cried. The brothers shook with fear.

Trembling, the brothers turned the donkeys round, and the steward and his men escorted them back to Joseph's house. They flung themselves on the ground in front of him.

'What did you think you were doing, stealing my precious goblet?' Joseph asked.

'What can we say?' said Judah. 'You won't believe us if we say we are innocent. We are guilty, it is true, though only God knows about the real crime we committed. Take us all, my lord, as your slaves.'

'No,' said Joseph. 'That would not be right. Only the one who stole the goblet. The rest of you can go back to your father in peace.'

Judah stepped forward. 'Our father is a very old man, sir,' he said. 'When we were about to return to Egypt, he said to us, "My darling wife, Rachel, had two sons. One was torn to pieces by a lion, and I've never seen his body. Now you want to take the other one away from me! If you do not bring Benjamin back safe, I will die with grief." So you see, sir, if Benjamin dies, it will kill my father. And it will all be my fault, because I promised to look after the lad till we got back. Let me take the blame, sir. Let Benjamin go home with the others. I'll stay here and be your slave. I can't go home without Benjamin, sir. It would kill my father. I couldn't bear it, sir.'

Joseph couldn't restrain himself any longer. 'Leave me alone with these shepherds,' he said to the steward and his men. When they'd left the room, he burst into tears. 'I am Joseph.' he said. 'Is my father really still alive?'

The brothers stared at him. They couldn't believe their ears.

'Come closer,' Joseph said. 'I am Joseph, your brother, the one you sold into slavery. God has brought great good out of the wrong you did me. God has helped me save countless people from starvation, including you and our whole family. God brought me here to save the world from famine. Look at me now – I'm the second most powerful man in Egypt! See this gold chain? The pharaoh himself gave me that. Go home and tell my father about me, and bring him down to Egypt, with your wives and your children and your animals. There are still five years of this dreadful famine to go. You'll be safer down here, and we can be near one another. Tell my father everything, and bring him to Egypt as soon as you can.'

Then he flung himself on his brother Benjamin's neck, and they both shed lots more tears. Joseph hugged all his brothers, one after the other, and they all cried.

They had a lot to tell each other.

The Reunion

JOSEPH'S BROTHERS hurried back to Canaan. As soon as they got home, they rushed into Jacob's tent. 'Joseph's alive!' they cried. 'He's not dead after all! And he's viceroy of Egypt as well, the second most powerful man after the pharaoh.'

Jacob's heart went cold. He didn't believe them. So they told him the whole story, and took him outside the tent. 'Look at all these wagons!' they cried. 'Joseph gave them to us, on the pharaoh's orders, to bring you and our wives and children down to Egypt.'

Jacob looked at the wagons and all the other presents Joseph had given them.

His eyes grew wider and wider. 'My son *is* alive.' he said. 'After all these years! I must see him again before I die.'

Within a short time Jacob and his entire family travelled down from Canaan to live in Egypt. When they got near where Joseph lived, Judah went ahead to tell Joseph they were coming.

Joseph rode out in his fine chariot to meet his father. When he caught sight of him, he got down from the chariot and ran and flung himself upon the old man's neck, weeping.

'I can die happy,' said Jacob, 'now I know you are still alive, now that I've seen your face again.'

So God's chosen family settled in the best land in all Egypt, under the pharaoh's protection.

3

MOSES AND THE MOUNTAIN OF GOD

The first chapter of this book contained stories taken from the book of Genesis about the beginnings of the world, of how God made everything very beautiful and very good, and how human beings spoiled everything through their violence and their pride. The second chapter told of God's plan to choose a people who would work with him to put the world back to rights. But the stories in that chapter were not about a people, but just about a family, about Abraham and Sarah, their son Isaac and his wife Rebekah, Isaac and Rebekah's sons, Jacob and Esau, and then about Jacob's sons, especially Joseph. These are the ancestors of the people of Israel, who believed themselves to be the people of God.

The stories about the creation of the world and Abraham and Sarah and their family are the first parts of a great story that stretches over the first books of the Bible. Now, in this chapter, we move on to the next phase. Abraham and Sarah's family becomes a great people. The people of God are born! The trouble is, they are in the wrong place. God has told Abraham that his people will live in the land of Canaan and have it as their own. He has told him they will have their freedom there, and will not be pushed around by some other nation that does not know God. At the start of this chapter, however, we find the people of God not in Canaan but in Egypt, and not free either, but slaves of a cruel king known as the pharaoh.

How will God get his people out of Egypt? How will he teach them the way to live in his Land? How will he give them the knowledge and the wisdom they must have if they are to work with him, share his vision for the world and keep him company? The stories in this chapter, mostly taken from Exodus, answer those questions.

When the people of Israel composed the stories about their ancestors, Abraham and Sarah and their descendants, they didn't turn them into great, strong heroes, performing fantastic feats, nor even make them especially good. When they told the stories about their own beginnings as a people, they didn't change their tune. So if you read the stories in this chapter, you won't find that the people of God are particularly brave or good. However, first you will find stories about some extremely brave women, and then you will discover someone who becomes a real hero, one of the greatest heroes in the Bible: Moses. One of the stories about Moses tells of God speaking to him face to face, as one speaks to a friend. We don't find anyone else in the early books of the Bible quite as close to God as Moses.

The Brave Midwives and the Pharaoh

IN THE DAYS OF JOSEPH, when a famine held the whole world in its grip, Jacob and his huge family came to live in Egypt. So many children were born in Egypt that after a bit they weren't just a family any more, they were a people. Israel, the people of God, had arrived!

The trouble was, the people were in the wrong place. God didn't want them in Egypt. God wanted them to live in Canaan further to the north. He'd made that quite clear to Abraham long before.

The king of Egypt, the pharaoh, thought they were in the wrong place too. Many years had gone by since Joseph had saved Egypt and the rest of the world from the terrible famine. This pharaoh had never heard of Joseph. And he was quite different from Joseph's pharaoh. That king was wise, generous and just; this one was none of those things.

He heard about the people of Israel and how fast their numbers were increasing. 'There are more Israelites in the country than Egyptians!' he shouted. 'If we're not careful, when there's a war, they'll join our enemies and fight against us.'

He was wrong, of course. The Egyptians far outnumbered the Israelites, and the Egyptians were a strong and powerful people. Yet fear filled the pharaoh's mind, and soon his fear turned into hatred, and his hatred into cruelty.

He made all the Israelites his slaves, and he had them working morning, noon and night – men, women and children, building cities for him. He was trying to break them. But the more cruel he was, the more children they seemed to have. So his men drove them harder and harder, and harder and harder, till the pharaoh thought they wouldn't be able to take any more.

He was wrong. His plan didn't work. He had to try something else. What he came up with next was truly horrifying – one of the worst things anyone could try to do.

There were two midwives working in the Israelite slave camps, helping to bring the Israelite babies into the world. The pharaoh hated Israelite babies, especially boy babies. They'd grow into soldiers one day, he thought, Israelite soldiers who would fight against him. He summoned the midwives to appear before him.

Their names were Shiphrah and Puah. The pharaoh summoned them into his presence, and when this pharaoh issued a summons, no one dared disobey.

'What does he want to see *us* for?' said Puah. 'We haven't done anything wrong, have we?'

'It must be serious if he wants to see us himself,' added Shiphrah.

So there they stood, in front of the pharaoh, looking down at the floor in front of their feet, hoping he wouldn't hear their knees knocking.

The pharaoh didn't have much to say. He didn't use their names, or even say hello. 'When you're helping any of the Israelite women, see if the baby's a boy. If it is, kill him. If it's a girl, let her live.'

That was all. He turned on his heel and left, while two slaves hurried Shiphrah and Puah out of the palace. They held back their tears till they were safely outside. They cried at the thought of killing babies. They cried too because they were so angry. Killing babies, newborn babies! They were *midwives*! Their job was helping babies to live, not die. That was what God had put them on earth to do, and they had more time for God than for that dreadful pharaoh.

So they took no notice of the pharaoh. They just carried on doing their work, and the Israelite women kept having lots of lovely bouncing boy babies as well as lovely bouncing girl babies.

But the pharaoh had his spies in the slave camps. He summoned Shiphrah and Puah to his palace once again.

'Why haven't you obeyed my orders?' he roared. 'I told you to kill the babies if they were boys. You've been letting them live! They tell me you haven't killed a single one. Why not?'

Shiphrah looked at Puah and winked. Her knees weren't knocking this time. Nor were Puah's. They weren't afraid of the pharaoh any more.

'Well, Your Royal-Ever-So-Divine Highness,' Shiphrah began. 'It's like this. These Israelite women, they're just like animals, aren't they, Puah?'

'Oh yes,' Puah agreed, 'just like animals. They have their babies so quick, we can't get there in time, can we Shiphrah?'

'Never,' Shiphrah said. 'Someone comes to tell us Mrs So-and-So's having her baby, and we rush round as fast as we can, don't we Puah?'

'Ooh, *ever so* fast,' exclaimed Puah. 'But we're always too late.'

'Always too late,' added Shiphrah. 'We get there and someone comes out and says, "She's had it already." And all we can do is say, "Oh, bother!" and go on our way. Isn't that right, Puah?'

'Oh, bother,' repeated Puah, and coughed loudly to hide a giggle.

The pharaoh frowned. He didn't know much about babies. He didn't know much about women either, or about midwives, and he certainly hadn't got the measure of Shiphrah and Puah. So he thought they must be telling the truth, and he let them go.

When they got outside the palace, they laughed so much they both got hiccups, and they had to pat each other on the back, which only made them laugh even more and get more hiccups.

The pharaoh gave up the idea of using midwives to carry out his plans. The Israelite babies kept being born safely, and God was very proud of Shiphrah and Puah. He made sure they had families of their own and that they were regarded as great heroines among the Israelites.

If only that were the end of the story, but the pharaoh was too crazy, too cruel. If the midwives couldn't do his dirty work, then his own people, the Egyptians, would have to do it for him. He issued a command. 'Take every boy baby born to any of the Israelite women,' it said, 'and throw them into the river Nile.'

Moses' Brave Mother and Sister

THE ISRAELITES were living as slaves in Egypt, under a cruel pharaoh who wanted to have all their boy babies drowned in the river Nile.

One day one of the Israelite women, called Jochebed, had a baby. It was a boy. She and her family were overjoyed and terrified at the same time. He was a lovely baby, with great big brown eyes, and black hair that stuck out at all angles. But what if the Egyptians found out? They searched the slave camp regularly, looking for boy babies. Whenever they found them, they snatched them from their mothers and threw them in the Nile.

Jochebed and Miriam, the baby's older sister, kept him in the house for three months. Whenever the Egyptians came, they hid him, praying that he wouldn't start crying. They got away with it over and over again, but Jochebed knew it couldn't last. Sooner or later they'd find him. She came up with a desperate plan. She wasn't sure it would work, but it was the best she could think of. If the Egyptians wanted the babies in the Nile, then she would put her own child there. Only she wouldn't throw him in: she would make him a little ark – like Noah's, only much smaller and without the animals.

She made the ark out of strips of the papyrus reed that grew along the Nile, and made it watertight. Very early one morning, before anyone was about, she fed the baby, put him inside the ark and took him down to the river. She carefully hid the ark among the reeds. Miriam sat on the bank a little way off to keep an eye on him. When he got hungry and started crying, she would run and tell her mother.

After a few hours Miriam heard the baby beginning to cry. She got up and was about to run home when she saw the pharaoh's daughter coming down to the river to bathe. She was with her women slaves. Oh no! said Miriam to herself. Please God, don't let her find him! She hid behind a palm tree and watched. The princess got nearer and nearer. She reached the spot where the little ark was floating.

'Goodness me!' she said. 'What on earth is this?'

One of her slaves went to the floating basket and picked it out of the water for her. The princess opened the lid and looked inside.

Miriam's heart thumped. The daughter of that cruel pharaoh had found her baby brother. In a moment the princess would surely take him by the heels and hurl him into the river. She would no doubt obey her father's command, and enjoy doing so. Unless she thought the baby was Egyptian.

'Gracious!' exclaimed the princess. 'It's a baby boy, and he's crying for his mother! It's one of the Israelites' children.' Miriam heard what she said and gave up all hope. The princess had realized straight away that the little boy was an Israelite baby. She could hardly bear to watch as the princess took him out of the basket. But wait! What was she doing? She was giving him a cuddle! She was wiping the tears from his cheeks and rocking him to and fro to comfort him. Miriam couldn't believe her eyes.

Suddenly an idea came into her head. It was crazy, even crazier than the ark, but it might just work. She slipped out from behind the palm tree and went up to the princess. 'What a lovely baby!' she said. 'He must have been abandoned by his mum and dad. You'll need someone to feed him and look after him, won't you. Shall I go and fetch one of the Israelite women for you?'

The princess was tickling the baby's tummy. 'What a good idea,' she said.

Miriam went running off as fast as she could. The princess smiled. 'What have I done?' she said to her slaves. 'By agreeing to provide this baby with a nurse, I've just adopted him as my own son. An Israelite baby too. But he's so lovely! We can't leave him here to die. What *will* my father say?' Her face changed and she suddenly looked frightened. 'The pharaoh must never find out about this,' she said to her slaves. 'Do you understand?' The women nodded. 'Good. When this girl returns with someone to nurse the child, we'll go back to my part of the palace, where my father won't find him. He'll be our secret, won't you little one?' and she kissed him and held him to her cheek. She smiled again at her slaves. 'I think my bathing will have to wait till tomorrow.'

Just then Miriam came back, bringing her mother, Jochebed, with her. She bowed to the princess. 'This woman is willing to look after the baby for you,' she said.

Jochebed bowed low herself, and the princess put the baby into her arms. 'You must come back to the palace and look after this child for me,' she said. 'I'll pay you proper wages, of course. He's a lovely little boy, isn't he?'

Jochebed couldn't believe it. She grinned up at the princess through her tears. 'Yes,' she said. 'A lovely boy.'

So the baby grew up right inside the pharaoh's palace. His own mother was looking after him, and she was being paid for it too. The princess called him Moses. Her women-slaves kept their mouths shut. They loved the little boy too, so the pharaoh never did find out about him.

Moses Meets God in the Desert

MOSES GREW UP as a prince in Egypt. The pharaoh's daughter had adopted him, but his own mother, Jochebed, brought him up when he was small. Jochebed told him that he was not an Egyptian but an Israelite, and she taught him all the old stories of the Israelite people. Moses was safe in a palace, but Jochebed explained that the rest of the Israelites were living as slaves and were having a terrible time. The pharaoh was trying to break them by giving them too much work to do. Many of the pharaoh's people were as cruel as he was.

When Moses finally left the palace, he soon got into trouble.

One day he saw an Egyptian guard beating an Israelite slave as hard as he could with a stick. Moses looked about him. There was no one else in sight. He leaped upon the guard, killed him and buried his body in the sand.

The story got around about what he'd done, and someone told the pharaoh. It was time for Moses to get out of Egypt.

So he fled to the east, to the Sinai desert. There he settled down and married a woman called Zipporah, and they had a son, Gershom. Zipporah's father was called Reuel, and Moses used to look after his sheep and goats.

But God still heard the cries of his people, as the Egyptians worked them into the ground and beat them to death. God always had a sharp ear for people's sufferings, and he loathed tyranny and cruelty and bullying. He remembered what he'd promised all those many years ago to Abraham and Isaac and Jacob. He'd said that he would bless them and turn their descendants into a great nation, and that they'd live and prosper in a land of their own. He looked at his people, toiling away in the full heat of the sun. Something had to be done. He needed someone to help him carry out a new plan.

Moses was out with Reuel's sheep and goats as usual. Pasture was hard to find that day. He led the animals further and further from home, to the back of beyond, till he reached the holy mountain of God, Mount Sinai. Moses thought it was just another mountain. The desert was all mountains round there. However, there was a spring of fresh water, and the grass was good. He struck up a tune on his pipe, as the animals munched away.

Suddenly, he stopped. The pipe fell from his hand. What a strange sight! A bush, not far away, was burning. The fire inside it flickered and danced, all the colours of the rainbow. But there was no smoke, no ash. The fire was not destroying the bush, not even singeing it, not curling a single leaf, nor snapping a single twig! In

fact, the bush seemed more alive with the fire, and shone and
glistened with its flames. It was the most beautiful thing Moses had
ever seen. He had to investigate: he started walking towards it.

'Moses! Moses!' came a voice from the bush.

'Here I am,' he whispered.

'Come no closer!' the voice said. 'Take off your sandals, for you
are treading on holy ground. I am God, the God of your ancestors,
the God of Abraham, Isaac and Jacob.'

Moses stopped, amazed. Now he was closer to the bush, the fire
was not beautiful any more. It was like a furnace, and there, in the
middle of it, he could see the Israelites in Egypt. He shut his eyes.
When he dared to look again, the flames had changed shape, and he
saw the burning pain and love of God. He couldn't bear to look any

more. He hid his face in his cloak.

God's voice came from the bush once again. 'I have seen my people in Egypt, and heard them also. I have seen their bent backs, and the marks where they have been beaten. I have heard them crying out in anguish and moaning with pain in the dark hours of the night. I have come to rescue them and take them to the Land I promised them, a land flowing with milk and honey. I need your help. I am sending you to Egypt, to the pharaoh, to bring my people out of Egypt.'

Moses let the cloak fall from his face. He could not face the pharaoh, but he could face his God. He *had* to face his God and tell him it was impossible for him to return.

'I can't,' he protested. 'It's absurd. Why me?'

'I will be with you,' said God.

'That's all very well,' said Moses, 'but...' His voice trailed off. Desperately he tried to think of an excuse. 'Look,' he said finally, 'suppose I go back to Egypt and tell the Israelites you've sent me, and they say, "What was his name?" what shall I tell them?'

'Tell them, "I will be there as I will be there",' God replied. 'Tell them, "I will be there has sent me to you."'

That's not a name! thought Moses.

But God continued with a long speech about how he was going to rescue his people, and how the pharaoh would refuse to let them go, and how there would be all sorts of trouble, but in the end the Israelites would all escape and come to live in their own land, a land of milk and honey. Moses was only half listening. He was too busy working out some more excuses. He was sure to get killed if he went back to Egypt.

'But the Israelites won't believe me when I tell them I've seen you,' he said.

'I'll help you to convince them,' replied God.

'I'm no good at speaking out loud. I'm completely hopeless at it!'

'Then I will help you to improve.'

'Please, God, please! Send someone else!'

The flames of the bush shot up into the sky. God lost his patience. He wouldn't listen to any more excuses. 'You have a brother called Aaron,' he said. 'He will help you. He's on his way to meet you already. You'll be able to go back to Egypt together. We must get my people out of Egypt, and I need your help. That's the truth, and there's no arguing with it.'

So that was that. Moses would have to give up shepherding and return to Egypt.

God and the Pharaoh

WHEN MOSES RETURNED to Egypt, he discovered there was a new pharaoh in power. He was no better than the one before. He was still working the Israelite slaves to death.

Moses and Aaron went to see him. 'Thus says the Lord, the God of Israel,' they declared solemnly, "Let my people go! I wish them to come into the desert to hold a great festival for me."'

'Who is this nobody you call the Lord God?' sneered the pharaoh. 'I've never heard of him. I'll show you who's boss in Egypt. Get out!'

In the work camps, the Israelites were making bricks for the pharaoh. They had to make a certain number of bricks each day. It was far too many, and the work was killing them. But at least the Egyptian slave-drivers gave them the straw they needed for the job.

Now the pharaoh ordered that the Israelites would have to collect their own straw, but still turn out the same number of bricks. 'That should do it!' he cried. 'That will break them, you see if it doesn't.'

The slave-drivers had put some Israelites in charge of the work to make sure the proper number of bricks were made each day. But the people couldn't begin to manage it when they had to collect the straw as well. The Israelite foremen got the blame, and were savagely beaten as a result. They stumbled off to the pharaoh's palace to complain.

'You're lazy, and your people are lazy!' shouted the pharaoh. 'Tell your people to get on with it, or else!'

The foremen found Moses and Aaron outside the palace. 'A fat lot of good you've done!' they cried. 'Now the pharaoh's made things ten times worse, and there's nothing we can do.'

Moses felt completely helpless. What could he do? He was bitter, angry and frightened. He turned to God and prayed, 'Why have you brought such disaster upon your people, God? Ever since I came back to Egypt to confront the pharaoh in your name, he's brought nothing but disaster upon the people. And as for rescuing your people, you've done nothing!'

'I don't break my promises,' God replied calmly. 'I will save my people from the pharaoh. I promise I will. But it will take some time. I need to show him who's boss in Egypt first.'

And so began a long and terrible struggle between God and the pharaoh. The pharaoh clung on to his power for all he was worth. His country became ruined, just like the world before the Great Flood. But he didn't care, not at first, not until he began to suffer himself. Then he did get frightened and agreed to let the Israelites go. But as soon as things began to improve again, he became as stubborn as ever and went back on his promise. His religious

101

advisers told him he was fighting against a god and would have to back down. But he didn't listen. His political officials begged him to set the Israelites free. 'Can't you see?' they said. 'Egypt is completely ruined!' But he ignored them. He was on his own, struggling with God, and he wouldn't give up.

Everyone had deserted him. His own people were suffering terribly. The animals and plants of the country were destroyed; the land, the water, the air were polluted. Water was turned to blood, day was turned into night, hailstones the size of melons flattened the plants and the trees, and the land swarmed with frogs, gnats, flies, locusts and disease. It seemed in Egypt that the whole of

creation was being undone. Yet still the pharaoh would not give up; still he refused to set the Israelites free; still he thought he was greater than God.

Until one fearful night, when his firstborn child died. Moses had told the Israelites to get ready to leave Egypt. 'We are finally going to escape tonight,' he told them. 'But first each family must take a lamb from their flocks and kill it and eat it. Eat it with bitter herbs to remind you how bitter your life has been in Egypt. And mark the doors of your houses with some of the blood of the lamb.'

No one that night in any of the marked houses died. But in every Egyptian family the firstborn child died. Not just the pharaoh's child, not just the child of the rich merchant, but the child of the slave-woman who ground the corn, the child of the prisoner shut up in prison. Their animals lost their firstborn lambs or kids or calves as well.

A terrible cry went up throughout the land. Egypt was already ruined. Now it was drowned in grief.

The pharaoh summoned Moses and Aaron for the last time. 'Get your people out!' he cried. 'Go and worship your precious God. Go and have your festival. You have done enough.'

God Splits the Sea

AT LONG LAST the Israelite people were on the move! They had never known anything but slavery, but now the cruel pharaoh had let them go. They travelled as fast as they could towards the Egyptian border, their men, women and children, and all their animals, and reached the shore of the Red Sea. Soon they would be safe in their own land, the Land which God had promised to their ancestors, beyond the pharaoh's reach.

Then they heard a strange sound in the distance behind them. They turned round and looked in the direction from where they had come. At first all they could see was a cloud of dust, but then they could pick out the pharaoh in his fine chariot, with his charioteers and riders and foot-soldiers. They were coming after them!

The pharaoh had changed his mind again. He'd lost his own child, yet he found it more terrible still to lose his power. In his grief he'd told Moses and Aaron to get the Israelites out of Egypt, but now they were leaving, he couldn't bear to let them go. He couldn't stand being beaten. He'd show them and their God once and for all who was boss in Egypt. He, the great pharaoh of Egypt, would show them who really ruled the world. His soldiers would cut them to pieces. They were trapped between his army and the Red Sea. They had nowhere to hide, nowhere to run.

'What have you done?' the Israelites cried to Moses. 'You've brought us out here to die! It would have been better if we had stayed as slaves in Egypt. We won't be free at all, we'll all be dead.'

'Don't be afraid,' said Moses. 'Stand your ground. This will be the last battle between the pharaoh and God. Wait and see what God will do. You will all be safe.'

There were ancient tales of how, at the creation of the world, God had fought against the Dark Forces of Chaos; how he had slain a great Sea-dragon; how he had divided the waters to make the dry land; how he had defeated Chaos and brought order and beauty to the world.

'Don't be afraid,' repeated Moses. 'Our God is the world's Creator, not that pharaoh. This will be like the creation of the world all over again. A new world, a new freedom, a new order. Watch!'

He stretched his hand out over the sea. It split into two. The water piled up to right and left, and the dry land appeared in the middle. 'A new creation,' he murmured. The sounds of the Egyptian army were getting louder and louder. 'Come on!' he shouted. 'We have to get to the other side of these waters of Chaos before that old dragon of a pharaoh catches up with us. Quick!'

The people hesitated. The strip of dry land looked so narrow, and the walls of water on either side so high. Could they possibly make it across to the other side? Then the yelling of the pharaoh and the shouting of the soldiers reached them, and they remembered the beatings and the killings. They rushed forward.

The walls of water seemed ready to crash down on them at any moment. Behind them the pharaoh whipped on the horses of his chariot. He and his soldiers plunged onto the path between the waters. 'We'll catch them now!' the pharaoh shouted. But when his soldiers had gone some way from the shore, their chariot wheels started to get bogged down in the mud. Then their horses stumbled and fell, and the foot-soldiers got tangled in the mass of chariot wheels and flailing horses' legs. They panicked. 'This is God we are fighting against!' the soldiers cried. 'Turn back!' ordered the pharaoh. They tried to turn round, but it was no good. They fell over each other in a chaotic heap of bodies.

Meanwhile, the Israelites moved on, half walking, half running, dragging along their animals as best they could. Mothers carried babies in their arms. Small children rode on their fathers' shoulders. The old and the sick were carried on makeshift stretchers, or on people's backs. Somehow they made it to the far shore, every single one of them. No one was lost. Not a single animal was left behind. They could hear the shouts of the Egyptians, coming from the middle of the sea. No longer were they shouts of anger and violence but cries of terror. Above all the noise, they heard the pharaoh give one last cry. 'This is my world, my land, my sea!' he shouted. 'I am the boss round here!'

Moses stretched his hand over the sea. At once the two walls of water collapsed on one another. The strip of dry land was gone. The surface of the sea shone smooth and calm, and a deep silence fell upon the place.

The Mountain of God

MOSES LED HIS PEOPLE on through the Sinai desert towards the Mountain of God, the holy mountain where long ago he'd met God in the flames of the Burning Bush.

None of the people had known freedom before. They'd been born slaves. Their parents had been slaves, and their grandparents, back as far as anyone could remember. They were used to being told what to do. They hadn't been allowed to think for themselves nor take any decisions. They didn't understand how to survive in a desert either, and they had no knowledge of that particular wilderness. They had no idea where the oases were, or the wells or springs, or how they could find any food.

They complained all the way. They said they would die of thirst, so God made a spring of bitter water sweet enough for them to drink, and in another place made water gush out of a rock. They said they had no food to eat and would die of hunger, so God gave them food which seemed to come straight from heaven, called manna – thin, flaky wafers that tasted as if they had been made with honey.

They needed to be taught, like children. Like children, they needed to learn to be independent, make their own plans and decide things for themselves. And what better teacher could they have than God? That was why Moses took them to Sinai, God's holy mountain.

They set up their camp at the foot of the mountain.

Dawn came on the third day, and with it strange, unearthly thunder and lightning, bright fire and smoke. A dense mist settled on the top of the mountain, and the people heard a long-drawn-out

sound, like the note of a ram's-horn trumpet. The sound kept getting louder and louder, and the whole mountain started shaking violently. Moses began to climb its steep slopes and disappeared into the mist. The people waited for him at the bottom. Eventually they could see him climbing back down again.

'I bring you the Ten Words of God,' he said. 'This is his teaching for you, so that you can learn how to be his people in his Land. These are the Ten Words and what they mean:

"'I am the Lord, your God.
I brought you out of Egypt,
out of its life of slavery.

"'You must be loyal to me.
I will be your God,
and you will be my people.
You must not make any images of me.
I am beyond your imagining.

You must not worship wood and stone,
for wood and stone do not think or feel,
hear or speak, as I do.
Other, stronger nations
will have larger palaces and finer temples,
will tell you their ways are best,
their gods are true.
Do not follow their ways,
for if you are like them
how can you remember me
or why I chose you?

'"Heap no shame upon my head.
Do not drag my name through the mud,
or make people think I am nothing,
or worse than that,
a tyrant like that pharaoh.

'"Remember the Sabbath day
to keep it holy.
On that day your family must do no work,
neither your children,
nor your slaves,
nor the strangers living in your midst,
nor your animals.
You were slaves in Egypt, remember,
where they worked you to death,
every day of the week.
It must not be like that with you.
You are a free people

and must live in freedom
and give freedom to all.
Even I rest on the Sabbath.
I wish you to share my rest.

"'Honour your fathers and mothers.
They deserve much better than they knew in Egypt.
Give them back their dignity.

"'You must not murder anyone.

"'Husbands and wives must be faithful to each other.
You must not commit adultery.
You must treat each other with honour,
For you are not slaves any more.

"'You must not steal.
You must not drive anyone into poverty.
You must not make anyone look a fool,
or rob them of their freedom and their dignity.

"'You must not spread gossip,
or false rumours about someone.
You must not tell lies to get another into trouble.

"'You must not want more and more things.
You must not want what your neighbour or your friend has.
You must not make others poor
to make yourselves rich.
Let all live in freedom and honour."

'These,' said Moses, 'are the Ten Words of God. If you take them to heart and live by them, then you will be God's people, and he will be your God.'

More Teaching from God's Mountain

GOD HAD MUCH MORE to teach his people. He wanted them to put the world in good order again, as it had been when he'd first made it. Moses brought all God's teaching down the mountain. Parents taught it to their children, and they in turn learned to repeat the sayings, hundreds and hundreds of them.

'If your enemy's ox or donkey goes astray and you find it, take it back to them.

'If you see a donkey which has collapsed under its load, and it belongs to someone who hates you and whom you hate yourself, then you mustn't turn your back on him and just leave him to get on with it. You must help him unload the donkey and get the animal to its feet.'

'When you harvest your field, you mustn't cut the crops right up to the edge. Leave a strip round the edge for the people who don't have land of their own. And if you drop stalks of grain as you go, leave them for the poor and the people who don't have anything. The same with your vineyard. Leave some grapes for the poor and those who don't have any of their own to pick. Don't strip the vines bare.'

'When you build a house with a flat roof, put a parapet round the roof in case anyone falls off.'

'Make sure everyone can take part in your religious festivals. You'll have great feasts then and much wine. Make sure all your slaves join in, and the children or the old people with no one to look after them, and any strangers. You were once slaves in Egypt. You must never treat others as the Egyptians treated you.'

'You mustn't be cruel or unfair to the immigrants living among you. You know what it's like to be immigrants. You were immigrants once in Egypt.'

'Love your neighbour as yourself.'

'Love God with all your heart, with all your soul and with all your strength.'

The Golden Calf

NO ONE EXCEPT MOSES was allowed to meet with God on the summit of Mount Sinai. On all but one occasion, when a few others came with him, he went up on his own.

Yet God did not wish to remain high above his people, out of sight in the mist and beyond their reach. He wished to be among them, right in the middle of their camp. They were living in tents, and what was good enough for them was good enough for him. He told the people to make a tent for him out of reddened goatskins and rams' skins, with curtains made out of goats' hair. It was called the Tent of Meeting. God used to meet Moses there and talk with him face to face, as one speaks to a friend.

But God had ideas for a more splendid tent, which would commemorate the victory at the Red Sea and his meeting with the people at Mount Sinai, and which they could take with them when they journeyed on into the Land. It would be a sign that he was travelling with them wherever they went. The tent would be a place where everything was in perfect order, where everything was very good and very beautiful, just like the world when he first made it. The people had brought a lot of Egyptian treasure with them across the sea. He would ask Moses to urge them to give up some of that treasure to make the tent gleam and sparkle. Inside it there would be the ark of the covenant, a beautiful wooden box, covered in gold, containing two stone tablets bearing the Ten Words of God. In that beautiful tent, beside the ark, God could meet with them, and they could meet with him. Heaven would be on earth, and they could carry a little piece of it around with them.

That was God's wonderful idea, and he summoned Moses to the top of his holy mountain to give him the precise instructions.

Moses was gone a long time. So long that the people got fed up. In the end they gave up on him completely. They gave up on God also. They gathered in a great crowd in front of the tent of Aaron, Moses' brother, and demanded to see him. 'Make us a god,' they cried, 'a god we can see and touch, a god who will lead us on into our own land! As for Moses, we don't know what's happened to him.'

'Give me the gold earrings you brought out of Egypt,' Aaron replied. 'I'll melt them down and see what I can do.' There were so many pieces of jewellery that Aaron had enough gold to make an image of a calf. The people had heard stories of other peoples making statues of bulls or bull calves, and they believed those peoples worshipped them as images of their god. 'Wonderful!' they cried, when they saw what Aaron had made. 'This must be the god who brought us up from the land of Egypt.'

'Tomorrow,' said Aaron, 'we'll have a great festival, and we'll call the calf the Lord God.'

The next day the people got up early for the festival. They ate and drank and were very merry.

Up on the top of the mountain, in the middle of that strange mist where God was, Moses could hear and see nothing of what was going on below. But God could. 'Go down, quickly!' he said to Moses. 'The people have ruined everything! They have made a golden calf, and are worshipping it and saying, "This is the god who brought us out of Egypt."'

God was bitterly disappointed. After all he'd done for his people! When Moses had brought them the Ten Words from the mountain, they'd all said they would be loyal to God. 'All that the Lord God has spoken, we will do,' they'd said. And here they were, worshipping a calf. And to make it, they'd used some of the gold God had wanted for his new tent.

God's grief spilled over into anger. 'I've had enough of this people,' he said to Moses. 'I'll start all over again with you. I'll make a new people out of *your* descendants.'

Moses tried to change God's mind and soften his anger. 'You can't do that,' he said. 'Not after saving them at the sea and bringing them all this way. What would the Egyptians say? That you'd helped your people to escape, just so you could get rid of them in the desert! And what about your promises to Abraham and Isaac and Jacob? You promised to make *their* descendants into a great nation. You can't untangle the threads of the story of Abraham and Sarah, of Isaac and Jacob, of Joseph and Egypt and the pharaohs and the crossing of the sea. You can't unwind them and let them blow away in the desert wind. You must keep your word, God… or you cannot be God.'

God relented. He would not start all over again with Moses.

Yet when Moses got to the foot of the mountain and saw the people dancing round the golden calf, his own anger boiled over. He was carrying two stone tablets bearing the words of God. He raised them above his head and smashed them on the ground. Then he took the calf they had made, melted it down, ground it to powder, mixed the powder with water and made the people drink it. So much for their precious god! It would give them a tummy-ache and nothing more.

'What did you think you were doing?' he asked his brother, Aaron.

'Don't be angry,' said Aaron. 'You know what the people are like. They didn't know where you were, and they asked me for a god to lead them. So I got their gold and threw it in a furnace, and that calf came out.'

'You have done a wicked thing,' Moses said to the people. 'A very wicked thing. I'll have to return to God to make a new start.'

Making a New Start

THE MOUNTAIN WAS very steep. The desert ravens spread their wings, rose on the warm air and swung across its slopes with perfect ease. For Moses it was a hard climb. The mist hiding God still shrouded the summit. Before, he had found that mist strangely warm. This time, after the golden calf had been made and the people had danced round it, proclaiming it their god, Moses found the summit icy cold.

He turned to God. 'Can you bear to go on living with this people?' he said quietly. 'If you can't, then blot my story out of your record. Let it be as if I had never lived.'

'I do not punish the innocent,' replied God, 'and you are innocent. I will go on ahead of the people and make ready the Land for them. But I will not keep them company any more.'

'But that will mean we will not be your people!' cried Moses. 'We need you *with* us, right in the midst of us, in order to be your people. I know they've done a terrible thing, but mercy can work miracles, and forgiveness achieve the impossible. All things are possible for you, God, my friend.'

There was silence. The air grew a little warmer. 'All right,' said

God. 'I will live with them. I will go with my people.'

Moses wanted to be sure. There would have to be another new beginning. The stone tablets bearing the words of God lay smashed on the ground. No one could read the words now. And what about the new tent, the little piece of heaven on earth? The last time, when God gave his people the Ten Words, he had come with thunder and lightning, fire and smoke, earthquake and the blast of a ram's-horn trumpet. If there was to be a new start, God would have to come again with all his glory.

'Show me all your glory, God,' Moses said.

'You cannot see that,' said God. 'You and I are friends, Moses, but I must remain a mystery, even to you. I am God after all. But I will show you my goodness, and you will hear my sacred name. I will hide you in a crack in the rock, and as I pass by, I will cover you with my hand. You will see all my goodness, all the things I will give my people in the Land, grain and wine, herds and flocks, dancing in the streets, and life like a watered garden. That will be my glory. I will pass by, and you will see me as I disappear.'

The cold disappeared and the mist felt comforting again. A distant flock of white storks flew past the mountain, wheeling high in the warm air, flickering like stars as they turned. And God himself passed by, shielding Moses with his hand in the crack of the rock.

After that God gave Moses the Ten Words once again, and he carried them down the mountain to the people. The new Tent of Meeting would be made after all.

As he came down from the presence of God, Moses' face shone with all he had seen and heard. He didn't realize it himself, but his skin was shining so brightly that the people could hardly bear to look at him.

The Death of Moses

GOD MOVED ON from Sinai with his people. They were in the desert many years together. In the end all of those who had crossed the Red Sea died in the desert… except for three men: Joshua, Caleb and Moses himself. When they came to the very edge of the Land, the one that God had chosen for them, Moses gave to those who had been born in the desert all the teaching their parents had received at Sinai. Then he gave them his blessing. They were ready now to cross over the Jordan river and enter the Land.

They were beside a mountain called Nebo. 'Come up to the top of the mountain,' God said to Moses. 'I want to show you something.'

So Moses climbed up the mountain. He was a very old man, but he still had enough energy for the climb, and his eyes were strong. On the top of the mountain he could see as clear as could be. He looked across the Jordan valley and saw the Land, the one promised to Abraham so long ago, the one the people had so nearly lost when they made the golden calf. Below him, on the other side of the Jordan, was the great oasis of Jericho: a large, inviting splash of green in the hot landscape. But Moses could see far beyond Jericho. It was as if he had been given God's eyesight! He could see the whole Land from top to bottom, from north to south, and right across to the Great Sea, the Mediterranean.

And there, on that mountain top, the great Moses, the friend of God, died. The people would have to cross over the river without him.

4

LIVING IN GOD'S LAND

The first quarter of the Bible is taken up with a long story about the people of God, the people of Israel. It begins with a poem and stories about the creation of the world and the first human beings, and then has a wonderful collection of stories about their ancestors, Abraham and Sarah and their children, grandchildren and great-grandchildren. The first two chapters of this book covered those parts of the story.

Next, the story tells how the people of God find themselves slaves in Egypt, and how God and his friend Moses rescue them. It speaks of a sea split in two; of a journey through a dry, stony desert to the holy Mountain of God; of God's Ten Words, and of a great deal of other sayings which Moses brings down the mountain; of the people turning their backs on God and making a new god out of gold. That hurts God a great deal, but still he travels on from Sinai with the people. He has promised to give them a Land of their own, and he cannot go back on his promises.

Yet they take so long to get there that by the time they reach the Jordan valley, which marks its boundary, all but a tiny handful of those who escaped from Egypt and came to God's mountain have died. The people of God are now formed by the new generation that has been born in the desert. Moses hands on to them the teaching he received from God at the holy mountain. Chapter three of this book covered all that.

Now the people are ready to cross the Jordan and begin their life in the Land. Moses will not go with them. He dies on the top of a mountain the far side of the valley. But Joshua, who has also survived since the escape from Egypt, will take over the leadership.

That is where we pick up the story in the next chapter of this book, with stories from the books of Joshua, Judges, Samuel and Kings.

The Fall of Jericho

THERE WAS A PROBLEM with the people of God, the Israelites, coming to live in the Land promised to them by God: the Land was not empty. Many people were already living there and had been living there for a very long time, as long as anyone could remember, and much longer still.

When God's people crossed over the Jordan river, the first things they saw in front of them were the palm trees and the fields of Jericho, and the great walls of that city rising above them.

The Israelites were not like their parents, who had come out of Egypt as frightened slaves, unable to look after themselves. The ones who crossed the Jordan had been born in the desert. The desert was a tough place, and it had made them hard also, as hard as rock. They were ready for anything.

They had a new leader, Joshua. He'd been trained for the task by Moses. Joshua had sent two spies into Jericho, and they'd come back saying the inhabitants were terrified of them.

And God was still with them, camped in the middle of them, in the Tent of Meeting, a little piece of heaven on earth. In the desert they'd made a golden box. 'The ark of the covenant of the Lord of Hosts' they called it. It lived in the Tent of Meeting and contained the Ten Words of God. With the ark in their midst, with God on their side, they were ready for anything.

The people of Jericho were indeed very scared, just as Joshua's spies had reported. They'd seen the Israelites massing on the far side of the Jordan, but they hadn't dreamed they would be able to get across. The river was in flood, the water deep and the current strong. But they'd walked across it as if they were walking on dry ground! A story had reached Jericho many years before about the Israelites walking on a strip of dry land across the Red Sea when they escaped from Egypt. The great pharaoh, the king of Egypt, had pursued them into the sea with his army, but just as the last of the Israelites reached the other side, the waters had collapsed and every one of the Egyptians had been drowned.

And there they were, this strange, desert people, who could walk through water, camped between their city and the river, on the very edge of their land.

They left their fields as quickly as they could. They drove all their animals inside the stout city walls. They shut the gates tight, barred them with thick planks of timber and waited for the siege to begin.

It was the strangest siege imaginable. The Israelites left their camp and marched round the city in a long procession. There were armed soldiers in the procession, plenty of them, but they didn't do anything except march slowly round the walls. In the middle of the procession were seven priests, dressed in fine robes of gold and blue, purple and crimson red. They wore bright turbans on their heads, and gold chains and precious stones flashed in the sun from their shoulders and their chests. Behind the priests, at the very heart of the procession, came other men carrying a gold box on long poles. The box shone more brightly than the sun. In front of it the priests blew seven trumpets made out of ram's horns.

That was all. The Israelites processed round the walls of the city, with the priests blowing their trumpets, and then they went back to their camp, taking their gold box with them! The people of Jericho couldn't make it out at all, but they still didn't feel it was safe to

leave the city. In fact, the procession left them feeling more uneasy still. What would the Israelites do next?

The answer came the next day. They did exactly the same! And the day after that, and three days after that. For six days the Israelites processed round the city walls, with their shining gold box on its long poles, and the seven priests blowing their ram's horns. And still nothing happened. No attack, no war cry even. Just the slow procession, the Israelite soldiers saying nothing, looking straight ahead, and the continual sound of the ram's horns. Each time they would go once round the walls, and then they would return to their camp near the river. What was going on? Well, if necessary they could put up with this for weeks, months even. A spring brought fresh water into the city, and they had plenty of food stored away.

Then came the seventh day. The sun was hidden behind clouds. This time the procession started early, at dawn, and wound its way round the city seven times. Then it came to a halt. The people of Jericho watched from the walls as the Israelites turned to face them. They braced themselves for an attack. Their hands gripped their weapons tightly. Someone who appeared to be the leader of the Israelites turned and said something to the line of troops and to the priests. It was Joshua. They couldn't hear what he said, but as soon as he'd finished, the priests blew a long-drawn-out note on their ram's horn trumpets. It was not like the sound they'd made before. It was the same as the noise the Israelites had once heard at the holy mountain of Sinai, just before God had given them the Ten Words. It seemed not to come from the priests or their trumpets at all but from heaven. At the same moment the sun came out from behind the clouds and burst in one blinding flash from the ark, and the Israelites gave a great shout. It was not a war cry, but the shout of triumph they made when God showed himself in their midst. Till then they'd kept silent during their processions round the city. Now it was as if the sound had been building up inside them all that time, and it exploded from them in one huge, earth-shattering cry.

It didn't shatter the earth, but, together with that mysterious blast of the ram's horns, it broke the ancient walls of Jericho. For thousands of years they'd withstood storm and earthquake. But they couldn't stand that shout, nor that bellowing of the ram's horns, nor the burst of light from the ark. They collapsed as if they had been made of straw.

The Israelite soldiers clambered over the rubble, went into the city and killed every person and every animal inside it: men, women and children, old people, babies, cattle, sheep and donkeys. Except for a woman called Rahab and her relatives, because when Joshua's spies had entered the city, Rahab had given them shelter and information, and then had helped them escape.

A fearful silence settled over the place.

At the beginning, when they were not yet a people but only a family, God had told their ancestor Abraham to be a blessing to all those he met. 'Remember, Abraham, be a blessing!' God had said. The Israelites at Jericho seemed to have forgotten that entirely.

Eluma, a Woman Despised

IT WASN'T EASY LIVING in the Land of God. It wasn't all collapsing walls and battles won without a fight. The Israelite tribes did not have the best fields, nor the strongest towns. The people already living in the Land had those. And there were serious threats from outside the Land also, particularly from the Philistines, who lived beside or near the Great Sea.

Many years after the time of Joshua, the Philistines gained control of the Land and held power there for a generation. It was a long time, and to the Israelite tribes it seemed it would go on for ever. The days of Moses and Joshua were long gone. They needed a new leader, a new hero.

There was an Israelite couple who lived close to the heart of Philistine territory. The husband was called Manoah, and his wife Eluma. They had no children. The years went by, but still no child arrived. Their childlessness was very hard for them to bear, particularly for Eluma. The other women in the village all had children.

Manoah felt ashamed of his wife. He believed it was all her fault. It was her job to have children and bring them up, and she wasn't doing it. It was her job to produce a son in particular, for if they had no son, who would look after them when they were old, and what would happen to his farm and to his family line when he died? Everything would simply disappear. There would be nothing left. That's what Manoah thought anyway.

Eluma felt even worse. Her husband despised her. She thought the other women must despise her too. Certainly she despised herself. Every day, when the other villagers were praying for God to send someone to rid them of the Philistines, Eluma prayed for a child.

'Please, God, please. Give me a child,' she prayed. 'You are the God of life. Without a son I'm as good as dead, and so is Manoah.' She prayed that prayer every day, but still no child arrived. She kept on praying, but her hope was shrinking to nothing, and her God seemed in another world, a world shut off from her own, where her words could not be heard, and her pain could not be felt.

Then one day her little room filled with light. It was the very light of God! God spoke to her, spoke with her face to face. And what words he said! The words she'd longed to hear for so long, for so many years, and words more extraordinary than ever she'd expected to hear.

'You will have a child,' God told her. 'A son. Indeed you are already pregnant. I have a special purpose for him, so you must take special care of yourself. When your son is grown to a man, he will begin to save Israel from the Philistines.'

A child. A son. A hero! Eluma went to tell Manoah. She thought he would think she was stupid if she said God had been speaking to her. So she told him it was a man of God instead. But she tried to describe him. 'He looked like God,' she cried. 'He told me I'm pregnant, and he gave me special instructions about the child.'

Manoah wanted to see this 'man of God' for himself. Eluma was quite overcome by it all, but Manoah didn't see that. He didn't even notice how pleased she was to be expecting a child, nor did he share her joy. He just wanted to know what was going on. 'Excuse me, God,' he prayed. 'That man you sent. Could you send him again? I want to meet him and hear him for myself.'

God heard Manoah's prayer, but instead of appearing to him, he met Eluma once more, when she was on her own in the fields. Eluma ran straight away to Manoah.

'That "man" who came to me the other day,' she cried. 'Well, he's appeared to me again!'

Manoah was furious. It wasn't right for any man to meet with his wife, certainly not without his permission, and without him being there. Who was this man, and what was he up to? 'Take me to this man of yours!' he shouted.

So Manoah strode off behind his wife to where God was waiting.

Blinded by jealousy and suspicion, Manoah couldn't see who it was. God was in front of his eyes, but he couldn't recognize him. He couldn't even be polite.

'Are you the man who spoke to this woman here?' he asked rudely. 'Suppose what you said is true, and she has a son. What are your special instructions about the way we must bring him up?'

'I have already told "this woman", as you call her,' God replied. 'She knows what to do.'

This is outrageous! thought Manoah. This stranger has the cheek to talk to me as if my wife is more important than me. I'll have to sort him out and find out what's really going on between them. I've got an idea. If I invite him to dinner, then I'll have a chance to watch him closely and ask him some awkward questions. He cleared his throat and put on his most polite voice. 'Please stay a while and have a meal with us,' he said. 'My wife will prepare us a nice, tender goat stew.'

God's eyes twinkled. He winked at Eluma. 'I think a sacrifice to God, to show your thanks to him for the promise of a child, would be more appropriate,' he said.

Manoah began to wonder. Who *was* this stranger? 'What is your name?' he asked.

'My name is beyond telling,' God replied.

That should have settled it. That should have made Manoah realize who he was speaking to, but he didn't. At least he went ahead and prepared the sacrifice, as the 'man' had suggested.

The fire of the sacrifice flickered and danced, all the colours of the rainbow. Suddenly Manoah and Eluma saw the mysterious stranger as if caught up in the flames. He shone with the bright glory of God. Then the flames leaped up as high as heaven, and the stranger disappeared.

At last Manoah realized who the stranger was. Eluma had

known all along, of course. 'We will die!' cried Manoah. 'We have seen God!'

'What do you mean, die?' Eluma replied. 'Of course we won't die! We're going to have a son. We're going to have a son!'

And so they did, and Eluma called him Samson.

Hannah, a Woman Without a Child

WHEN SAMSON GREW UP, he did break the Philistines' grip on God's Land, for a time at least, but he was not the man to make God's greatest plan come true. God wanted all the families of the earth to find blessing through the descendants of Abraham. Samson was not the man for that job. God needed a different leader, someone who would understand his ways and see things the way he saw them.

Sometimes it seemed that God chose the most difficult path! He wanted a new, great leader for his people, and he chose Hannah to be his mother. But Hannah couldn't have children, or she thought she couldn't. She was married to a man called Elkanah. He had another wife as well, Peninnah. Peninnah had children, but Hannah had none.

Every year Hannah and Elkanah, with Peninnah and her children, used to go on a private, family pilgrimage to a shrine at a place called Shiloh, about fifteen miles from their village. They would worship God and offer sacrifices to him, and eat wonderful meals and drink lots of wine. It should have been marvellous, but Hannah dreaded it. There they were, thanking God for all his blessings, when God had not blessed her with a single child. The whole thing made Hannah feel empty and useless. And Peninnah always made things much worse. She would stand there with her children running round her ankles, and the latest baby in her arms, telling Hannah God must be punishing her for something she'd done wrong. 'That's why you haven't got any children like me,' she would say. It was a dreadful idea, that God would punish anyone like that, but Hannah couldn't get it out of her head. Elkanah did his best, but he didn't really understand. Mind you, life wasn't easy for Peninnah either. She had Elkanah's children, but he didn't love her. He only loved Hannah. But Hannah couldn't have any children.

The meals they had at Shiloh were always difficult, but one year Peninnah was even worse than normal, and Hannah couldn't take it any more. She couldn't eat a thing. She felt completely alone and burst into tears.

'What's the matter, Hannah?' Elkanah asked. 'I know it's hard not having a child, but you mustn't let it spoil things. And anyway, am I not worth more than ten children to you?'

Let it spoil things! Hannah said bitterly to herself. Can't you see, things will always be spoiled for me until I have a child? You can't possibly make up for me not having children. You should know that. Of course, *you*'ve got children, haven't you – Peninnah's. It doesn't seem to matter to you whether I have them or not.

But she didn't say any of this out loud. Instead, she got up, left the family meal and went to pour her heart out to God.

Eli, the priest of the shrine, was sitting near the entrance of the temple. Shiloh was a very important place in those days, and Eli was a very important man. Everyone agreed with that, including Eli himself.

The tears streamed down Hannah's face as she prayed, and she couldn't stop herself shaking. She spoke the words of her prayer silently. Her lips moved, but she made no sound. Eli watched her closely.

> 'My God, my friend,' she prayed.
> 'Look at me!
> See my misery!
> Remember me;
> do not forget me.
> Give me a child,
> a son,
> and I will give him back to you.
> I will dedicate him to you
> for his whole life.
> That is my solemn vow.'

It was an extraordinary prayer. This woman who wanted a child so desperately was willing, if she had one, to give him away to God. But Eli didn't even realize she was praying. He called across to her. 'You're drunk, woman!' he shouted. 'Go and sober up, and stop making such a nuisance of yourself!'

That would have been enough to silence many women, and many men too. But Hannah was made of sterner stuff. 'I'm not drunk,' she protested, 'just extremely upset. I've been pouring out my troubles to God, that's all.'

Eli felt a little ashamed. 'Then go in peace,' he said. 'And may God grant you what you have prayed for.'

And God did. He did see her misery. He did not forget her. Soon she had a son, and she called him Samuel.

When Samuel was three years old and Hannah had stopped breast-feeding him, she took him to Shiloh with her, together with a young bull, some flour and some wine as presents for God. She held Samuel's hand and led him to Eli. 'Do you remember me?' she said. 'I was the woman you saw praying. I was praying for a son. Here he is! I vowed that if I had a son, I would dedicate him to God. So keep him. He can live here in this holy place and keep God company.' Then she let go of Samuel's hand.

So Hannah returned home without her son. Every year, when she and the rest of the family went to Shiloh for their annual pilgrimage, she would take him a new robe to wear. Eli would bless her and Elkanah and say, 'May God give you many more children to thank you for giving Samuel to him.'

God did. Hannah had three more sons and two daughters.

'Samuel! Samuel!'

SHILOH WAS A HOLY PLACE. The Tent of Meeting was there and the ark of the covenant too. But holy places need holy men and women if they are to shine with the holiness of God. The priests of Shiloh, Eli and his sons, were not holy men. His sons were just out for what they could get. They had no respect for God, nor for those who came to worship at the shrine, nor for the women they worked with. Eli was old and had lost his eyesight, and when he told his sons off, they refused to listen. Eli himself felt out of touch with God. The people who came to Shiloh no longer found God there. No longer did he speak to them face to face as one speaks to a friend, as he had with Moses. He seemed shut up in a silent and invisible heaven.

Things had begun to change, however, when Hannah had come

to Shiloh to meet with God and had found his generosity. She hadn't seen God, nor heard his voice, for Eli had interrupted when he thought she was drunk. But she had poured out her soul to God, and he had filled her to the brim with joy by giving her a son. Then she had added her own generosity to God's. She had given her son, Samuel, back to God. Samuel was at Shiloh, the living proof of the generosity of God and of the generosity of a remarkable woman.

Samuel was still a young boy. One night he lay asleep inside the temple, near the ark.

'Samuel! Samuel!' He heard a voice speaking inside his head.

He woke up. 'Here I am,' he said. It must be Eli calling me, he thought. So he ran to find out what Eli wanted. 'Here I am,' he said. 'You called me.'

'I didn't call you,' said Eli. 'Go back to bed.'

So Samuel went back to bed.

'Samuel!' The voice came a second time.

Again Samuel got out of bed and went to Eli. 'Here I am. You called me.'

'I didn't call you, my son,' said Eli. 'Go back to bed.'

'Samuel!' The voice came a third time, urgent, insisting.

A third time Samuel got out of bed and went to Eli. 'Here I am,' he said. 'You called me. Really you did.'

Suddenly Eli saw the truth. The strange voice must be the voice of God! He said to Samuel, 'Go and lie down, and if you hear the voice again, say, "Speak Lord, for your servant is listening."'

Samuel went and got back into bed. God came and stood beside him. 'Samuel! Samuel!' he said.

'Speak, for your servant is listening,' replied Samuel, and, Bother! he thought. I missed out 'Lord'. He was just about to say it again, properly, when God started speaking once more.

'I'm about to do something extraordinary in Israel,' God said. 'The news of it will make people's ears tingle. Eli and his sons are the most powerful men in Israel, but I'm going to take their power away from them. The sons are wicked men, and Eli is too weak to stop them. People who come to Shiloh should find my generosity. Instead all they find is the greed of Eli's sons. I need someone to take their place, someone who comes from my generosity and knows it. I need you. You must show me to the people.'

The silence of the night returned. The distant barking of a fox was the only sound to be heard. The little boy lay on his bed, his eyes wide open, unable to say anything. He got no more sleep that night.

In the morning he got up as usual and opened the doors of the house of God to let in the sun. What could he say to Eli? He hoped he wouldn't have to say anything. Then he heard a voice calling him. 'Samuel, my son!' He recognized the voice at once. It was Eli's.

He went over to Eli. 'Here I am,' he said.

'What did God say to you last night?' asked Eli. 'Tell me everything.'

Samuel told him what God had said. He was shaking as he spoke, thinking that Eli would explode with anger.

He finished, and there was silence. Eli did not get angry. Instead he got up and went quietly over to his seat at the entrance to the temple. He watched the sun as it rose above the hills to the east. 'It is the Lord,' he said quietly. 'It is God. Let him do whatever seems best to him.'

King Saul

GOD FIRST APPEARED to Samuel when he was a young boy. After that, God spoke with him many times. When Samuel grew up, people heard about the things he was doing at Shiloh, and came to consult him there. If they couldn't seem to hear God speaking for themselves, they would come to Samuel, and he would tell them what God was saying. Samuel could see things through God's eyes. He knew God's mind.

Meanwhile, the Philistines remained their enemies, and the Israelite tribes were still very frightened of them. With Samuel as their leader, they were sometimes able to keep the Philistines at bay. At other times, however, the Philistines attacked their towns and villages, and caused them terrible suffering. And Samuel was getting old. Everyone knew he wouldn't be around for ever, and then what would happen? His sons were scoundrels, no better than the sons of Eli had been. Would God be able to find another leader like Samuel? The people didn't know, so they decided to make plans of their own.

'Give us a king,' they said to Samuel. 'All the other nations have kings. How can we become a proper nation, if we don't have a king?'

'But God is your king,' said Samuel. 'That's what makes you different from other nations.'

'No, we want to be like the others,' the people replied. 'Give us a king!'

'A king will take all your best land for himself, and your best slaves and your best animals,' protested Samuel. 'You'll have to give him a tenth of your grain and your wine and olive oil. You'll have to fight his battles, and plough his ground, and cook his meals and bake his bread. He'll want more and more. He'll make you poor, to make himself rich. He'll not let you live in freedom and honour. You'll all become his slaves.'

'We want a king!' the people shouted, 'We want a great king over us, like the other nations. We want a king to fight our battles.'

So they got one, and this is how it happened.

A rich man called Kish had a son named Saul. He was still quite young. His beard hadn't started growing, but he was very tall. He was already taller than anyone else in the land, and he was very handsome too.

One day some of Kish's donkeys went missing. He said to Saul, 'Take one of the servant boys and go and find them and bring them back.'

So Saul chose his favourite servant, and the two boys put some food in their bags, took some leather bottles of water and went off in search of the donkeys. They carried on looking for them for nearly three days, but still they couldn't find any trace of them. In the end Saul became worried. 'We'd better go back home,' he said to his friend, 'or else my father will start worrying about us.'

The servant boy pointed to a town on a hill nearby. 'There's a man of God in that town,' he said. 'Let's go and find him. He'll be able to tell us where the donkeys are.'

'But we haven't got anything to give him,' Saul replied. 'We'll have to give him a present, and we haven't got anything. All our food's gone, and we haven't got any money.'

'Oh yes we have,' the servant boy said triumphantly. 'Look!' He reached into the bottom of his bag and pulled out a small heap of silver.

'Excellent!' cried Saul. 'Let's go!'

As they were climbing up the track towards the gates of the town, they met some girls walking towards them, carrying jars on their heads. They were coming out to the town well to fetch some water.

'Is the man of God in the town?' the boys asked.

'Yes,' the girls answered. 'You've come at just the right time. There's going to be a great feast, and the man of God is going to bless the food before everyone starts eating. If you hurry, you'll just catch him.'

The boys ran on up the track. As they were going through the town gates, the man of God bumped into them. He was none other than Samuel himself. The boys had never met him before, and they didn't know who he was.

Now the day before, Samuel had heard God speaking in his ear. 'Tomorrow,' God had said, 'I will send you a young man whom you must anoint king over my people Israel. I cannot bear to see how my people are suffering at the hands of the Philistines. I've heard their cries of terror, their wailing grief, their sobbing in the dark of the night. This young man will save them and give them back their freedom.'

The moment Samuel set eyes on Saul at the entrance into the town, God whispered to him, 'This is the young man I told you about. He shall be king over my people.'

Saul, of course, didn't hear any of that. He was just interested in getting his father's donkeys back and returning home. 'Excuse me,' he said to Samuel, 'do you know the way to the house of the man of God?'

'I am the man of God,' Samuel replied. 'Come with me and join me in the great feast. You can stay the night in the town and go back home tomorrow. Don't worry about the donkeys. Your father has found them already. There are more important things than donkeys to think about. You are the man the people of Israel have been waiting for.'

Saul was glad to hear about the donkeys, but he couldn't understand that last bit at all. 'What do you mean?' he asked. 'My tribe is the smallest of all the tribes of Israel, and my family is the humblest of all the families in the tribe. We are nobodies!'

Samuel said nothing, but led the two boys into the hall where the feast was to be held. All the great people of the town were there, but Samuel gave Saul and his servant boy the seats of honour. Then he ordered the cook to give Saul the best portion of meat. Saul's eyes grew wide when it was put in front of him. It was fit for a king!

What was going on? Saul couldn't understand it. He'd never been treated like this before. And when it came to bedtime, beds were laid out specially for him and his friend up on the flat roof. It was very warm at night, and the roof was the coolest place to sleep. It was the place reserved for honoured guests.

'What's all this about?' Saul said to his friend before they went to sleep.

'No idea,' his friend answered. 'But I'm not complaining!'

Next morning, just as the sun was coming up over the hills, Samuel called up to Saul and his friend. 'Get up!' he shouted. 'It's time to go.'

They went down the stairs into the street, where they found Samuel waiting for them. They started walking down the road together, but as they were approaching the gates of the town, Samuel said to Saul, 'Tell your servant boy to go on a bit and wait for you. I have something very important to say to you.'

Saul's friend carried on, till he was round a corner. Then Samuel took out from his pocket a small flask of olive oil. It was holy oil, and very special. He stretched up his hand and poured it over Saul's head. In a most solemn voice he declared, 'God has anointed you king over his people. You will reign over the people of God and save them from their enemies.'

And that is how Israel came to have a king.

David the Shepherd Boy

THINGS DIDN'T GO according to plan. Saul did his best, but his best never seemed good enough for Samuel. He grew up to be a brave warrior, but somehow he never seemed to be able to get things quite right. The Philistines still troubled the people also. In the end God wanted to start again. He decided he would find another king for the people, someone truly after his own heart.

'I want you to go to a small town called Bethlehem,' God said to Samuel. 'Take some holy oil with you, find a man named Jesse and ask to see his sons. I have chosen one of his sons to be king in Israel. I will point him out to you, and you will anoint him.'

'But I can't do that!' Samuel protested. 'If I anoint one of this man's sons, that'll make two kings in Israel at the same time. That's one king too many. Saul will kill me!'

'Just do it,' replied God. 'Go to the town and tell them you've come to offer a sacrifice or something.'

'But...' said Samuel.

'No buts,' said God.

So Samuel went to Bethlehem. As he got near the town, the people working in the fields spotted him. The first thing they noticed was his fine clothes. They looked at one another in amazement. 'No one posh ever comes to our town,' they said. Then one of the women recognized him. 'It's Samuel!' she cried. 'What's *he* here for? What have we done? We just want to be left alone to get on with our work.'

The elders of the town approached Samuel, trembling with fear. 'Do you come in peace, sir?' they asked.

'In peace,' Samuel answered. 'I have come to offer a sacrifice to God. I want you all to come to the sacrifice. Oh, and by the way, is there someone called Jesse in the town?'

One of the men coughed nervously. 'That's me, my lord,' he said.

'Come to the sacrifice, and make sure you bring all your sons with you,' said Samuel.

The men were still uneasy, but they did as they were told. The whole town gathered for the sacrifice.

Jesse and his sons were there. Samuel asked Jesse to present them to him, one by one. The eldest, Eliab, came first. He was tall and handsome, the very image of a king. This must be the one, Samuel thought.

'No, he isn't,' God whispered. 'I don't judge people by what they look like. It's what they're like inside that I'm interested in.'

Jesse presented the second eldest.

'No,' whispered God to Samuel. 'Not him either.'

So Jesse presented the third eldest, then the fourth, then the fifth, then the sixth and the seventh. Seven sons! Everyone in those days thought seven sons was the perfect number to have.

'None of those,' said God.

Samuel was confused. He addressed Jesse in his most solemn voice. 'God has not chosen any of these. Do you have any more sons?'

What's going on? thought Jesse. What does he mean, God has not chosen any of them? Chosen them for what? I thought we were just going to have a sacrifice. But he didn't dare say any of this to Samuel.

'Do I have any more?' he replied. 'Well, yes, one, sir. But you won't be interested in him. He's the youngest of the lot. Only a lad. He's down in the fields, sir, looking after the sheep.'

'Go and fetch him here,' ordered Samuel.

So Jesse sent Eliab to fetch the lad. He and the rest of his sons hopped about from one foot to the other and bit their nails. What was going on? And where was Eliab? He'd been gone for ages. Samuel just stood there in his fine clothes, saying nothing, staring in the direction where Eliab had gone. It was all very unnerving.

Eventually, they could see Eliab coming back, almost running, with his youngest brother beside him. Jesse presented the boy to Samuel. 'This is my youngest, sir. He's only a lad, as I said. I'm sorry, sir, but I did warn you.'

'This is the one!' God said to Samuel. 'Get out your holy oil, pour it on his head, and anoint him king over Israel.'

And that's precisely what Samuel did. Jesse and the older brothers could not believe their eyes. Nor could the rest of the town.

Then Samuel went home.

No one dared tell Saul what had happened. So only Samuel and the people in Bethlehem knew there were now *two* kings in Israel!

David and Goliath

DAVID THE SHEPHERD BOY sat and wondered. Samuel had anointed him king over Israel, but he was still looking after the sheep. His family kept quiet about what had happened, and so did all the other people of Bethlehem, where he lived. King Saul and the people of Israel beyond Bethlehem didn't hear anything. It was as if nothing had happened, except that now the brothers were jealous of David. They couldn't understand why Samuel hadn't picked one of them.

The people had chosen Saul as king to rid them of their enemies, the Philistines. But Saul was not succeeding: peace did not come. One day the Philistine army marched towards the watercourse called Elah to fight the Israelites in battle. They pitched camp on one side of the river bed, with the Israelite army on the other side. It was summer, and the river bed was bone dry.

The armies drew up their battle lines, shouting their war cries, facing one another across the valley. Saul waited for the Philistines to make the first move. He didn't have to wait very long. A man called Goliath stepped forward from the Philistine ranks. The armies fell silent. Goliath was huge, over two metres tall and very broad. He had a helmet of gleaming bronze on his head, a heavy coat of mail, and bronze greaves protecting his legs below the knee. He carried a sword, a javelin and a heavy spear. The Israelites had never seen anyone like him. He came swaggering down the hillside with his shield-bearer in front of him. He stopped and planted his feet firmly on the ground, and looked at the lines of Israelite soldiers from one end to the other. He shook his sword and spear at them and yelled, 'What have you come here for? Take a good look at me – I'm a Philistine! Now look at your king, Saul.' He roared with laughter, the cruel, mocking laughter of a man who'd always got his own way, and who enjoyed frightening, hurting and killing others. 'All right,' he continued. 'If you want a fight, you can have one. Choose a man to come down here and fight me. We will decide the battle, just the two of us. If he kills me, then you win. If I kill him, then we win, and your people will become our slaves.'

Silence fell over the valley. Saul and the Israelite soldiers were terrified. They had no one who could fight a man like that. They shifted uneasily, blinking in the sun. Then they turned and ran back to their tents.

Goliath went back to the Philistine ranks laughing. The whole Philistine army joined in his laughter. The valley shook with their mockery.

David's three eldest brothers were in the Israelite army. They'd thought David was too young to go and fight. He was still back home, about twelve miles away to the east, looking after the sheep.

Day after day at the watercourse, every morning and evening, Goliath came out from the Philistine ranks and shouted his challenge to the Israelites. Day after day the same thing would happen. No one from the Israelite side would dare come forward, so Goliath would return with that terrible laugh, and all the Philistines would join in. The Israelites felt smaller and smaller, and more and more terrified of Goliath. Goliath knew it and loved it.

Back in Bethlehem Jesse was waiting for his sons to come back from the battle. Weeks went by, and still they didn't come. Someone told him the two armies were still encamped facing one another. They didn't tell him about Goliath.

He realized his sons must be running short of food. 'Go and take this grain and these loaves to your three brothers,' he said to David. 'And take these cheeses for their officer. Find out how they are and bring me back something to show me they are safe. Be as quick as you can.'

When David reached the camp, the two armies were just taking up their positions as usual. He left the food with the man looking after the supplies, and went to find his brothers. He'd just finished greeting them when Goliath came out from the Philistine ranks and yelled his usual challenge. David turned. He heard what he said, and heard his laugh too, as well as the mocking cheers of the Philistines as the Israelite soldiers fled to their tents.

'Have you seen that man?' some of the soldiers said to David.

'Saul's going to give great riches and his own daughter in marriage to anyone who manages to kill him. He'll be a great hero.'

'Who does that Philistine think he is?' David said. 'We are the people of God! He's not just making you look like fools and cowards. He's trying to make the living God look like a fool and a coward too. Listen to those Philistines! They think our God is *nothing*!'

His brother Eliab heard what he was saying. 'Who do *you* think *you* are?' he cried. 'You're just a kid! This is grown-ups' work. Go back home and look after the sheep, and leave the fighting to us.'

But Saul got to hear about what David was saying and sent for him.

'I'll go and fight that Philistine for you,' David said.

'You can't,' Saul replied. At last he had a volunteer, but he was surely far too young. 'You're only a boy,' he told him. 'That Philistine's an experienced fighter.'

'But I'm a fighter too,' said David. 'Back home I've saved some of our lambs from the mouths of lions and bears. If God can help me kill a lion or a bear, then he can help me deal with that Philistine. The stupid bully thinks our God is nothing. Well, I know different!'

Saul hesitated. He looked at David more carefully. Then he said, 'Very well. Go down and fight him, and may God go with you! Here, take my armour to protect you.'

David put it on. He'd never tried on armour before. He could hardly walk! He was quick and agile, like a gazelle. This armour made him heavy and cumbersome, like an old, over-laden camel.

So he took it off and went out to meet Goliath in his shepherd's tunic, with his shepherd's bag, his shepherd's staff... and a sling. The Israelites watched him go, their hearts pounding. As he reached the bottom of the river bed, where the winter rains had washed the stones smooth, he bent down, chose five good stones and put them in his bag.

Goliath came lumbering down from the Philistine lines to meet him, his shield-bearer going in front of him. Goliath couldn't believe his eyes. After all this time was this the best the Israelites could do? He was just a boy! No armour either. No weapons even. (Goliath didn't spot the sling.) This was an insult! He, the great Goliath, deserved to fight against their greatest champion, and they sent him a shepherd boy with a stick.

'So you think I'm a dog, do you, and you can beat me with a stick? Come any closer,' he roared, 'and the lions and vultures will have you for breakfast!'

'You believe no one can touch you with your great sword and javelin and spear,' David shouted. 'But I've got the living God with me, the God you think is nothing. You don't know who you're up against, Goliath. Yes, the lions and the vultures will soon have plenty to feed on, but it won't be me!'

Goliath was enraged. How dare the kid speak to him like that! He gave a great shout and started to run forwards in his armour. David darted towards him, took one of the stones from his bag, put it in the sling, swung the sling as fast as he could and sent the stone spinning. Goliath didn't see the stone coming, but felt a sudden, sharp pain just above the knee. He stumbled forwards and fell flat on his face. His armour was so heavy, he couldn't move. He lay there, his face in the dust, his knee screaming with pain, while his shield-bearer scampered back up the hill to the Philistine ranks. David ran over to him. Goliath's helmet had fallen off when he hit the ground, but his sword still hung at his side. David stood over him, took the great sword from its sheath, raised it above his head and brought it crashing down on Goliath's neck.

The battle was won.

David on the Run

AFTER DAVID DEFEATED GOLIATH, things went remarkably well for him. He became a national hero, a commander in Saul's army, a member of Saul's court and the best friend of Saul's son Jonathan. Soon he married Saul's daughter, Michal, as well. Above all, he was the man after God's own heart. Whereas Saul couldn't put a foot right, David couldn't put a foot wrong.

But that became the root of the trouble – Saul grew jealous. He still didn't know about the anointing at Bethlehem, but he knew very well how popular David was. He decided to get rid of him.

One day Saul's jealousy boiled up into a great rage. David was playing the lyre, and suddenly, without any warning, Saul sprang up and hurled his spear at him, meaning to pin him to the wall. David leaped to one side, and the spear hit the wall instead. He ran out of the room and out of the palace.

He ended up hiding with a few of his soldier friends in caves in the desert, and Saul came with his army to hunt him down.

One day David and his men were in a cave overlooking the Dead Sea. They had gone right to the back of it, where it was pitch dark, and were keeping very quiet. Saul was coming! They could hear his men marching along the track that followed the shore – three thousand of them.

As Saul's soldiers got closer, the wild goats went scampering over the rocks. Their feet sent small stones tumbling down across the mouth of the cave. David and his men nearly jumped out of their skins. Then they could hear someone scrambling up towards the cave. They huddled back even further into the darkness.

A figure appeared in the light at the cave's entrance. He was unusually tall. It was Saul! What was he doing? He was on his own. He didn't look around the cave at all, but turned to face the entrance and squatted down. He had come to relieve himself!

David's men couldn't believe it. 'Now's your chance,' they whispered to David. 'You've got him!'

David crept forward, his sword in his hand. He came up behind Saul, and without making a noise cut off a corner of Saul's robe. Then he crawled back to his men.

Saul got up, left the cave and climbed down to the road.

'I shouldn't have done that,' David said to his men. 'Saul is the anointed king, specially chosen by God to lead his people Israel. I should have left him completely alone.'

Just as Saul was about to move on along the road with his soldiers, David went to the mouth of the cave and stood blinking in the bright sun. 'My lord the king!' he shouted. Saul and his men turned and looked up. Saul stepped forward a pace, and David bowed himself to the ground. Then he stood up and called out, 'Why do you hunt me, as if I'm your enemy? Look what I've got in my hand!' He held up the triangle of cloth he had cut off Saul's robe. 'I could have killed you back there in the cave. My men urged me to kill you, but I didn't. You are the anointed king of Israel, chosen by God to lead his people. I am not your enemy. See how few of us there are up here! I'm no more a threat to you than a dead dog – than one of the dog's fleas! And you come against me with three thousand soldiers. May God judge between you and me and decide which one of us is in the right.'

Saul could hardly see: his eyes were full of tears. 'Is that your voice, David, my friend?' he said. He didn't wait for the answer. He knew who it was. 'You are a better man than I,' he continued. 'I have done you harm, and you have repaid me with good. May God reward you.' His eyes cleared. He looked at the corner of his royal robe that David was still holding in his hand. 'You will be king of Israel,' he called. 'I know that now. You deserve to be king more than me.

'About turn!' Saul shouted to his soldiers. 'We're going home.'

But once he was back home, Saul's jealousy returned. He couldn't bear to think of David becoming king. So he set out again with his three thousand men.

David was still hiding in the desert, a bit further to the west this time. He didn't trust Saul, despite what he'd said.

He heard that Saul was coming after him again, and he sent spies to find out where their camp was. The spies returned and said to David, 'Come with us. We've got something to show you!'

It was dark, but they knew that stretch of desert very well. The spies led David and the others along a narrow track and up to the top of a ridge. They peered over the edge. There below them were Saul and his men, sleeping out in the open in the warm night air, snoring their heads off. David looked hard to see if he could see Saul. The moon came out from behind a cloud. There he was, right in the middle of his army, with his commander Abner lying beside him. Both of them were fast asleep.

David turned to his men. 'I'm going down into the camp,' he said. 'Anyone coming with me?'

'I'll come,' a man called Abishai replied.

David and Abishai slid down the ridge and crept through the camp. The snoring stopped. David and Abishai carefully stepped over the soldiers and wound their way between them. The men were all in a deep sleep. None of them woke up.

Eventually David and Abishai reached the middle of the camp and stood looking down at Saul and Abner. Saul's spear was stuck in the ground at his head, with a jar of water beside it.

'Let me take his spear and pin him to the ground,' Abishai whispered to David.

'No,' David whispered back. 'He is God's anointed king. God may make me king one day in his place, but I will not take his power for myself, let alone take his life.' He paused, then gave Abishai a grin. 'But I can take his spear and his water jar.'

David and Abishai tiptoed their way out of the camp and climbed back up to the top of the ridge. 'Hey, Abner!' David shouted. 'Wake up, Abner!'

Abner stirred. 'Who's that?' he said drowsily.

'You haven't been looking after your king, very well, have you, Abner? Where's the king's spear and the king's water jar, Abner?'

Saul and his soldiers were all wide awake now. Saul called out, 'Is that you David, my friend?'

'It's me, alright,' David replied. 'And I still want to know why you've driven me away from God's Land. What harm have I done you? Don't let me die here, out in this wilderness.'

'I have done wrong,' Saul cried. 'I have been a fool. Come back, David. I will never harm you again.'

But David still didn't trust him. 'Send one of your men to collect your spear,' he shouted. 'I spared your life tonight, because I know how precious it is. My life is precious too. May God save me and bring me through in the end.'

'My blessing be upon you, David,' Saul answered. 'You will do great things. You will succeed in the end.'

David and Bathsheba

DAVID NEVER DID GO BACK to Saul's court, and Saul never caught him either. In the end Saul was killed in a battle with the Philistines. After that there was a war between the supporters of Saul's family and the supporters of David. David's side was victorious, and the people proclaimed him king over all Israel. David made a city called Jerusalem his capital, and with great ceremony he brought the ark of the covenant there. Finally he managed to defeat the Philistines. Most important of all, God gave him solemn promises, like the ones he had once given to Abraham:

'I took you from the pasture, David,
from following after the sheep,
to be a ruler over my people, Israel.
I have been with you,
always by your side.
Now I will make you as famous
as the most famous people on earth.
My people have always been under threat,
ever since they came to this land of mine.
Now I will plant them firm,
and they will dwell secure.
No more shall wicked men oppress them.
No more will they tremble with fear.
I will give you rest from all your enemies.'

Those were God's promises. But God needs people to work with him, or else his promises are words left hanging in the air. Now he needed David to keep his people safe, to plant goodness, truth and justice in the Land, so that it might indeed become God's Land.

David was good at winning battles and at getting his commanders to win them for him. But he was not good at everything.

It was the spring, and late one afternoon. King David's army was away fighting about forty miles to the east of Jerusalem, under the command of Joab, one of David's generals. They were besieging a town called Rabbah. David himself stayed behind in Jerusalem. Now he was king, he had everything. He had started out as a shepherd boy in a small village, the youngest in a large family, the one everyone ignored or kicked around, the one left to protect the sheep and goats from lions and bears. Now he was a king, in his own palace, with wives and servants, and a whole army fighting his battles.

The afternoon was hot. David went to bed for his usual siesta. He slept for a few hours, then got up, stretched and went for a stroll on the palace roof. He glanced down at the houses beneath the palace walls and caught sight of a woman bathing. He stopped and looked at her. She was very beautiful. He wanted her. He must have her.

He summoned a slave. 'Who's that woman?' he asked. 'Go and find out.'

The slave returned, bowed low and said, 'She's Bathsheba, my lord, Uriah's wife.'

'Uriah's away fighting in the army, isn't he?' David replied. 'Go and get the woman for me.'

The slave did as he was told. In a few minutes he was back, dragging Bathsheba with him. David took her and slept with her. Afterwards Bathsheba ran back home.

A few weeks passed. The army was still away fighting. David had almost forgotten about Bathsheba. But then one day she sent one of her own slaves to the palace with a message for the king. It was very short. 'I'm pregnant,' it said.

It was a brave thing for Bathsheba to do. She couldn't know how the king would take the news, or what he would do.

David knew exactly what to do. He must get Uriah back to Jerusalem, back to his home and his wife. Then when the baby was born, Uriah would think it was his, and all would be well.

So he sent a messenger to Joab, telling him that Uriah must return to Jerusalem at once and present himself before the king in the palace. A few days went past. David grew increasingly nervous, but when finally Uriah arrived, he didn't show it. 'My friend!' he said. 'How good to see you! How is the campaign going?'

They talked for some time about the war. Then David got up and said, 'It's getting late. Go down to your house, relax with your wife and enjoy yourself.'

Uriah left David's presence. As soon as he'd gone, David summoned a slave. 'Follow Uriah,' he ordered, 'and give him this bribe.' He coughed. 'I mean this present.'

Uriah did not go home. Instead he slept at the entrance to the palace with the palace guards.

The next morning one of the guards reported to David, and he summoned Uriah once more. He did his best to hide his anger. He put on his kind, friendly voice. 'Why didn't you go home and relax?' he said.

'How could I?' Uriah replied. 'Joab, my commander, and Your Majesty's army are camped out in the open, and the ark of the covenant is there with them. How can I possibly go home to eat and drink and sleep with my wife. I swear I will never do that!'

David had to think again. 'Stay in Jerusalem today,' he said to

Uriah, 'then I'll send you back tomorrow.' But the next day he didn't send him back. Instead, he invited him to dine with him at the palace. 'Keep giving Uriah wine,' he whispered to a slave. 'I want to get him drunk.'

It still didn't work. David got Uriah drunk all right, but Uriah still didn't go home. Drunk or not, he couldn't think of doing such a thing. He slept again in the same place, with the palace guards. Again one of them reported to the king the next morning.

Right, said David to himself. If the man won't co-operate, I'll have to get rid of him.

He wrote a letter to Joab, the commander of the army. As Uriah was leaving Jerusalem to return to the camp, David gave him the letter. 'Give this to Joab,' he said.

Uriah wouldn't have dared open a letter meant for his commander, sealed with the king's own seal. It took him a couple of days to reach the Israelite camp. He handed the letter to Joab.

Joab dismissed him and opened the letter. 'When you next attack Rabbah,' it said, 'put Uriah in the front line where the fighting is fiercest. Then when he's in the thick of it, order the other soldiers to fall back so he's left on his own. I want him killed.'

Joab did as his king ordered. The plan worked. Several officers were killed, and Uriah was among them.

Joab sent a full report back to David. 'If the king gets angry about the loss of his men,' he said to the messenger, 'just tell him that Uriah is dead.'

The messenger went back to Jerusalem as fast as he could. He entered the palace to report to the king. 'The men of Rabbah came out from the city and attacked us, Your Majesty,' he said. 'Then we drove them back closer and closer to the walls. But their archers shot at us from the walls. Some of your Majesty's officers fell.' He paused and looked David straight in the eye. 'Uriah, one of your officers, is dead.'

David sighed. 'That's war,' he said calmly. 'People get killed. Tell Joab not to worry about it. He must renew his attack on the city and destroy it.'

Bathsheba heard about her husband's death. She loved him, and he had loved her. Now he was dead. She cried and cried, wailing with grief.

As soon as he could, David had her brought to the palace. This time, with Uriah out of the way, he could keep her. He married her and put her in his harem. In due course her baby was born. David could smile again. It seemed only right that he, the king, should have his own way.

David and Nathan

DAVID THOUGHT he'd got away with his plan to steal Bathsheba, but God knew very well what he'd done. God always took the side of people who suffered at the hands of those in power. When David took Bathsheba and slept with her, God was outraged. When her husband was killed and she cried and cried, God wept also. He couldn't let David think he'd done nothing wrong.

He sent a friend of his called Nathan to the king. Nathan was a prophet. Prophets spoke in God's name. 'Thus says the Lord!' they would say, and everyone would have to listen, whoever they were, even kings. Prophets spoke God's mind, saw things through God's eyes and delivered God's words to the people. They were not the servants of the king; they were the servants of God.

So Nathan came to David. The king acted as the chief judge in the land, and Nathan pretended to bring him a legal case for him to decide upon.

'There were two men in a certain town,' he explained. 'One was rich, with many flocks and herds, and the other was extremely poor, almost destitute. He only had one little ewe lamb. He loved that little lamb. It grew up with his children. They all loved it. The man used to give it some of his own food and drink. It would sleep beside him; it was like a daughter to him. Then one day a traveller came to stay with the rich man, and the rich man had to find something special for his guest to eat. He had more than enough animals of his own, but he didn't take one of them. No, he went and took the poor man's ewe lamb and served that up instead.'

David exploded in anger, 'As the Lord God lives, that rich man deserves to die!' he cried. 'He shall pay back the poor man four times over. What a thing to do! Completely without pity.'

Nathan looked straight at the king. 'You are the man!' he said.

There was a long silence. Then Nathan began to speak again, quietly, but with devastating effect. 'Thus says the Lord,' Nathan said, 'I gave you everything. You had everything, including plenty of wives. All Uriah had was Bathsheba. And you took him from her, just because you wanted her. You have ruined everything! With my help you rose from nothing to these great heights of power. Well, now I have seen how you use your power. This is the beginning of your fall, David. You have ruined everything, and everything will be ruined!'

God was right. Bathsheba's child died. She had another son, Solomon, but soon after he was born David's family fell to pieces, and a few years after that the country itself collapsed into the violence of civil war.

Elijah and the Contest on Carmel

SOLOMON SUCCEEDED his father, David. He became famous for his wisdom, wealth and power, and for building God a fine temple in Jerusalem. But there was another side to Solomon. He spent seven years building a house for God, but he spent thirteen building a palace for himself, and he made sure he finished the palace first. He surrounded himself with all the trappings of power. For some of the people of the land, for those who were already living there when the Israelite tribes came out of Egypt, Solomon was almost as bad as any king could be. Even the backs of the Israelites began to bend under the weight of his power. He also gathered a huge harem of foreign wives, who persuaded him to worship their own gods and build temples for them. He began to forget the God who long ago had brought his people out of Egypt.

After his death the kingdom split into two, and there was war between the tribes, fighting between men who had forgotten they were blood brothers. From then on, both in the northern kingdom, called Israel, and in the southern kingdom, called Judah, it was not kings but prophets who kept the rumour of the God of Abraham alive. The kings were usually more concerned with their own power than with the power and the honour of God.

One hundred years after David, Ahab was king of the northern kingdom of Israel. He had his kingdom under his thumb – except for a prophet named Elijah.

Ahab had a fine new capital city, which his father had built, called Samaria. He had married a wife called Jezebel, a princess from a foreign city called Tyre, on the coast of the Great Sea. One of the gods they worshipped in Tyre was known as Baal. Jezebel wanted Baal to be worshipped in Samaria too, so Ahab built a temple for him in Samaria, and he and his court worshipped there. Then Jezebel started killing the prophets of the God of Abraham.

Elijah was not afraid for himself, but he was afraid that the worship of the God of Abraham would be wiped out. He feared the people would forget the God of their ancestors, the God who had given them the Land, the God who was on the side of the poor, the helpless and the vulnerable. Instead, they would worship the god of the king and queen, the god of those in power, the god of those who lived in fine palaces.

Baal was a god of rain and lightning, rider of the clouds and master of the storm, and brought fertility to the Land, so his worshippers believed. Elijah declared there would be a terrible drought in the Land.

'I am God's man, not the king's,' he cried. 'I obey the Lord God, not the king. As the Lord God lives, I swear no rain will fall on the Land, no drop of dew will form, until I say so. We will see who is God in this Land. We will beat Baal at his own game. We will show you who it is who brings the rain, who it is who makes the crops grow and turns the pastures green!'

Then Elijah turned on his heel and left. He went to live far away from Ahab and his royal city.

The drought came and held the land in its grip for over two years. It was terrible.

Ahab became worried about his horses and mules. If his servants didn't find fresh pasture for them soon, the animals would die. He was more concerned about them than he was about his people. Yet some of the people were down to their last meal. That was the truth, and Elijah knew it. So did God.

God worked out a plan. He would bring the drought to an end, and he and Elijah between them would show the people what was what.

'Go and meet Ahab,' God said to Elijah.

Elijah set out. One of Ahab's servants called Obadiah was scouring the country at the time, looking for pasture for the king's horses and mules. Obadiah didn't follow the religion of the court – he was still loyal to the God of Israel. When Jezebel had started killing God's prophets, he had rescued a hundred of them and hidden them in caves in the hills, with stocks of food and water.

During his search for pasture, Obadiah bumped into Elijah.

'Go and tell your master I am here,' Elijah said to him.

'I can't do that!' cried Obadiah. 'Ahab will kill me! He blames you for the drought, and has been hunting high and low for you. You can't order him about, he's the king!' He paused for breath, then launched once more into his protests. 'People come to *Ahab*. They don't tell *him* to come to *them*. Anyway, if I do go back to him, and he agrees to come, by the time he gets here, you'll be gone, and then he'll blame me, and that'll be me done for. Haven't you heard what I did for the prophets of God, one hundred of them? I risked my life for them. And now you want me to lose my life, just because you, a single prophet, want to play a stupid trick on the king.'

'As the Lord God lives,' Elijah replied calmly, 'I swear I will meet Ahab here today. Go and fetch him.'

Obadiah shook his head, but did as he was told.

Despite what Obadiah had said, Ahab did come to meet Elijah. Elijah was waiting for him, as he'd promised.

'You are the ruin of Israel!' Ahab cried.

'No, you are!' answered Elijah. 'You have brought this catastrophe upon the country yourself, you and Jezebel, by claiming it is Baal's Land and not the Land of the God of Abraham, the Lord God who brought our ancestors out of slavery in Egypt. We will show you what's what, God and I. Summon all the people to meet with me on Mount Carmel and tell all the prophets of Baal to be there.'

Mount Carmel was a long high ridge, jutting out into the Great Sea. It was the first place in Israel to catch the rains that blew in from the sea, and usually it was lush and green, and strewn with flowers. But now it was parched, hard, unyielding, dull brown – as dry as the rest of the Land.

The people assembled on the mountain. Ahab was there, and the prophets of Baal too, but Jezebel stayed behind in the palace.

'How long will you dance to Baal's tune?' Elijah shouted to the people. 'You must choose today who you will follow. You must decide who is God in Israel – Baal or the Lord, the God who brought you out of Egypt.'

There was silence. The people shifted uneasily from one foot to the other and kept their eyes on the ground.

'Yes,' Elijah cried. 'Look at the ground! See what a desert it has become. Let's see now which god can make the lightning strike and bring you the promise of rain. We will have a contest.'

There were two large, round, stone altars on Mount Carmel. One was dedicated to Baal. The other one was dedicated to the God of Abraham, and that hadn't been used for some time. It was neglected, damaged, overgrown.

'We will slaughter two bulls and lay them on wood on the altars,' Elijah continued. 'But we will not set fire to the wood. We will call upon our gods to do that. Whichever god manages to set fire to his sacrifice, he will be God in Israel. Do you agree?'

'We agree,' the people replied.

Elijah had chosen bulls for the sacrifices on purpose. Was not Baal sometimes called 'the Bull', and was he not sometimes pictured with bull's horns? Well, his God would make sure Baal went up in smoke!

'You go first,' he said to the prophets of Baal.

The four hundred and fifty prophets of Baal prepared their altar, placed one of the bulls on the wood and called upon Baal to set fire to it. 'O Baal, answer us!' they cried. Nothing happened. 'O Baal, answer us! O Baal, answer us!' they shouted. Nothing happened. They shouted it all morning, dancing a strange, limping dance, till the fire of the noonday sun burned down on them. Nothing happened.

'Shout louder!' Elijah suggested. 'Perhaps your god is lost in thought. Perhaps he's gone off somewhere. Perhaps he's relieving himself or having a siesta!'

The prophets shouted louder, and louder still, and worked themselves up into such a frenzy, that they cut themselves with knives till they were covered in blood. And still they limped their limping dance. And still nothing happened. The sun shone down out of a clear, untroubled sky, empty of clouds, empty of rain.

Eventually Elijah had had enough. 'My turn,' he said.

'Come closer now,' he called to the people. 'Watch and see what will happen.'

The people moved forward. They watched as Elijah rebuilt the tumbledown altar of the God of Israel and dug a trench round it. He laid the wood for the sacrifice on the altar, slaughtered the second bull, cut it up and arranged the pieces on top of the wood. Then he ordered the people to fill four huge jars with water and pour the water over the sacrifice and into the trench. Three times he ordered them to do it, twelve jars of water in all. The bull, the wood, the altar and the ground around it were completely soaked, and the trench was full to the brim. 'All that precious water!' the people said to themselves. 'It's all we had! What's the madman playing at?'

Finally all was ready. Elijah stepped forward and prayed this prayer out loud:

> 'O Lord God, answer me!
> Answer me,
> that the people may know that you,
> the Lord,
> the God of Abraham, Isaac and Jacob,
> are indeed God in Israel.
> Let them know that you are the true God of the lightning,
> rider of the clouds and master of the storm,
> the one who brings life to the Land and all who dwell in it.'

Immediately a bolt of lightning fell from the clear sky. It ate up the bull, the wood, even the stones of the altar and the soaked earth around it, and licked up the water in the trench. It was all gone. There was nothing to see, except for a strange, unearthly light, flickering and dancing. There was no smell of burning, just the scent of heaven. The people prostrated themselves, bending their faces to the ground in worship. 'The Lord, the God of Abraham, he is God!' they cried. 'The Lord, he is God!'

'Then we must rid the Land of these wretched prophets of Baal,' Elijah cried. 'Seize them!' The people grabbed them, dragged them down into a dried-up river bed beneath the ridge, and there they slaughtered them.

A deep silence fell over the place. 'I can hear the rumble of distant thunder,' said Elijah. He and a servant of his went back to where the altar had been, just below the top of the ridge, to wait for the storm.

Elijah squatted down on the ground, his head between his knees.

'What can you see?' he asked his servant.

'Nothing,' the servant replied.

'Go and have another look,' Elijah said.

Five more times the servant went up to the top. Five more times he returned saying the sky was still clear.

Then after the seventh trip he came running back down. 'There's a tiny cloud in the west!' he cried. 'No larger than someone's hand.'

'We'd better tell the king to leave the mountain before his chariot gets stuck in the mud,' said Elijah.

The cloud grew and grew till it covered the sky and turned it black with thunder. The lightning fell, and then the rain – buckets and buckets and buckets of rain!

The drought was over. The Lord, the God of Abraham had brought life once more to the Land and all who dwelt in it – plants, animals and people. All, that is, except the prophets of Baal, whose blood turned red the stream of water rushing down the river beneath the Carmel ridge.

Elijah on the Run

AHAB TOLD JEZEBEL what had happened on Mount Carmel. That is, he told her how Elijah had mocked the prophets of Baal and had ordered them to be killed. He didn't tell her how the Lord, the God of Abraham, had beaten Baal in a great contest. He didn't tell her about the altar of God which Elijah had rebuilt, nor about the bull he had laid on top of it, nor about all the water poured over it. He didn't say anything about the lightning that God had sent out of a clear sky to eat it all up, nor about the people shouting, 'The

Lord, the God of Abraham, he is God!' He just told her about the prophets of Baal.

Jezebel had thought Ahab was stupid to go to Mount Carmel in the first place, let alone take all the prophets of Baal with him.

'You idiot!' she shouted. 'If you'd got rid of that troublemaker, Elijah, when you had the chance, none of this would have happened. Four hundred and fifty prophets – good, loyal men – dead! How will we get in touch with Baal now? Leave this to me. As for Elijah, I'll deal with him, you see if I don't!'

She sent a messenger at once to Elijah. 'A message for you from Her Majesty the Queen,' the messenger said. He cleared his throat and put on his most solemn, giving-messages-from-the-queen kind of voice. 'I swear,' he declared. 'I mean,' he added hurriedly, 'that's what the message says. It's not me doing the swearing, you understand, it's Her Majesty the Queen.' He coughed and picked up his official voice again. 'I swear by the great god Baal that by tomorrow you will be as dead as the prophets you killed at Carmel!'

He tossed his head, turned on his heel and left.

Elijah was petrified. When Jezebel said you were going to die, you were going to die! He would have to leave at once, get right away from Jezebel and the centre of her power. He would have to go to another centre, to the heart of God's power.

He took a servant with him. They left immediately and travelled for several days, always going south, until they reached a town on the edge of the desert, called Beer-sheba. There Elijah said goodbye to his servant. He would go on alone.

He went a day's journey into the wilderness. It was the same part of the desert where long ago an Egyptian slave, Hagar, had gone with her son, Ishmael. Elijah knew the old story well. Hagar had been the slave of Sarah, Abraham's wife. Wandering in the desert

with her son, Hagar had despaired of finding food and water, had placed her child in the shade of a bush and had sat at a distance, unable to watch him die. For Elijah, also, it seemed that the desert was a place of death: hard, unforgiving, silent and uncaring. Its loneliness hit him in the face. He sat down under a bush and prayed that he might die. 'Enough!' he cried 'Now, my Lord God, take my life. I am no better than my ancestors who came out of Egypt into the desert and failed you so grievously.'

Hagar had not been concerned for herself. All she'd thought about was her child. But Elijah could think of no one but himself. He felt very sorry for himself, and disappointed too. He had a journey to complete, and now he wouldn't make it.

Yet God had found Hagar and her child in that desert and shown them how to defeat its cruel hunger and its thirst. So now God found Elijah. He knew very well where Elijah was heading. He touched the sleeping prophet gently on the shoulder.

'Get up and eat!' God said. 'It's breakfast time.'

Elijah sat up, startled. He looked about him. There *was* breakfast! A cake and a jar of water. He ate and drank a little, but the despair of the desert lay heavy on him still. He didn't have the strength to move on. He would die under that bush.

God woke him a second time. 'Get up and eat!' God repeated. 'Or your journey will be too much for you.'

Elijah ate and drank some more, and now the despair left him. He remembered why he had come to this desert.

He travelled on until he came to Mount Sinai, the holy mountain behind the desert, in the back of beyond. Sinai was the place where God had met his people after bringing them out of Egypt, and had appeared to them with strange, unearthly thunder and lightning, bright fire and smoke, and the long-drawn-out call of a ram's horn. It was the place where God had talked with Moses face to face, the place where he'd hidden Moses in a cleft of the rock and passed him by, dressed in all the finery of his goodness. It was the place where God had been so hurt by his people's disloyalty, when they'd made a golden calf and started worshipping it as their god. God had threatened to start all over again with Moses and form a new people from Moses' descendants. When Elijah reached the mountain, he climbed some way up its slopes, then hid himself in that same cleft in the rock, the very spot where God had passed Moses by. He waited for God to appear before him, as once he had appeared to Moses. He waited for God to speak to him face to face, as one speaks to a friend, as once he had spoken with Moses, and make some solemn, earth-shattering pronouncement.

A quiet voice spoke. 'What are you doing here, Elijah?' the voice said.

It was the voice of God! Elijah recognized it at once. What the voice said was a bit disappointing, though. Elijah hadn't expected to be asked that. Still, if God wanted to know why he was there, he would tell him.

'I've been a fantastic supporter of yours, O Lord, Most High God,' Elijah cried. 'But I'm the only one left. All your people have turned their backs on you. They've thrown down your altars and killed your prophets with the sword. I'm the only one left who's still loyal to you, and they're out to take my life too.'

That should do it, Elijah thought. I know I've exaggerated a bit, but I mean to remind God of the golden calf that drove him into such a fury on this very mountain and made him vow to start again with Moses. Moses stopped him then. But Moses is not here now. I'm here instead, and God can start all over again with me.

'Come out of the cave,' the voice called again, louder this time. 'Come and stand out in the open. Come and stand in the presence of God!'

This is more like it! thought Elijah. But then a sudden, mighty wind struck the mountain. It seemed strong enough to break it in pieces. Elijah cowered back in the cave.

God was not in the storm.

Then an earthquake shook the mountain as if it was a rag and drove Elijah even deeper into the darkness of the rock.

God was not in the earthquake.

Then came a raging fire.

God was not in the fire.

The storm, the earthquake and the fire were all but empty show, and now they were gone. Huddled deep inside the cave, Elijah still waited.

A stillness settled on the mountain, and a strange, soft, gentle, drawn-out whispering sound, like a distant echo of heaven.

Elijah knew that sound. It was the sound of God. Now God would speak to him face to face, as he had with Moses. He came out of the cave, that cleft in the rock where God had passed Moses by, and stood at its entrance. Like Moses at the Burning Bush, Elijah hid his face in his cloak. He waited.

God did not appear to him, but for a second time on the mountain Elijah heard his voice. 'What are you doing here, Elijah?' God said.

Now that was *really* disappointing! Hadn't God heard him the first time? He'd better tell him again, only in a louder voice. 'I have been a fantastic supporter of yours, O Lord, Most High God,' he shouted. 'But I'm the only one left. All your people have turned their backs on you. They've thrown down your altars and killed your prophets with the sword. I'm the only one left who's still loyal to you, and they're out to take my life too.'

It was time for God to do some plain speaking. If Elijah thought he was going to start a new people with him, the people of Elijah instead of the people of Abraham, then he had better think again. God spoke plainly. 'You still have work to do, Elijah,' he said. 'I'm not going to give up on my people just because of an Ahab and a Jezebel. You can't escape from the world of their ugly, scheming power. I want you as my prophet again, back in the thick of it, speaking my mind, making sure my word is heard.'

That was all. But it was enough. Enough to bring Elijah to his senses, enough to turn him once more into a prophet of God. Back into the thick of things he went.

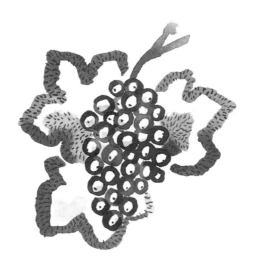

Elijah, Ahab and the Vineyard

KING AHAB HAD two palaces: one in his new capital, Samaria, and one in a place further north called Jezreel. Next to the Jezreel palace was an ancient vineyard. It was owned by a man called Naboth. Naboth's family had worked that piece of land for years, centuries even. They didn't own it. Like the rest of the Land, it belonged to God. That was their firm belief. It was God's Land, and when the Israelites had settled in it, he had allocated a portion of it to each of the tribes. Naboth's family had been given the plot that now lay outside Ahab's palace walls. Since Naboth didn't own it, he couldn't sell it. It had to remain as part of the family's inheritance, passed on from one generation to the next, for ever and ever.

But Ahab cared nothing for such beliefs, while his wife Jezebel, coming from the very different world of Tyre, where kings and queens did what they liked, did not begin to understand them.

Ahab wanted that vineyard. He set his heart on it, and so one day he approached Naboth. 'Give me your vineyard,' he said. 'It's right next to my palace, and I want to have it as a vegetable garden. I'll give you a better vineyard in exchange for it, or else pay you good money for it, if that's what you would prefer. I can't say fairer than that.'

'You can't have it,' answered Naboth. 'God forbid that I should give you the inheritance of my family! My ancestors came out of Egypt, and God gave their children this vineyard when they entered the Land with Joshua. It's not mine to give you. And anyway, the Land is God's, not yours. If you think you own it, you'd better think again.'

Ahab went back to Samaria and sulked. He lay on his bed, turned his face to the wall and refused to eat.

'What's the matter?' Jezebel asked.

'I wanted to get my hands on that vineyard at Jezreel, the one that belongs to Naboth. It's just by the palace. But he wouldn't let me have it. I made him a very generous offer, but he flatly refused to sell it to me.'

'For goodness' sake!' Jezebel cried. 'You're the *king*! You can have whatever you like. How dare Naboth refuse you! Who does he think he is? Anyway, you stop being so miserable; I'll get that vineyard for you.'

Jezebel dictated some letters. They read as if they came from the king, and they were sealed with his royal seal. She gave them to a messenger to take to Jezreel and hand to the elders and nobles of the town. She knew those men in Jezreel. They would not defy the king, like Naboth. They would do anything, if Ahab commanded it.

This is what the letters said: 'Proclaim a solemn fast. Get the word around that a terrible catastrophe is about to overtake the town, because of what someone has done, and that's why you are having the fast. Then call an assembly of all the men of the town. Give Naboth a seat of honour, where everyone can see him, and get two men who don't mind telling lies. Tell them to bring false charges against Naboth. They must say to his face, out loud, so everyone can hear, "You have cursed God and the king!" Then take him outside the city and stone him to death.'

Jezebel knew it would work, and it did. It all went according to plan – the fast, the assembly, the seat of honour for Naboth, the false charges, the judgment, the dragging outside the city walls and the stoning. The elders and nobles sent a letter to Jezebel in Samaria, giving her the news she wanted. It said simply, 'Your Majesty, no doubt you will be pleased to hear that Naboth has been stoned to death.'

The queen read the letter and went at once to tell the king. 'I told you I would sort things out, didn't I? Well, I have. Naboth's vineyard is all yours. The man's dead. It serves him right for defying the wishes of the king. So you can stop sulking now. Go down to Jezreel, take possession of the land, pull up the vines and plant your precious vegetables.'

Jezebel didn't tell Ahab how she'd done it, and he didn't ask.

But God knew exactly what she had done. So he sent his friend, the prophet Elijah, down to Jezreel.

Ahab was in the vineyard, pacing it out, when Elijah arrived.

The king stopped in his tracks. He didn't like Elijah. Elijah had already caused him a lot of trouble. 'Oh, so my old enemy's tracked me down again, has he?' sneered Ahab.

'I have found you alright,' Elijah replied, 'and so has God! "You must not murder anyone." That is one thing the Ten Words of God say. "You must not want what your neighbour has. Let all live in freedom and honour." That's another. "You must not tell lies to get another into trouble." That's a third. God will not allow your kind of tyranny in his Land, Ahab, nor the tyranny of your queen. You are in for trouble, you and Jezebel!'

Before this, when Jezebel had threatened to kill him, Elijah had run for his life, all the way back to Mount Sinai far to the south. He had forgotten what it meant to be a prophet of the God of Abraham. Now he had come to his senses. He was a prophet again, and there was nothing any king or queen could do about it.

Ahab never did plant his vegetables in Naboth's vineyard.

5

THE PEOPLE OF GOD UNDER THREAT

Over seven hundred years before Jesus of Nazareth was born, the two small kingdoms of Israel and Judah, where the people of God lived, were overrun by the Assyrians. The Assyrians came from a country to the north-east, from an area around the river Tigris. They were great traders, and created some wonderful buildings and works of art, but they also had the strongest and most ruthless army. They brought the kingdom of Israel to an end, while the little kingdom of Judah to the south only survived by the skin of its teeth.

The first pieces in this chapter date from the time when the Assyrians were beginning to pose a threat. They come from a prophet called Amos, whose words are found in the Bible in the book of Amos. Amos tries to look at the people of the kingdom of Israel through God's eyes. He sees them for what they are. He sees the greed of the rich people and the suffering of the poor. He tells them that if they do not change their ways, disaster will overtake them. Amos was a fine poet, and this chapter includes some of his poems, as well as a story about his confrontation with a priest called Amaziah.

Another poet-prophet was Hosea. His poems, which we can read in the book of Hosea, were composed just a few years after Amos's, after the Assyrians had invaded the kingdom of Israel and inflicted terrible suffering on its people. Hosea was the earliest person in the Bible to speak of the love of God, and this chapter includes his most famous poem on that subject – one of the most beautiful poems in the whole Bible.

One hundred years after the Assyrians destroyed the kingdom of Israel, it was Judah's turn. This time it was not the Assyrians but the Babylonians who invaded. They had taken over the Assyrian empire and were as ruthless as the Assyrians had been before them. Some people in Jerusalem, the capital of Judah, believed the city was safe. It was the city of God, they said, and could never be captured. In the Bible there are some poems, or songs, which express that belief, and you will find two of those, or parts of them, in this chapter. They are from the book of Psalms. We don't know who wrote them, nor exactly how old they are, but they were composed to be sung in the temple in Jerusalem.

However, not everyone agreed with those psalms. The prophet Jeremiah was living in Jerusalem at the time the Babylonian army invaded the country. The people were hoping God would save them. Jeremiah said it was too late and told the people that they should surrender. Not surprisingly, this got him into trouble. As well as some of Jeremiah's poetry, you will find in this chapter a story about him being put in a pit to die. The story will tell you how he escaped. The poetry and the story are from the book of Jeremiah.

Jeremiah predicted that Jerusalem would be captured and destroyed. He was right. Many people were killed and many more taken hundreds of miles into exile in Babylonia. The Babylonians took the people's cattle, their sheep and goats also, and destroyed their crops, so that the people left behind in Judah had almost nothing to eat. This chapter includes another of the psalms about the destruction

*of Jerusalem, as well as some poems from the book of Lamentations
about the suffering of the people in Judah afterwards. The book of
Lamentations is sometimes called 'The Lamentations of Jeremiah',
but in fact we don't know who composed them. Some of them,
perhaps all of them, may have come from women.*

*Among the exiles in Babylonia were two prophets, who dreamed
bright dreams about how God would lead his people back to the Land
and make all things well again. The first of them was a very great
poet, but we don't know his or her name. The poems are found in the
book of the prophet Isaiah, but they are clearly not composed by him.
Isaiah lived in Jerusalem back in the time of the Assyrians. These
poems were composed in Babylonia one hundred and fifty to two
hundred years later. This chapter includes two of them. The other
prophet of the exile represented in the chapter is Ezekiel. He had been
a priest in Jerusalem when the Babylonians came. Years later, in exile,
he had some striking visions of how God would restore his people and
make their Land a garden of delight.*

*Yet the dreams of those great prophets of the exile did not quite
come true. Some of the exiles eventually went back, but there was no
triumphant march home, as the first of the prophets had spoken of, nor
was the Land a garden of delight. Instead much of it was still in ruins.
Yet a new temple was built in Jerusalem, and eventually, under the
direction of a man called Nehemiah, the walls of the city were rebuilt
as well. We will hear part of Nehemiah's story, as he tells it himself in
the book of Nehemiah.*

*After the exile the people of God came to be known as Jews. They
still did not have their freedom. The Babylonians had been conquered
by the Persians, and the little country of the Jews was part of the
Persian empire. Later the Persian empire was taken over by the
Greeks under Alexander the Great, and nearly one hundred and*

*seventy years before Jesus was born, a Greek king tried to wipe out
the worship of God and destroy his people's way of life. It was too
dangerous for anyone to criticize the king openly, but a brave Jew
wrote a book about him, in which he included some old stories about
some dreadful kings of the Babylonians. That book is in the Bible
and is called Daniel. Its two most famous stories are at the end of
this chapter.*

'Let Justice Roll Down Like Water'

One hundred years after the time of Elijah, another
prophet came to the northern kingdom of Israel, whose
name was Amos. Amos was from a small place called
Tekoa, a few miles south of Jerusalem, in the kingdom
of Judah.

The king in Israel at the time was called Jeroboam.
The country was going through difficult times, and
from time to time enemy soldiers invaded parts of
its territory. There were others in the kingdom who
wanted Jeroboam's throne too and were plotting
against him.

But the people who were having the hardest time
were the peasant farmers. Their families had worked
their farms as long as they could remember, right back
from the time, so they believed, when God had given the
Land to the Israelite tribes who crossed the Jordan with
Joshua. But more and more of them were being driven
into poverty. Rich men who lived in the cities bought up

their land and every year demanded some of its produce as rent. When the harvests failed, when there was a drought or a plague of locusts or the crops got diseased, then the farmers couldn't pay and still have enough to live on. Then they'd have to sell their wives and children and themselves into slavery. They became the slaves of the men who owned their land. Often they were treated like dirt. Yet if they took their case to the courts in the cities, they'd find the rich men in control there too, and there was nothing they could do.

Some of them were forced off the land altogether and had to survive in the cities as best they could. But life for them there was even harder. The merchants who sold them grain to make their bread would use false weights, so they didn't get a fair amount for their money. And the prices the merchants charged were often exorbitant, sometimes for grain that was little better than dust.

Amos saw all this and was enraged.

ONE AUTUMN Amos came to the ancient shrine of Beth-El. It was a holy place, for long ago one of the ancestors of the people of Israel, Jacob, had met God there. The men of Israel were gathering for an important religious festival. It was going to last a week. There would be much eating and drinking, as well as prayers and songs and sacrifices. God would be in their midst, as he was when their ancestors came out of Egypt, and would join them to defeat all their enemies. At least, that is what the men believed, or what they hoped.

Amos watched them eating and drinking, and thought of the peasant families in the countryside who didn't have enough to eat.

He listened to the prayers of the festival and to the special songs being sung, and he remembered the desperately poor people in the cities.

'Just listen to them!' he said quietly to God. 'They don't care about the poor people at all. They don't spare them a thought. *You* care about them, God. You always care about them. How can I speak the truth, God? How can I make them take any notice?'

Amos fell silent. Then an idea came to him. He would start by telling the people things they wanted to hear, and then, when they were on his side, he would say what he really wanted to say. He would tell them what was on God's mind.

He began to preach, and the people gathered round to listen.

'Thus says the Lord God,' he cried,
'"the people of Damascus are in for trouble.
They overran part of Israel, beyond Lake Galilee,
and ploughed its people into the ground.
Their brutality spells their ruin,
their violence will drive them to destruction."'

The people cheered. This was just the sort of thing they liked! For centuries, not just in Israel, but in Egypt and Mesopotamia also, prophets had cursed the nation's enemies. They had put words to a nation's fear and hatred. Prophets were holy men and uttered holy words, words full of the power of the god in whose name they spoke. That was what the people believed. And here was Amos denouncing Damascus for invading Gilead. Wonderful!

'Thus says the Lord,' Amos continued,
'"the people of Gaza are in for trouble.

178

For they raided towns in Israel and Judah
and carried off their peoples
to sell in the slave-markets of Edom.
Their ruthlessness will be their undoing;
their cruelty will be their downfall.'"

The people cheered louder still and started dancing, singing and clapping. Then they fell silent as Amos spoke again.

Five more of their enemies he denounced. 'This prophet is like a lion,' they cried, 'prowling round our borders, picking off our enemies as if they were sick goats or lambs, tearing them to pieces with his words. Marvellous!'

But then Amos motioned once more for silence.

'Thus says the Lord,' he shouted,
'"You people of *Israel* are in for trouble!
For you have sold the poor into slavery,
taken away their freedom and honour,
when they owed you but a trifle,
the price of a pair of sandals.

You have trampled their heads
into the dust of the ground!

"'You have overturned justice
and put up bribery in its place!
When the wretched and abused
come to the courts for God's justice,
they are shoved to one side
and denied all mercy!

"'You love to sell your grain;
you cannot wait to sell.
Yet your weights are false!
The poor do not get what they pay for,
while the grain you sell them
is but the sweepings off the floor.

"'You work to death the men and women on your land,
and the children too,
while you yourselves lie back on beds inlaid with ivory,
and loll around on soft couches!
You feast on lambs and calves
that they have reared
but never get to eat themselves;
you drink gallons of the wine
they have produced
but which they never taste!

"'And here you are
at Beth-El,

the house of your God,
lying beside the altars,
wrapped warm in the cloaks of the poor,
while they shiver through the night's cold.

"'Do you not see the ruin
you have brought upon God's Land?
Do you not see the ruin
that awaits you,
if you do not mend your ways?

"'Let justice roll down like water,
like the torrent that roars down the parched river bed
when God's rain has fallen on the hills.
Let righteousness flow like a spring that never stops,
that even in the heat of summer
brings life to the dry ground.

"'If still you oppress and bully and treat with contempt,
then this festival of yours is a sham,
and you are spitting in the face of God.
Your greed will spell your ruin,
your lack of mercy will be your downfall.
Your land will be overrun,
and you will be herded into exile!'"

The people did not dance after that, nor did they sing or clap their hands. They listened to Amos in stunned silence.

Amaziah, the priest in charge of the sanctuary, heard everything Amos had said. Something will have to be done about this troublemaker! he said to himself. He sent a message to the king, Jeroboam. 'Amos is plotting against you,' he said, 'denouncing you in front of all the people. He is saying terrible things. The land itself cannot bear the words he has uttered.'

That should fix him! he thought. But he didn't wait for an answer from the king. He wanted Amos to leave immediately, before he could say any more.

'Get back home to Judah and do your prophesying there!' he ordered. 'Don't you dare come to Beth-El again. This is the king's sanctuary, and we can't have people speaking against the king and his country here.'

'Well I never!' Amos replied. 'And I thought it was God's land and God's sanctuary!' He moved closer to Amaziah. 'Look,' he said, 'I don't take orders from you. You have prophets here on Jeroboam's payroll, paid to say what he wants to hear and to obey your commands. Well, I'm not one of those prophets, Amaziah. God ordered me here. God showed me the truth of this land. God gave me the words to say. How could I not speak them? I owe my loyalty to God, not to you, nor to the king. I tell you this, Amaziah, when this land is overrun, your family will be among the first to suffer. And when the people are dragged into exile, you will be among them, and you will die on foreign soil, far from this precious sanctuary of yours.'

Not many years later the invasion came. The Assyrians, the most powerful and ruthless of all the nations in that part of the world, overran the kingdom of Israel and took its leaders into exile. Amaziah was never heard of again.

But some remembered the words of the prophet Amos, wrote them down and kept them safe.

Hosea and the Love of God

A little after Amos, in the northern kingdom of Israel, nearly two thousand, seven hundred and fifty years ago, there was a prophet called Hosea. He was a wonderful poet, and he wrote a most beautiful poem about the love of God.

Israel at the time was suffering terribly from the Assyrians. They'd invaded the kingdom, turned most of it into provinces of their empire and carted off many of the leaders among the people to Assyria, along with much of the country's treasures. Only the strongly fortified city of Samaria was left, and the towns and villages in the hills around it. Where could the king of Israel get help? Some people thought he could get it from Egypt and from the pharaoh there and his army. Hosea thought seeking help from Egypt would only end in disaster: it would put the Assyrians in a rage, and they would come back and destroy the rest of the kingdom. Some people believed they would be saved if they prayed to the ancient gods of the land, the gods which had been worshipped there for centuries and centuries, long before the Israelite tribes came from Egypt. Hosea believed their only hope was to turn to the God who had rescued them from Egypt and given them the land.

ONE DAY HOSEA was praying to God. He was keeping very still and quiet. Suddenly he knew with all his being just how much God loved his people, and how much they had hurt him. Words flooded into his mind and seemed to come from God himself. It was as if he could hear what God was saying.

And this is what Hosea heard God say:

'When Israel was a child,
I loved him,
and out of Egypt I called my son.

'Now they call for help
to the powers that enslaved them.
They dither about,
turning now to Egypt,
crying to them to come to their rescue,
now to Assyria,
protesting their loyalty,
handing over their wealth.

'And still they sacrifice to gods who are not gods,
and pray to gods who are no use to them.

'Yet it was I who cared for them in the desert.
It was I who carried them in my arms when they got tired.
Yet they did not even recognize who I was!

'I was like a father, a mother to them,
their farmer too, and they my favourite cow!
I took the yoke off their shoulders,
removed the ropes from their jaws;
I took them away from the toil and struggle of the plough
and led them to fresh pasture,

where they could eat to their heart's content.
Such love and gentleness I showed them!

'They will get no help from Egypt;
Assyria will be their king.
The sword will devour their cities
and eat up their villages.

'I am the only one who can help them,
and yet they cannot think what to do,
nor find the strength to do what is right.

'Look at them,
how wretched, how helpless they have become!

'How can I give you up, O Israel?
How can I deliver you to the enemy,
hand you over to their destruction?
I cannot do it.
My heart leaps back in horror.
Compassion overtakes me.
I love you too much!

'I will not release my anger,
for I am God and not a man;
I am the holy one in your midst,
the God of all creation,
come to live among you.'

Jerusalem will Never be Taken!

The Assyrians destroyed the northern kingdom of
Israel, and they did not leave the people of the southern
kingdom of Judah alone either. They captured many
of their towns and took much of their treasure. Yet they
did not capture Jerusalem. They besieged it, but they
did not take it. Some believed Jerusalem could never be
taken. They sang ancient songs in the temple that king
Solomon had built, which went like this:

'GOD IS OUR REFUGE, our stronghold.
With God we can be safe when trouble comes.

'God's wings shelter us against the biting cold of the night,
the stinging rain, the lashing of the storm

or the burning heat of the sun.
God is like a mother bird to us.
Snuggled up among her feathers,
against the warmth of her body,
against the strong beating of her heart,
we can hide from all that would harm us.

'So we will not fear,
even though the world should pitch and roll
on its foundations,
and the mountains be tipped into the sea.

'Jerusalem is God's city,
where earth and heaven meet.
With God in her midst,
she can never be shaken!
A stream brings life to the city,
whose waters never fail.
It is a gift from God,
welling up from the ground,
water from the hidden rivers of Eden.

'God is with us!
God fights for us!
The God of Abraham, Isaac and Jacob is still with us,
our refuge, our stronghold!

'Go outside Jerusalem
and walk around her walls.
See how strong they are!

See how many towers there are,
as strong, as fine, as majestic, as glorious
as God himself!

'God is our God for ever and ever.
God will never abandon us.
Always we will have God's care.'

Jeremiah Speaks the Truth

The people of Jerusalem sang their fine songs in the
temple. Yet a century and a half after Amos another
prophet, Jeremiah, tried to bring the people face to face
with some very uncomfortable truths.

By the time of Jeremiah, the Assyrian empire had
fallen. Now the Babylonians were the threat. Twice
they laid siege to Jerusalem. The first time the siege
lasted for three or four months, and ten years later it
dragged on for eighteen months. In the middle of it
the Babylonian army left, to deal with a threat from
the Egyptians to the south. The people breathed a great
sigh of relief. But Jeremiah knew they would come
back. He knew Jerusalem would fall. Long before,
he had tried to tell the people what they were doing,
and how much it displeased God. They thought God
was on their side, but Jeremiah believed they had
rejected God and driven him away. This is what he
had told them:

'THUS SAYS the Lord God:
"People of Jerusalem,
you are like a wife to me,
and I your husband.
I remember how once you loved me,
when first we were married.

"'I brought you out of Egypt
and led you through the terrors of the wilderness.
I took you through a wasteland
of dark ravines,
where no one lived,
which no one crossed.
I brought you into a good land,
a special land,
a land of plenty,
full of fruit, like Eden.

"'Yet see how you have ruined it!
See how you have forgotten me!
I am not welcome there any more.
You have left me in the wilderness,
in a wasteland of dark ravines.

"'You have given up what is true
and chased after what is false.
I have been like an ever-flowing stream,
bringing you cool water in the heat,
fresh water even in the drought.
I have been an ever-present source of life for you,

yet you have abandoned me
and gone chasing after the false god Baal.
By the sweat of your brow
you have dug pits in the rock to hold water,
but you have left them unplastered,
and the water has leaked out,
leaving nothing but mud.
Your precious Baal is like that,
a cracked, stinking pit
that holds no water
and gives no life.'"

But the king and the people had taken no notice. There were other prophets who told them what they wanted to hear. 'God would protect them from harm,' they said. 'Remember the ancient songs,' they said. 'Jerusalem can never fall,' they said. Jeremiah knew he would have to do something dramatic to drive his message home.

ONE DAY HE BOUGHT a narrow-necked water jar, made of pottery. He gathered together some of the priests of the temple and some of the leaders of the people. 'Come with me,' he said. 'I want to show you something.'

He led them through one of the gates in the city walls and down to the bottom of a small valley. He was carrying the jar in his hands. Suddenly he stopped, and the men gathered round him. He put the jar down and looked round at them. Then with one hand he took the jar by the neck, raised it high above his head and brought it crashing down onto the ground. It broke into a hundred pieces. Then he cried:

'Thus says the Lord God:
"Like this jar
will this city be broken and its people,
smashed to pieces by the Babylonians,
shattered beyond repair."'

The time came when no one inside Jerusalem could go outside its walls, and no one could get in to help or bring them food. The Babylonians were besieging the city for the second time, and their army was camped outside its walls. The king and the people were getting desperate, longing for God to come and save them. But Jeremiah knew it was too late. God, he believed, had gone over to the enemy. The only thing for the king to do was surrender.

'Thus says the Lord,' he declared.
"'See, I am setting before you the way of life
and the way of death.
Those who stay inside the city shall die,
by sword, by famine, by disease.
Those who go out,
who surrender to the Babylonians,
will at least survive.

"'I, your God, do not live in this city any longer.
I am not welcome here.
You have driven me out
and into the enemy camp.

"'If only you,
O king of Judah,
and you, the fine people of the palace,
had looked after the weak and the hurt,
the immigrants who have no power,
the children and women who have none to look after them.
If only you had made this city a place of justice,
where all could live in freedom and honour,
then you would have been safe.

"'But now it is too late.
This fine city,
of which you are so proud,
will be destroyed and burned with fire.
You have ruined it already;
soon it will become but a heap of ruins.'"

Not surprisingly, some in Jerusalem found Jeremiah's words of warning unbearably harsh. Three of the most powerful officials in the palace heard him preaching and went to Zedekiah, the king.

'The man's a traitor!' they cried. 'He's telling people to surrender to the Babylonians. We can't put up with such talk. We need to encourage the people to fight, and Jeremiah's telling them to give themselves up. The morale of the soldiers and people is bad enough as it is. With him around it'll be destroyed altogether. We've got to get rid of him.'

The king was exhausted. 'Do with him what you like,' he replied.

So the officials arrested Jeremiah and threw him into a water pit. The water was gone; it had all been drunk. There was just mud in the bottom, thick mud. Jeremiah sank down into it. He couldn't climb out, for the pit was far too deep. It was dark and cold too, and the stench was vile. He had no water, no food. The officials left him there to die.

But Jeremiah did have some friends in the palace. One of them was a man from Ethiopia, called Ebed-melech. He went to king Zedekiah to tell him what the officials had done.

'Jeremiah is a prophet!' Ebed-melech said to him. 'He is here to speak God's mind, see things through God's eyes, deliver God's words to the people. We have to listen to him! Your officials have done a terrible thing. The man will die of hunger in that stinking pit.'

Zedekiah looked up at him. 'All right,' he said weakly. 'Take three men with you and get him out.'

Ebed-melech ran off and fetched three of his friends, and they went to the pit with old rags and worn-out clothes and some rope. They tied the clothes and rags to the rope and lowered them down to Jeremiah.

'Bunch the clothes and rags under your armpits, so the rope doesn't cut into you,' they called down. 'Then wrap the rope round you, under your arms, and hold on! We'll pull you out.'

Jeremiah was saved from the pit, but the king kept him under arrest. And still the siege went on.

Jerusalem Falls

Twice the Babylonians besieged Jerusalem. Twice they captured it.

The first time, the king, named Jehoiachin, his family, his palace officials and his officers gave themselves up to the Babylonians and were taken into exile in Babylon, along with many others from Jerusalem and the rest of the kingdom.

The second time, it was much worse. The siege lasted far longer. The people had carefully stored extra food before it began, but it ran out, and in the end they had nothing left. The new king, Zedekiah, sent for Jeremiah. They met in secret, at one of the entrances to the temple.

'I NEED YOUR HELP,' said Zedekiah to Jeremiah. 'Things are desperate, as you see. I don't know what to do for the best. I want your advice.'

'If I give it, you won't take any notice. You won't like what I have to say, and you'll have me killed for being a traitor.'

'I promise I won't put you to death,' replied Zedekiah. 'I know there are some people who want to get rid of you, but I won't hand you over to them. I swear it.'

Jeremiah paused. Then he spoke. 'Thus says the Lord God,' he said, '"If you surrender to the Babylonians, then your life will be spared, this city will not be destroyed, and your children will be safe. If, however, you do not surrender, then the Babylonian army will capture the city and burn it with fire, and you yourself will not escape."'

'But if I surrender, my own people will think I have betrayed them. They'll be out for my blood!'

'God wishes you to surrender,' said Jeremiah. 'Obey God and you will be safe. Otherwise disaster will overtake both you and the city.'

'Don't tell anyone about our conversation,' Zedekiah said. 'If you do, you will die.'

Jeremiah kept quiet, but Zedekiah did not follow his advice. 'Thus says the Lord God,' Jeremiah had said. But Zedekiah didn't take any notice of that.

One dark night, when there was no moon and a strong wind blew against the city, enough to drown out the sounds of escape, some of Zedekiah's soldiers came to him with a plan.

'Your Majesty,' they said. 'There is no food left in the city, and the cisterns are empty of water. If we stay here we will all die. You will die. But we have a plan. We can make a small hole in the walls, in a place where the Babylonian soldiers won't see us. They won't hear us either above the roar of this wind. We can take to the desert and make for Jericho and beyond. We'll get there before they realize we've gone.'

This is a better plan than Jeremiah's, Zedekiah said to himself. He took up his sword. 'Let's go!' he said.

His soldiers made the breach in the walls and crept out, Zedekiah and his sons among them. There a large orchard immediately outside the walls, and they slid quickly among the trees. They got past the Babylonian camp and made for the desert.

They knew the hills of the desert well, and its dark dry river beds. They thought no one had seen them escape, but they were wrong. As they approached Jericho and the sun began to rise the other side of the Dead Sea, they heard the sound of Babylonian soldiers behind them. They quickened their pace, but they hadn't eaten properly for weeks, and their legs were heavy.

The Babylonian commander shouted to his troops, 'Capture their king and his sons. I want them alive!'

Zedekiah's soldiers heard the shout. They scattered in all directions and left Zedekiah and his sons to their fate.

The Babylonians were soon upon them. 'We are taking you to the king of Babylon,' the commander told them.

The king of Babylon was in a place called Riblah, three hundred miles to the north. When they got there, Zedekiah and his sons were thrown down at his feet.

'Look up at me!' the king shouted to Zedekiah. 'I will show you what happens when you do not surrender to me.' He turned to his soldiers beside him. 'Kill this man's sons, and then blind him,' he ordered. 'Put him in chains and take him to Babylon.'

There was no king in Jerusalem now, nor any soldiers to defend it. The Babylonian army made breaches in the walls and stormed into the city. The temple stood there gleaming in the sun. The soldiers burst in and stripped it of its treasures. They took all the sacred vessels, all the gold, silver and bronze. Then they set the place on fire. The king's palace they burned also, and all the other great houses of the city. Then they demolished the city walls and left Jerusalem in ruins.

Some of the priests from the temple and some of the palace officials were tortured and executed. As for the rest of the people, many of them were taken into exile. They started out on the long journey to Babylonia, under the guard of armed soldiers. Some of the people put their belongings on ox carts, while the women and children sat on top of the baggage. But most of the adults had to walk, sacks slung over their shoulders containing some of their possessions and provisions for the journey. Some of the smaller children rode high on their fathers' shoulders, while others who were bigger walked with their parents. Not all of them managed to finish the journey.

A handful of people remained in the Land, but they had a hard time too. The countryside was ruined and empty.

Others escaped to Egypt. They took the prophet Jeremiah with them, although he did not wish to go. Egypt was the country where the people of Israel had been born. Now some of them were back there again, back where they started. Was this the end of it all?

Sad Songs of Lament

The temple and the rest of the city of Jerusalem lay in ruins, but the people living there did not stop praying to God. They still gathered for worship in the place where the temple had stood. The Babylonian soldiers had wrecked it, but they had not robbed it of its holiness. For the people of Jerusalem it was still a place where they hoped to find their God. It was still a place where they could pour out their hearts to him, show him their pain and express their anger and their bewilderment.

Some poets (we don't know their names) composed

new songs to sing to God, beautiful songs, but full of sharp distress.

'We will speak to God as Moses did on Mount Sinai,' they said. 'Moses was the friend of God. He poured out his heart to God and hid nothing from him. Well, we are the friends of God also. We will not hide anything from him. We will not pretend that things are better than they are. We will show God what we really feel and tell him all our misery. If we are straight with him, then he can be straight with us.'

And these are the songs they sang:

WHY, O GOD, do you seem so angry?
We are your flock,
you our shepherd.
So you have been from the beginning.
Why, then, why
do you seem to have abandoned us,
left us to the mercy of wild animals,
to be torn apart and left for dead?
Why, God, why?

Remember us, your people.
Remember too your temple, your dwelling place.
Pick your way through its ruins.
See what the enemy soldiers have done!
They have trampled all over it,
bellowing and shouting.
They have hacked it to pieces,
smashed all its carvings

and burned it with fire.
They have raised their standards
and the emblems of their gods
on the very spot
that has marked your presence for so long.
They have defied you.
They have insulted you.
They have dishonoured you.

How long, O God, how long
will they continue with this mockery?
Why do you hold back?
Why do you sit back and do nothing?

You are the Creator of the whole world, God!
Think how you made things out of that dark heap of water!
Think how you split one thing from another
and put everything in its place.
Think how you defeated the Dark Forces of Chaos.
It was you who made the sun and the moon.
The day is yours; the night is yours.

Winter and summer,
they are of your making.

Yet these enemies, these fools
have dragged your name through the mud,
treated you like dirt,
shamed you, as if you were nothing.
Remember that.
Remember us also.
We are like a dove
caught on the ground,
surrounded by lions.
Do not forget us.
Do not forget us.

The Babylonian soldiers had not only wrecked the city.
They had wrecked the countryside around it also.

By the time Jerusalem was captured, all supplies of
food inside the walls were gone. As soon as they could,
the people of the city who were left behind by the
Babylonians went out into the fields to find food. The
sight that met their eyes made them weep. Their flocks
and herds were gone, and their crops had been stripped
to feed Babylonian soldiers, or else had been trampled
into the ground or burned. There was nothing to eat.
They walked over the next ridge of the hills and down
into another valley. It was just the same: nothing but
devastation. The Babylonian army had returned to
Babylon. But now a new enemy had arrived: famine.

And the city itself seemed so empty, and yet was so

full of grief. So many people had gone, killed by the Babylonian soldiers or taken off to Babylon. There were no children playing in the streets any more. The temple was destroyed, and the old priests and prophets left in the city had no words of comfort to give.

So the poets wrote yet more songs of lament. They poured their distress into these songs, but they also sang of the love and mercy of God. They knew that only God could save them now.

HOW LONELY the city sits!
Once she was full of people.
Once she was renowned.
Once she was like a princess.
Now she is like a widow,
with none to care for her.
Now she is like a slave,
toiling in the slave gangs.

Bitterly, bitterly she weeps in the night,
her cheeks running with tears.
There is no one to comfort her.
All her friends have betrayed her.

The roads to the city,
that once were thronged with pilgrims
on their way to the festivals,
are empty now,
for no pilgrims come.
The roads themselves weep with loneliness.

The gates to the city,
where once people met
and talked the business of the day,
lie now in ruins.

Her rulers were like stags,
wandering in the desert,
finding no pasture,
their strength gone,
too weak to escape their pursuers.
Her priests groan in despair.
Her prophets find no vision from God.
No one makes music;
there is no dancing in the streets.
Her children are gone,
taken from her into captivity.
All that was her glory has vanished.

'Look, O Lord God,' the city cries,
'see how worthless I have become!

'Look, those of you who pass by,
see my agony!
This is God's doing!
He has set my bones on fire.
He has tripped me, trapped me,
laid me low in endless distress.
He has put a yoke on my shoulders
that has broken my back.

'For these things I weep,
with none to console me.
My children are devastated.
The enemy has prevailed.

'I know the Lord God is in the right.
I ignored him and went my own way.
Yet still, you peoples of the earth,
see my pain!
My children, the girls and the boys,
have all gone into captivity.
Look, O Lord God,
see to whom you have done this!

'Yet this I will bring back to mind,
in this I will find hope:
the enduring love of God never ceases,
the bond between us is too strong,
his compassion, his mercies never come to an end
but are new every morning.
Great, O God, is your faithfulness!'

Dreaming of Home

The exiles in Babylonia were hundreds of miles from
home. They felt hundreds of miles from God too. They
felt forgotten by him, abandoned, as if he did not care
about them any more.

Babylon itself was a magnificent city. Jerusalem was a mere village by comparison. Running through the heart of Babylon was a long, straight, broad street – a great processional highway. At times of festival the king would ride along this highway, and the images of the Babylonian gods would be paraded along it, glittering in their gold and silver. When the king returned from the destruction of Jerusalem, he and his gods rode along it, while the people of the city clapped and cheered. The highway was a symbol of Babylon's power – a reminder of the glory of her kings and the overwhelming might of her gods. That is how the Babylonians saw it, at least, and they wanted the exiles from Jerusalem to think of it in the same way.

THERE WAS A PROPHET from Jerusalem among the exiles, a great poet, who saw things differently. One day he sat underneath some trees, looking across the great river Euphrates to the walls of Babylon. A massive bridge stretched across the river, and on the far side of it was a beautiful gateway, covered in glazed bricks, shining in the sun. The great highway went through that gate. The poet remembered the stories of people from Judah and Jerusalem being dragged along that street behind the king of Babylon and his gods, when first they were brought into exile. He shut his eyes and prayed.

A vision came into his head – a vision of another highway, much longer than the one in Babylon, a magnificent road that stretched all the way back to Jerusalem. And on that road were the exiles. They were going home! And God was leading them!

He composed a poem to recite to his fellow exiles:

God speaks in heaven among the gods,
among the members of the divine council.
He addresses the powers of heaven:
'Comfort, oh comfort my people.
Tell them of my love,
tell them they have suffered enough,
endured far more than they deserved.'

A voice rings out in the council:
'Prepare a triumphal highway for the Lord God.
Lift up the valleys, flatten the hills!
Clear away the rocks and stones,
fill every pit and pothole!
Make the highway straight,
straight across the miles of desert,
straight across the ancient wilderness,
all the way to Judah and Jerusalem!
Then the glory of God will be revealed,
and all the world will see it!
The Lord God has spoken.'

A second voice rings out:
'Cry out, prophet!' it says.
'But what shall I cry?' I answer.

'The people are like wild flowers,
blown by the hot desert wind,
their petals fading,
their leaves withering away.
The people are withered to nothing by the anger of God.'
'Wild flowers may fade and wither,' the voice replies,
'but the word and the love and the promises of God stand
    for ever.'

A third voice cries, more loudly still;
it speaks from heaven to Jerusalem:
'Rouse yourself, rouse yourself, O Jerusalem!
Climb to the top of a high mountain.
Look towards the wilderness and see.
Lift up your voice and shout with all your might,
lift it up, do not be afraid;
cry to the cities of Judah,
"Here is your God!
See, he is marching along his highway.
He has won back his people.
See how they follow in his triumphal train.
Our God is like a shepherd,
bringing his flock back home,
carrying the newborn lambs in his arms,
gently leading the ewes that are with young."
Rouse yourself, Jerusalem!
Look towards the wilderness and see.'

The poet-prophet composed many beautiful poems
to encourage his people and bring them out of their

despair. On another day, when he was in prayer, he found himself thinking of the people left behind in Jerusalem. He knew what they must be feeling. And he knew how astonished they would be when God brought the exiles back. God had been like a husband to them. They must be thinking he had abandoned them, just when they needed him most. But soon he would come back and gather them up in his arms once more.

The prophet composed another poem and recited it to the exiles. He pretended that Jerusalem was a woman and that he was speaking to her.

SING, O barren one,
and burst into song!
You who have no children,
you who have longed for them
and had no end to your longing,
shout aloud for very joy!
For like Hannah of old,
who waited so many fruitless years
and bore the taunts of Peninnah,
you will have more children than ever you dreamed of.
For your children in exile
will come streaming back to you,
and you will have to enlarge your tent,
stretch out its curtains
and lengthen its ropes
to make room for them all.

Do not be afraid.
You feel abandoned, humiliated, ashamed,
like a widow with none to care for her.
Yet you will forget all that sorrow,
for your Creator,
the God who made you,
he is your husband.
The Holy One of Israel,
the God of all the earth,
he is your redeemer.
He will turn your disgrace quite all to grace.

You are like a wife forsaken,
grieved and broken in spirit,
like a woman abandoned by her husband.

God breaks into your silence;
once more you hear his voice:
'For a moment I forsook you,
but now with great compassion
I will embrace you.
For a moment my anger came between us,
but now in everlasting love
I will have compassion upon you.
The bond between us is too strong!

'Remember Noah, Jerusalem.
Remember how I promised after the Great Flood
never to destroy the earth again.
So now I promise,

I will not be angry with you any longer.
The mountains may disappear
and the hills vanish,
but my love for you will not disappear,
my promise to care for you and give you peace
will never vanish.
I am the Lord, your God, who loves you;
I cannot hide my compassion from you.'

A Valley Full of Bones
and a New Garden of Eden

Among the exiles in Babylonia was a prophet named
Ezekiel. When he lived in Jerusalem, he had served as
a priest in the temple. The Babylonians had laid siege
to Jerusalem twice, and Ezekiel had been taken to
Babylonia after the first siege. Over ten years later news
reached the exiles of the second siege, and they learned
of the final capture and destruction of the city and its
temple. Their despair was now complete. All hope was
gone. There was nothing to look forward to any more.

Ezekiel himself was devastated by the news, but
he wasn't surprised by it. He had already had a vision
of God leaving the temple, deserting Jerusalem and
arriving in Babylonia. God had been driven into exile
himself, not by the Babylonian soldiers but by his own
people. They had not been faithful to him. They had
not loved him as they should have done. In God's own

temple they had been worshipping other gods. The temple had to be destroyed so a new one could be built in its place. Jerusalem had to be smashed so that a new city could be built, with God at its centre. That is what Ezekiel believed.

So when the terrible news came of the result of the second siege, Ezekiel did not despair. There could be a new start now. God would bring life again to his people.

ONE DAY some of the exiles came to Ezekiel to discover if he had anything new to say to them. They sat down in front of him, their eyes fixed on the ground. They looked so weary, so downhearted. There was a dead look in their eyes, and they could hardly speak.

'What hope is there for us now?' one of them asked.

'I will tell you,' said Ezekiel. 'Let me tell you the new vision I have had.'

'I felt the hand of the Lord God upon me,' he said. 'God picked me up, took me out of my house and set me down in a wide valley.

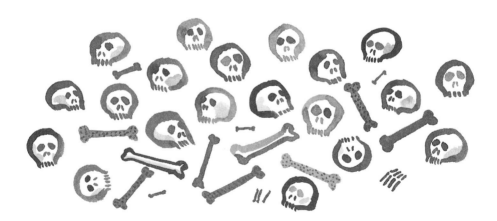

It was full of bones. They lay scattered all over the ground. It was as if a vast army had perished there many years before. The bodies had not been buried. The wild animals had eaten the flesh; the vultures had picked the bones clean. So all I could see was bones, dry bones, bleached by the sun. There was no life in them at all, but death all around. Surely no chance of life – just piles of bones. God led me among them, from one end of the valley to the other. There were thousands upon thousands upon thousands of them, pile after pile of dry bones.

'God said to me, "Can these bones come to life again?"

'"O Lord God," I answered. "Only you know that."

'Then he said to me, "Prophesy over these bones, Ezekiel. Say to them: 'O dry bones, hear the word of the Lord God. Thus says the Lord God: "See, I will bring the breath of life to you, and you shall live. I will lay the flesh upon you once more and put the breath of life within you, and you shall live. Then you shall know that I am the Lord God.'"

'So I prophesied as I had been told, and as I did so, suddenly I heard a rattling noise, coming from all over the valley. The bones were coming together again! Then flesh formed on them. But they were not breathing yet. They lay on the ground, row upon row of lifeless corpses, as far as my eyes could see.

'God spoke to me again. "Prophesy to the breath of life. Say to it, 'Thus says the Lord God, Come from the four winds, O breath of life, breathe upon these slain, that they may live.'"

'I prophesied as I had been told, and the breath of life came blowing from all the corners of the earth, like four winds swirling and playing over the valley floor. It entered the corpses, and they started breathing. Then slowly, stiffly, they stood up on their feet, a vast multitude of people!

'And God said to me, "These dry bones are the people of Israel. The people say, 'All our hope is gone. We might just as well be dead and buried. We are no more than heaps of dry bones. We are cut off, buried in the dark despair of exile, left to rot, like corpses in their graves.'

'"So prophesy to the people, Ezekiel, and say to them, 'Thus says the Lord God: I myself am going to open these graves of yours and lift you out of your darkness. I will stand you on your feet again and bring you back to the land of Israel. I will put my spirit, my breath of life within you, and you shall live once more! I will put you back on your own soil and give you rest. Then you shall know that I, the Lord God, keep my promises. What I have spoken, I will perform!'"'

On another day Ezekiel spoke again to the exiles.

'I have had a vision of a new Jerusalem,' he declared, 'and a new temple. We will go back there one day soon and rebuild the city. We will build a new temple at the heart of it, and God himself will return from exile to dwell there once more. It will not be like the old temple or the old city. They were corrupt and had to be destroyed. God will give us a new spirit, and we will be his people once more, and he will be our God. The land will come to life again. You remember the Dead Sea? Nothing can live in its waters, and its shores are desolate. I tell you, when God returns to Jerusalem and his new temple, the Dead Sea and the desert around it will become like the Garden of Eden! Let me tell you what I saw in my vision.

'I saw the glory of God, coming towards Jerusalem from the east. There was a noise like the noise of huge waterfalls, and the whole earth shone with the light of God. This shining, bright, roaring, cascading presence of God came to the city, reached the temple and then moved inside. The whole temple was filled with the glory of

God! I tell you, Jerusalem will have a new name. It will be called, "The Lord God is There".'

'A guide from heaven brought me to the entrance of the temple. A stream of water was coming from it, flowing from the heart of the presence of God. The water was little more than a trickle, but my guide led me on towards the east, through the hills of the desert, and I saw it was up to my ankles. Then he led me on further, and it was up to my knees. Then it came up to my waist, and then it was deep enough to swim in. It was a huge river now, too wide to cross.

'We turned back, my guide and I, and I saw trees growing on the banks of the river. The desert had become a garden!

'The guide said to me, "Do you see this? Wherever this river goes, it brings life. It is flowing down towards the Sea of Death, and when it gets there, it will turn it into the Sea of Life! The waters of the sea will become fresh and will teem and swarm with fish. People

will stand on its banks fishing. It will be a place for kingfishers and for the spreading of nets. On the banks of the river all kinds of trees will grow, trees that will bear fresh fruit every month of the year. Their leaves will not wither, nor will their fruit fail. Their fruit will be for food, an everlasting supply, and their leaves will be for healing. It will be like the Garden of Eden!"'

The exiles looked up at Ezekiel astonished. They had ceased to have any hope for the future. Now they could dream bright dreams again. They had felt that God had abandoned them. Now they sensed he was very close.

Rebuilding Jerusalem

The Babylonians had left Jerusalem and its temple in ruins and taken many of its people into exile. But while these exiles were living in Babylonia, hundreds of miles away from home, a new empire was emerging in that part of the world. Its king was called Cyrus. Soon his empire stretched from the Mediterranean Sea in Turkey as far as north-west India. The day came when Cyrus marched into Babylon, while the people of the city cheered and danced. Even the Babylonians had had enough of their own king. The Babylonian empire was no more. The Persian empire had taken its place. In Babylon Cyrus declared himself 'king of the world, king of the four rims of the earth'.

The next year King Cyrus made a solemn decree allowing the exiles from Jerusalem to go home if they wished. He ordered them to rebuild the temple there and make the city a holy place once more. The Babylonians had looted the temple when they had captured the city, taken all its sacred vessels to Babylon and placed them in the temples of their own gods. Cyrus ordered them to be given back to the exiles so they could take them with them on their journey home. But the ark of the covenant, that ancient golden box containing the Ten Words of God, which once had lain in the holiest part of the temple, had disappeared. It was never heard of again.

A year after their return, the exiles laid the

foundations for a new temple. It was a great day! The priests were there in their special robes. They blew silver trumpets, they clashed bronze cymbals, they sang holy psalms, and all the people shouted a great shout to welcome God back home again. Most of them shouted for joy, but for some old people the ceremonies brought back painful memories. They had lived right through the exile. They could well remember the time when they were children in Jerusalem. Their minds went back to the old temple gleaming gold in the sun, before the Babylonians had arrived. They remembered the terrible times when the city was besieged, and what the Babylonian soldiers did when they captured it. They thought of all their friends and the members of their families who had lost their lives. They could almost hear again the sounds of the soldiers wrecking the city walls and hacking the temple to pieces and burning it with fire. They looked at the foundations of the new temple, and a lump came into their throats. They couldn't join in the shouting, or share the joy of the rest of the people, but wept with a loud voice, their tears and their crying full of pain.

Rebuilding the temple was not easy, but eventually it was done. Yet Jerusalem still had no walls to surround it and keep it safe. Many of its buildings were still in ruins or empty. It was not even the capital city of that part of the Persian empire. And some of the powerful people in the regions around didn't want Jerusalem to be strong again either. They thought they might lose some of their power if it was rebuilt. The priests and the other leaders in Jerusalem didn't know what to do. Until one day a man called Hanani had an idea.

Hanani had a brother called Nehemiah, who was an important man in the court of the great king of Persia. Nehemiah was the chief of the king's cup-bearers, the taster of the king's wine, the guard of the royal apartments. Most people couldn't get anywhere near the king. But Nehemiah could. He attended on him every day. Hanani thought that if they went and spoke to Nehemiah, he might persuade the king to help them.

So Hanani and some of his Jerusalem friends travelled all the way to Susa, the city where the king had his winter palace, to see Nehemiah. They kept the purpose of their journey a strict secret, afraid that the men in charge of the regions they were travelling through might stop them, or even kill them, if they knew.

In the book in the Bible named Nehemiah, Nehemiah himself tells the story of what happened next.

ONE DAY I WAS WORKING in the palace of the great king, when some men arrived from a long journey to see me. Among them was my brother Hanani!

'How good to see you!' I cried. 'But why have you come all these hundreds of miles to see me? And why do you all look so sad? How are things in Judah? And Jerusalem – what's the old place like now?'

So they told me everything: the broken-down walls, the gates destroyed, the shame and disgrace of it all. I was overcome with grief and prayed fervently to God:

'O God,
you are the God of the heavens,
you are the God of love,
enduring, unbreakable love.
Open your ears, O God,
and hear my prayer.
Open your eyes and see my grief.
See the grief and shame of your people,
the humiliation of your holy city,
the ruin surrounding your temple.
Give me success today
when I go to the king.
Fill the king with your kindness,
that he may show me some mercy
and listen to my request.'

So that day, when the king sat down to his meal, I brought in his wine as usual. He looked at me and said, 'Nehemiah, why is your face so sad? You're usually such a cheerful man.'

'O king,' I replied. 'May you live for ever! The city where my ancestors lie buried is in ruins, its gates destroyed by fire. That is why my face is so sad.'

'What do you want me to do?' the king asked.

'If it pleases you, Your Majesty, and if I have found favour in your sight, send me to Judah, to the city of my ancestors, so that I may rebuild it.'

The queen was sitting beside the king. She and I had always

understood one another. I glanced across at her. She leaned over and said something quietly to the king. He turned towards me. 'How long will you be gone?' he asked.

My heart leaped. He had agreed to my plan! I gave him some idea of how long it would all take, and then I asked, 'If it pleases you, Your Majesty, could you give me some letters which I can show the governors of the regions I will have to travel through, and the governors of the regions around the city of my ancestors, so that they may know I have your backing? And could you give me a letter to show to the man in charge of your royal forest, so that he can give me timber for the new gates?'

'I will give you all the letters you need,' the king answered, 'and I will order some of the officers in my army and some of my cavalry to go with you, to make sure you get there safely.'

I wanted to clap my hands and dance for joy, but that was not the way to behave in front of a king. So instead I bowed very low and thanked him with all my heart. I thanked God too, for his hand of blessing had been upon me, and his love had held me tight that day.

And so Hanani and his friends and I set off for Jerusalem, with the king's soldiers and cavalry, and the king's letters, bearing the royal seal, safe in my bag. When we came to the regions near Judah the governors weren't at all pleased to see us. They didn't want Jerusalem rebuilt at all. But when they read the king's letters and saw the number of soldiers we had with us, they realized there was nothing they could do. So they let us travel on, and at last we arrived in Jerusalem.

I wanted to inspect the whole circuit of the walls, to see just how bad things were and how much work needed to be done. But I didn't want everybody knowing about it. So one night I got up quietly, took just a few men with me and rode out of the city.

We turned left and followed the old circuit of the walls, riding by the light of the stars and a half moon. The hooves of our donkeys fell soft on the dusty ground. An owl hooted in the distance, and another one answered from nearby. We could see it silhouetted on the top of the damaged wall, its large head bobbing from side to side, its eyes watching us intently.

When we came to the steep valley on the eastern side of the city, we could go no further. The ancient terraces, where olive trees once had grown, had collapsed, and the stones of their walls had tumbled down into the valley, completely blocking our path. So I got off my donkey and climbed up the slope as best I could. Halfway up I surprised a pack of jackals out for a night's scavenging. They looked at me for a moment, their eyes glinting in the moonlight, and then they turned and ran. I continued climbing until I reached the place where the great city wall had been. There was virtually nothing left of it. All I could see were piles of stones, overgrown with thorn bushes, nettles and thistles. I scrambled down again and got back onto my donkey. I signalled with my hand to the men, and we turned the animals round and went back the way we had come. We slipped into the city just before the dawn began to lighten the eastern sky.

There was much to do and no time to waste. I called a meeting

of the heads of the families of the region of Judah, together with the priests of the temple and the city officials.

'Look around you,' I said to them. 'This city, once so fine, is still in ruins. It's a disgrace. It's our spiritual home and was once our capital. Look at it now!

'Yet I bring you good news! God's hand of blessing has been upon me. I have letters from the king in Susa, urging me to rebuild the city and granting me enough timber from his royal forest to make new gates.'

All those who heard me were amazed. 'Let's start building at once!' they cried.

Our enemies in the nearby regions didn't like what we were planning one bit. Their leader was the governor of Samaria, the region to the north of Judah. His name was Sanballat. 'What is this you're up to?' he and his friends said. 'Are you preparing to rebel against the great king?'

'God will give us success,' I replied, 'and he is the God of heaven and the whole earth. We are his servants, his friends, and we are going to start building whether you like it or not. There is nothing you can do to stop us.'

And so we made a start. Teams of men began to make pairs of strong wooden gates, while others began work on the walls. Some women were able to come and help too.

In some places the wall just needed to be built up again to the proper height. But on the northern side of the city, and on the southern side, where I had seen the jackals, we had to clear away the rubble and start from scratch.

Sanballat's men reported to him that we had made a start on the rebuilding, and he was furious. But he didn't think we would succeed. 'What can those feeble Jews do?' he said to his soldiers and his friends. 'How can they build strong walls out of piles of rubble? When the Babylonians set the city on fire, the stone of the walls got burned too. It will just crumble to pieces when they try to use it again.'

'Yes,' said one of his friends. 'The walls they're building will be so weak that when a fox climbs up on top of them, they'll all come tumbling down.' They roared with laughter.

When they saw the progress we were making, however, they stopped laughing and became very angry again. Right round the city the walls were up to half their height already! The gaps were being filled, and soon the whole circuit would be finished. So Sanballat summoned together the leaders of all the regions surrounding Judah and said, 'We must join our armies together and march on Jerusalem and stop it being rebuilt. If Jerusalem is strong, then we will be weak. If Jerusalem stays a ruin, we can remain in power.'

Things did not look good for us. We had enemies to the north, to the south, to the east, to the west. But I had commanded all the men of Judah who were capable of bearing arms to come to our aid. In some places the city was overlooked by higher ground. Sanballat's spies would be able to see inside the walls from there. So in those areas of the city I massed as many people as I could, armed with swords, spears and bows and arrows. I wanted our enemies to think we had a huge army guarding the whole city. 'Do not be afraid!' I said to them. 'Remember God is with us, and God is far greater than Sanballat! Fight for your families, for your sons, for your daughters, for your wives, for your homes.'

My plan seemed to work. The attack we'd expected from Sanballat didn't come. But we couldn't be too careful. Until the walls and gates were completely finished, we were very vulnerable.

So from then on half the people worked on the rebuilding, while half stayed on guard with their weapons in their hands. Even the builders were armed. Those carrying the smaller stones on their shoulders, or baskets of debris on their heads, steadied them with one hand and held a weapon in the other. And each of those laying the stones or fixing the timbers had a sword strapped to his side. I set trumpeters at intervals along the walls, ready to blow the alarm. 'If you hear one of the trumpets sound,' I said to the leaders of the people, 'then you and your people must come running at once. It will mean we are under attack.'

We worked from the breaking of the dawn until the stars came out in the evening. The people from the other towns and villages of Judah did not go back home at night. They stayed inside the city, in case our enemies came to attack us after dark. While some kept watch, we slept in our working clothes, our weapons by our side.

After just fifty-two days the walls and the gates were finished. Our enemies were astonished we had done it so quickly. Indeed, they were amazed we had done it at all. 'They must have had God helping them,' they said.

They were right.

Now God's holy city was secure and strong. God's holy people could live in safety once more, gathered around God's holy temple.

Daniel: God in the Flames

Thanks to Nehemiah the city of Jerusalem was rebuilt and became strong again. Yet it did not remain safe for ever. The Persian empire was conquered by Alexander the Great, and from then on the whole of the eastern Mediterranean area became influenced by Greek culture. Cities were built on the Greek model. The Greek language was introduced. Greek ideas, Greek ways of thinking, Greek religions, Greek dress, Greek sports and Greek forms of government were all brought in.

In the ancient holy city of Jerusalem the Jews held on to their old ways, but a Greek king called Antiochus arrived, who wanted to make Jerusalem like the other Greek cities in his empire. When the people there rebelled, he punished them severely. His soldiers massacred many of them and took others into slavery. They burned parts of the city and tore down its walls. That was terrible enough, but even worse was to follow. Antiochus issued a decree: he made it illegal for the Jews to practise their religion, to celebrate their ancient festivals, or even to possess a copy of their sacred writings. And he tried to turn their temple into a Greek temple, where his own birthday would be celebrated and the Greek god Zeus would be worshipped.

Some Jews went along with what he wanted. Some rebelled and decided to form an army to fight against him. Others said they should not fight, but called upon the people to stand firm, stick to their Jewish ways, remain loyal to God and trust in him to deliver them.

Somebody, or perhaps several people in this third group, was responsible for writing the book of Daniel. It is the latest book in the Old Testament to have been written.

It was very hard for the Jews to trust in God in those days. Antiochus seemed so strong, while sometimes God seemed to be so small, unable to do anything to help. So the author or authors of Daniel wrote their book to encourage their fellow Jews to remain loyal to their faith. They knew some marvellous stories about great heroes of the past who had also faced persecution. Their ancestors had handed down these tales for a hundred or two hundred years before Antiochus came on the scene. The author or authors of Daniel thought they fitted their own situation perfectly; just the thing they were looking for. So they retold a number of them in the first part of their book, and two of them are included here.

The stories tell of a hero called Daniel and his three friends: Shadrach, Meshach and Abednego. According to the stories, these four Jews were taken from Jerusalem to Babylonia at the time of the exile, four hundred years before Antiochus. They came from rich and powerful families, and the Babylonian king, named Nebuchadnezzar, wanted them to be trained in his court to help him run his empire. They made such an impression on him that he put them in some of the most powerful positions in the land. So far, so good. But then things turned very nasty.

KING NEBUCHADNEZZAR, the great king of Babylon, king of kings and lord of lords, ruler of the world and all that was in it, was nervous. A lot of the people running his empire were foreigners, people who'd been deported to Babylon, like Daniel and Shadrach,

Meshach and Abednego. Would they stay loyal to him? Would they do things the way he wanted, or would they try to get the better of him? He wanted to test them, to make sure.

So he ordered a statue to be made. When it was finished, it was huge, thirty metres high. It stood upon the dusty plain, its gold head shining in the sun. The head looked remarkably like Nebuchadnezzar's.

He commanded his officials – all his governors, counsellors, treasurers, judges and officers – to assemble beneath the statue. Daniel wasn't there, but Shadrach, Meshach and Abednego were. To one side there was an orchestra, the king's musicians. There were horns, pipes, lyres, trigons (a special kind of lyre), harps and drums, and other instruments too.

One of the king's heralds shouted out in a loud voice, 'O all you people gathered here,' he began, 'hearken to this! When you hear the sound of the horn, pipe, lyre, trigon, harp, drum and entire musical ensemble, you are commanded by the king to fall down and worship this magnificent statue which king Nebuchadnezzar, king of kings and lord of lords, ruler of the world and all that is in it, has

made. If you do not obey His Majesty's orders, if you do not fall down and worship the statue, you will be in deep trouble – the very deepest of deep trouble. In fact, you will be in a burning fiery furnace, which His Majesty has got burning already – you will be thrown into it, right into the middle of the flames, immediately, straight away, without delay!'

The herald turned to the orchestra and nodded. The players started up. The music was solemn, royal and commanding – music designed to bend the knee, curl the back and press the forehead to the ground. At once the people prostrated themselves before the statue – everyone, that is, except Shadrach, Meshach and Abednego. They remained standing. How could they bow down to Nebuchadnezzar's statue and still be Jews? How could they do it and remain loyal to their God? Their God was greater than any statue. Their God was far greater than Nebuchadnezzar. Who did he think he was? They remained standing, their heads held high.

They stood out a mile, of course. The Babylonians noticed them at once. They hated those Jews. Who did they think they were? They were foreigners after all, from some stupid little country called Judah. They didn't deserve the power the king had given them. Such power gave them the right to order Babylonians about, and that was not how things should be. Now was their chance to get rid of them! They went over to where Nebuchadnezzar was sitting on his great throne and bowed low before him.

'Your Great High Most Colossal Majesty,' they said, 'may you live for ever! You gave an order, O king, that when the orchestra started to play, the horns, pipes, lyres, trigons, harps, drums and the entire musical ensemble, everyone should prostrate themselves and worship your golden statue. And you said, Your Majesty, sir, that if anyone did not do that, they would be thrown into a burning fiery furnace. Well, sir, you know those three Jews you have put in charge of the great province of Babylon, that Shadrach, Meshach and Abednego, sir. Well, sir, they have not prostrated themselves. They have remained standing bolt upright. They are taking no notice of you, sir. They refuse to serve your gods or worship your statue. We thought you ought to know, sir.'

Nebuchadnezzar was very angry. He ordered Shadrach, Meshach and Abednego to be brought over to him at once. 'Is this true?' he demanded. 'I will give you one more chance. If you are ready to fall down and worship my statue, as soon as the orchestra starts to play, then well and good. I will let you off this once, for I am a kind and generous man. But if you will not prostrate yourselves, then you will be thrown at once into the burning fiery furnace. What god is there who could save you from my power then?'

The three friends looked the king straight in the eye. 'Your Majesty,' they said, 'we will not try to defend ourselves. We know full well that we have not obeyed your command. We are ready to take the consequences. If our God, the one whom we serve, is able to save us from the flames and deliver us from your hand, O king, then he will save us. But if he cannot rescue us, then we still refuse to serve your gods or worship the statue you have made.'

Nebuchadnezzar's face turned bright purple and twisted with rage. 'Stoke up the furnace!' he shouted. 'I want it seven times its normal heat.'

When it was ready, he looked across to where some of his soldiers, his very strongest men, were standing. 'You men over there!' he cried. 'Tie up these Jews with ropes and throw them into the furnace!'

The soldiers did as they were told. The furnace was so hot that as they pulled open its door and lifted up the three Jews to throw them in, the flames caught them and killed them. Shadrach, Meshach and Abednego, the ropes bound tightly round their bodies, fell into the heart of the fire.

Everyone was silent. The only sound was the roar of the furnace.

Then Nebuchadnezzar peered into the flames. His expression changed. What he saw astonished him. He leaped up from his throne.

'Did we not throw three men, bound with ropes, into the fire?' he asked.

'Yes, Your Majesty,' his counsellors replied.

'But I see *four* figures there,' he cried, 'walking about in the flames, unbound, unharmed, untouched! And the fourth figure looks like a god!'

He was right. God had joined his friends in the fire.

Cautiously the king approached the entrance to the furnace. He called into the flames, 'Shadrach, Meshach and Abednego, servants of the Most High God, come forth!'

The three men did as they were told. They came out of the fire. Everyone gathered round, amazed. They were completely untouched by the fire! Their hair was not even singed. Their clothes were intact. There was no smell of fire on them.

'Blessed be the God of Shadrach, Meshach and Abednego!' the king declared. 'They risked their lives to remain loyal to their God, and he has delivered them. I therefore issue this solemn decree: Any people who say anything against the God of Shadrach, Meshach and Abednego will be torn apart, limb from limb, and their houses demolished. There is no other god who can come to the rescue as their God has done.'

It was a fearful decree. Nebuchadnezzar was still a tyrant. He still thought he could tell his people what to think, what to believe and which god to worship. Still he meant to punish most terribly anyone who disobeyed him. He hadn't learned very much at all from seeing God in the flames.

Yet Shadrach, Meshach and Abednego were still faithful Jews and friends of God. With their God they had been through fire and had survived. They had learned much about their God.

Daniel in the Lions' Den

A NEW EMPEROR came to power, a man called Darius. Daniel, the Jew, was in his court. Darius was not like Nebuchadnezzar. He seemed a just man, and he and Daniel got on very well together. Darius had a huge empire, far bigger than Nebuchadnezzar's had been. He felt as though he ruled the whole earth.

He divided his empire into one hundred and twenty provinces, and appointed governors or satraps, one to each province, to rule over it for him. Over the satraps he set three presidents. One of those was Daniel. Daniel was so good at his job, Darius started thinking about setting him over his entire empire. That idea did not please the satraps one little bit. They wanted to be left alone to get on with ruling their provinces the way they wished. They didn't want somebody else telling them what to do or sending reports on them to the king. What's more, Daniel was a Jew, which they thought made it much worse. And the other two presidents didn't like him either. The king was threatening to put him in a higher position above them. They didn't want anyone, let alone a Jew, having power over them. But how could they get rid of him? He was so popular with Darius. They would have to trap him somehow and trap the king as well.

The satraps and the two presidents got their heads together. They spent a long time scratching them for ideas. The trouble was, Daniel was too good at his job. He did everything the king asked. He treated everyone fairly too: he didn't take bribes; he didn't use his power to line his own pockets; he protected the poor. Everyone thought he was a wise and good man. If they went to the king with some trumped-up charge against him, Darius simply wouldn't believe them. They would go away with a severe reprimand, or worse, for telling lies. What could they do? They talked about it for hours and hours. No idea came. In the end they fell silent. They couldn't think of anything.

Then one of them shouted, 'I've got it! He's a Jew, isn't he, that Daniel? And he prays every day, three times a day, to his Jewish God, doesn't he? I've seen him. Well, if we get the king to pass a law saying it's illegal to pray to anyone except him – just for a bit, mind, say thirty days – then we can get Daniel good and proper. He'll never obey a law like that, and then we'll catch him in the act of praying to his God. We'll tell the king, and he'll have to chop his head off!'

'Or throw him into a den of lions,' said another.

'Brilliant!' they cried. 'A den of lions – that should finish him off! Let's go to the king straight away. Daniel's going to be breakfast for the lions!'

'O King Darius,' they said, 'Great Ruler of the whole earth, may you live for ever and ever and ever! We have met together, Your Majesty, your presidents, your satraps, your advisers and officials, and we are all agreed. May we humbly suggest, Your Majesty, that you issue a solemn decree saying that during the next thirty days if anyone prays to any god or human being besides you, Your Majesty, then they will be thrown into a den of lions. We will get the decree

written out for you, if you wish, Your Majesty, and you can sign it so that it cannot be changed.'

The satraps and the two presidents were back in two minutes with the decree written out in the special royal writing the king had invented. 'Sign here, Your Majesty,' they said.

Darius signed. It will be rather nice, he thought, having everyone praying to me for a bit. No harm can come of it, I'm sure.

Daniel got to hear about the order of the king. Everyone heard about it. But Daniel didn't take any notice. Three times a day he went upstairs in his house, as he always did, into a room which had a window facing west, towards Jerusalem. Three times a day he opened the window, knelt in front of it and prayed to God.

The satraps and the two presidents had been watching him for some time. They knew exactly where he prayed, when he prayed and to whom he prayed. The day after the king issued his decree, they got up very early and crept up to Daniel's house. Without making a sound they went round to the side of the house which faced west. They could hear Daniel praying. They looked up at the open window. Yes! There he was, on his knees, praying to his God.

They had him! He was trapped. They tiptoed away, and then, as soon as they were far enough from the house, they started running. They ran as fast as they could to the king.

'Your Majesty!' they cried, breathing heavily. 'Your Majesty! You know that decree you issued?'

'Of course,' Darius said.

'You signed it, did you not, Your Majesty?'

'I did.'

'And any decree you sign cannot be changed, can it?'

'Indeed it can't.'

'And you said, Your Majesty, that anyone who prayed to any god or human except you, during the next thirty days, would be thrown into a den of lions.'

'I did.'

'Well, Your Majesty, Daniel, that Jew from Jerusalem, is taking no notice of you, Your Majesty, or of your solemn decree. He is still praying to his God three times a day! We have seen him with our own eyes. Heard him too.'

Darius was heartbroken. 'Get out!' he shouted.

The satraps and the presidents hadn't expected that. They'd expected the king to issue an order at once for Daniel to be arrested and thrown to the lions. They hung about the palace waiting impatiently for him to act.

Darius spent the day trying to work out a way of saving Daniel. He couldn't think of anything. He was trapped by his own decree, caught by his own power!

In the evening, after the sun had gone down, the satraps and the two presidents came back.

'You cannot change the law, O king,' they said quietly. 'You have issued a decree. You cannot go back on it now.'

Darius put his head in his hands. 'Arrest Daniel,' he muttered, 'and throw him to the lions.'

A little later he went to the lions' den and watched as Daniel was thrown in. 'May your God keep you safe,' he said quietly, more to himself than to Daniel.

The den was a deep pit. Darius's men slid a large stone over the top of it so there was no way of escape. Darius himself marked the edge of the stone with his royal seal and the seals of his officials. If anyone broke the seals and moved the stone, they would be put to death.

The king went back to his palace with a heavy heart. His servants brought his evening meal to him, but he couldn't eat anything. He couldn't sleep that night either.

As soon as dawn came the next day, he rushed off to the den. 'Daniel, Daniel,' he cried, 'has your God been able to save you?'

He covered his face in his hands, not expecting to hear anything except for the purring of satisfied lions.

'O king, may you live for ever!' came a voice from below the great stone.

It was Daniel! The king couldn't believe his ears.

'God sent an angel to keep me company in the den and keep the lions' mouths shut,' Daniel called.

It *was* Daniel! The king was overjoyed.

'Quick!' he said to his men. 'Roll away the stone. Pull him out.'

They pushed the stone aside and pulled Daniel up into the sunlight. He was completely unharmed. He and the king embraced each other.

The king was not just filled with joy, however. He was angry too. The satraps and the two presidents had tricked him and made him look a fool. He was not having that. He gave another order to his men. 'Go and arrest those scoundrels, the ones who accused Daniel, and arrest their wives and children too, while you're about it. Throw the lot of them to the lions!'

The men obeyed the order, and before the satraps, the presidents and their wives and children reached the bottom of the pit, the lions had torn them to pieces.

Darius wrote another decree to all the peoples of his great empire:

> 'Everyone must tremble in fear
> before Daniel's God,' it said.
> 'For he is the living God,
> who saves,
> who delivers,
> who works signs and wonders
> in heaven and upon the earth.'

What he really meant was, 'Everyone must tremble in fear before Daniel and before me. For Daniel and I, the great king of all the world, can save and deliver, it is true, but we can also arrest and put to death. If you do not do what we say, then we will destroy you!' Like Nebuchadnezzar before him, Darius had not really learned anything about God and his ways.

6

FINE STORIES, FINE POEMS

This chapter is different from the previous ones. So far the stories and poems we have read have been parts of a larger story, or have followed a single theme. Now we have a little anthology, a small collection of works which do not have much to do with one another. We have included them in The Book of Books *simply because they are so good.*

The story of Ruth, with which this chapter begins, is one of the most beautiful stories in the Bible, and the story of Jonah that follows it is one of the funniest, but also one of the most profound.

After Jonah we come to the book of Job, written by an anonymous poet who is perhaps the greatest poet in the Bible. Job has something very significant to say about the world we live in, the hurt and pain people suffer, and the kind of God behind it all.

Finally we have two psalms, or sacred songs. For many Jews and Christians down the centuries the book of Psalms has been one of the most precious books in the Bible. Chapter five contained a few psalms, but it did not include the most famous one of all, Psalm 23. That Psalm, and another one, also very beautiful, will bring this chapter and our explorations of this part of the Bible (the Old Testament as Christians call it, or Tanakh *as the Jews refer to it) to a fitting conclusion.*

Ruth, Naomi and Boaz: Love Wins the Day

The book of Ruth is a short story (works are referred to as 'books' in the Bible even when they are only a few pages long) which is complete in itself. It is not part of a larger story.

Most of it is set in the town of Bethlehem. Bethlehem is famous now, because king David was born there, and much later Jesus was born there too. But in those days it wasn't famous at all.

This is a love story, a story of love triumphing against all the odds, a story with a very happy ending. It tells of how Ruth, a foreign woman from the country of Moab, meets a man in Bethlehem named Boaz and marries him. But it has even more to say about a remarkable friendship between Ruth and a woman from Bethlehem called Naomi. They are the main characters, and even most of the minor characters in the story are women too. That is unusual for stories in the Bible, and it makes us wonder whether the original storyteller was a woman. Unfortunately, we don't know the storyteller's name.

We don't know when the story was first told either. At the very end it mentions King David, so it can't have been composed before his reign. Most of the experts think it goes back a long way, to the eighth, ninth or even the tenth century BC. But it doesn't really matter when it was composed. What matters is that it is so beautiful.

IN THE EARLY DAYS, before the Israelites had any kings, a certain family lived in a town called Bethlehem. The father was called Elimelech, the mother's name was Naomi, and they had two sons, Mahlon and Chilion.

Elimelech's ancestors had all lived in Bethlehem, as long as anyone could remember. But the time came when they couldn't live there any more. The rains hadn't come. Their crops had failed. Other people's crops had failed too. There was famine in the town, famine in the whole region, famine throughout the land.

Most people in Bethlehem had just enough left to live on, but Elimelech and Naomi didn't. The name 'Bethlehem' meant 'House of Bread', but for them and their two sons it meant 'House of Death'. They had no choice; they would have to become refugees. They would have to go to a foreign country. They would have to walk there, all the way. When they got there, they wouldn't be able to buy their own land, yet someone might give them work. They might be able to help with the sowing and the harvesting in someone else's fields. They might be able to settle there. They might be able to live there, and not die.

So with heavy hearts they left Bethlehem and went to Moab, a country the other side of the Dead Sea. The Moabites spoke a different language. They had different customs, told different stories, worshipped different gods. But at least there was food in Moab. The family settled down as best they could.

It wasn't easy, and soon it got worse: Elimelech died.

At least Naomi still had her two sons. They both married Moabite women. Chilion married someone called Orpah, while Mahlon married a woman called Ruth. They lived together in Moab about ten years. Neither Orpah nor Ruth had any children.

Then Mahlon and Chilion both died.

Naomi was left in a foreign country with no man to protect her, no man to look after her and no way of surviving, as far as she could see. She would have to go back to Bethlehem. The famine there had come to an end. God had blessed his people with good harvests. That was the news that reached Naomi in Moab, and that was one good thing, at least. Naomi couldn't think of anything else that was good.

So she started out on the journey round the northern end of the Dead Sea, past the place where once Jericho had been, to Bethlehem. Orpah and Ruth set out with her. They walked for several miles without saying anything. Suddenly Naomi stopped.

'You can't come with me any further,' she said. 'Go back home to your mothers. You were good wives to my sons, and you've been kind to me. I hope the Lord God is kind to you in return. I hope he helps you find new husbands, good Moabite men.'

She kissed Orpah and Ruth goodbye, and they burst into tears. 'We want to come with you,' they said.

'You can't,' insisted Naomi. Her voice, her face, her body and spirit were full of bitterness. 'Why should you come with me?' she cried. 'I've got nothing to offer you. Go back to your own people. Get married again. You're young enough. I'm not. I've got no more sons to give you. There's no hope for me any more. God has turned against me. He's made the sweet taste of life all bitter in my mouth.'

Orpah and Ruth had lost their husbands too, but Naomi could only think of herself. She was sunk too deep in her despair. 'It's much worse for me than for you,' she concluded. 'Go back and leave me to carry on alone.'

Orpah and Ruth burst into tears once more. But behind her tears Orpah realized Naomi was right. There was no chance of marriage in Bethlehem, she thought. No chance for Ruth either. They were both still in their twenties, but most men married women much younger than they were. In Bethlehem they would be foreigners as well. Who would want them? How would they survive without men to look after them? Naomi was right. It was much more sensible for her and Ruth to go back and see if their mothers could find new husbands for them.

So Orpah kissed her mother-in-law goodbye and turned back to Moab. She thought Ruth would do the same.

But Ruth didn't do the sensible thing. Ruth clung to Naomi and wouldn't let go.

'Look!' Naomi said to her. 'Your sister-in-law's going back to her own people and her own gods. Go back with her.'

> 'Don't make me leave you all on your own!' she cried.
> 'Where you go, I will go.
> Where you live, I will live.
> Your people is my people,
> your God my God.
> Where you die, I will die.
> There will I be buried.
> I swear most solemnly,
> I swear by the Lord God,

the God of Israel,
even death itself will not separate us!'

Naomi said nothing. It was a fine speech, one of the finest speeches anyone could ever make, a speech brimming over with loyalty and love. Yet it was still not strong enough to lift Naomi out of her despair. She realized she could do nothing to persuade Ruth to go back home. Her daughter-in-law would have to come with her then. She turned once more for Bethlehem.

The two women walked on in silence. It took them two days to reach Bethlehem. In all that time Naomi kept her mouth shut. She only opened it again when they arrived at the town.

The women of Bethlehem flocked round them. Their eyes were all on Naomi. Was this *really* Naomi? Her name meant 'Lovely', and she *had* been lovely when she and her family had left for Moab all those years ago. But now she was hard and bitter. She didn't even seem pleased to be home. She didn't come running towards them, to throw herself into their arms. She didn't so much as look at them. She just carried on walking, looking straight ahead of her, her mouth set hard in a bitter line across her face.

'Are you really Naomi?' they asked.

'Don't call me Naomi,' she cried. 'I'm not "Lovely" any more. Call me Mara. That means "Bitter", and that name suits me now. God has turned me bitter. When I left here, I was full. I had everything: a husband and two fine sons. Now I've come back empty. I have no one. Why do you call me "Lovely"? Look what God's done to me!'

'I've come back empty,' she said. 'I have no one.' That wasn't true, of course. She had Ruth.

***

Back in Bethlehem Naomi had no energy to do anything. Ruth, however, refused to sit and wait for them both to starve to death. They had nothing to eat. Well then, she would go and find something.

'They're harvesting the barley,' she said to Naomi. 'I'll go down to the fields and do some gleaning. I'll pick up what the harvesters have left behind. At least, I'll see if anyone will let me do it.'

Naomi was sitting in the corner of the room, staring at the wall. 'All right, off you go,' she replied. There was no colour in her voice.

Ruth went through the gate of the town and followed the track down towards the fields. It was very early in the morning, but the men were already at work cutting the ripe barley. Behind them came the women bundling the stalks into sheaves. Ruth came to the edge of one particular field and noticed a young man who was obviously in charge of what was going on. She went over to him.

'Can I do some gleaning among the sheaves,' she said in her thick Moabite accent.

The young man looked her up and down. He recognized her at once. She was the Moabite woman who'd come back with Naomi. There weren't any other Moabites in Bethlehem.

'You can't do that, lady, without special permission, not glean right among the sheaves. I'll have to ask the owner when he gets here. Until then you'll just have to wait.'

The field belonged to a man called Boaz, and, as it happened, Boaz was a distant relative of Naomi's. Ruth didn't know either of those things.

She had to wait for several hours. By the time Boaz arrived, the sun was getting high, and the air was already hot.

Boaz greeted his workers. 'God be with you!' he called. 'God bless you!' they answered. Then Boaz spotted Ruth. He didn't know her. She wasn't from those parts. She was clearly a foreigner. What was she doing there? he wondered.

He turned to his foreman. 'Whose wife is that?' he asked.

'It's that Moabite woman who came back from Moab with Naomi,' the foreman answered. 'She asked to collect grain among the sheaves. I told her I'd have to ask you first. She's been standing here ever since.'

Boaz looked back at Ruth. So this was the woman who'd come all the way from Moab. He'd heard about her. It was astonishing her leaving Moab like that, all for a tired, bitter old woman. He went over to her and smiled. 'Of course,' he said to her. 'Collect as much grain as you like. But be careful of the men. Some of them can be rough with women. Stay close to my women instead, the ones making the sheaves. Follow them and pick up what they leave behind. I'll tell the men to leave you alone. And if you get thirsty, go to one of the jars over there and have a drink. The men have filled them specially. It's hot work down here.'

Ruth was overcome. 'Why are you being so kind to me, sir?' she said. 'I'm nothing special. I have no rights here. I'm a stranger, a foreigner.'

'Oh no,' said Boaz. 'You're very special. Everyone's talking about you – about all you did for Naomi after your husband died. How you left your mother and father behind, and the country where you were born. And how you came all the way to Bethlehem, to a people you didn't know. Oh yes, you're special all right! You've come here to find refuge beneath the wings of the Lord God of Israel. Well, I hope he rewards you handsomely.'

'I hope I'll continue to please you, sir,' Ruth replied. 'I didn't know what you'd say. But I'm not afraid any more. You've spoken so kindly to me, and I'm not even one of your workers.'

She worked all the rest of the morning close to Boaz's women. Then the time came for the midday meal. Ruth thought she would go hungry, but Boaz called her over. 'Come and sit with us,' he said. 'Have some bread and dip it into the wine.'

Ruth went over to where they were sitting, taking with her the little sack of grain she'd gleaned. 'Here, have some roasted grain,' Boaz said.

Roasted grain! That was a real treat, and Boaz was giving her mountains of it! She had more of it than she could eat, and bread too. She would have enough to take some home for Naomi. She wrapped it in a cloth and put it inside her sack.

She got up to start gleaning again. Boaz called across to his men. 'Let her glean right among the sheaves,' he said. 'And pull some handfuls out of the sheaves and leave them on the ground for her to pick up. And don't you dare tell her off.'

The men raised their eyebrows and looked at one another. No gleaner had got this treatment before. What was Boaz doing, the silly old fool? Was he in love with the woman or something?

But they'd better do as they were told, or they might not get paid.

Ruth carried on gleaning till the evening came. It was back-breaking work, but with the benefit of Boaz's orders to his men she picked up loads and loads of grain. By the end she had a huge basketful. It was as much as one of the men normally earned in two or three weeks.

Naomi's eyes grew wide when she saw what Ruth brought home. Then Ruth unwrapped the cloth and got out the spare bread and roasted grain. Naomi's eyes grew larger still.

'Wherever did you work today?' she asked. 'Someone's been extremely kind to you. God bless him, whoever it was!'

'It was Boaz,' said Ruth.

'Boaz!' cried Naomi. 'God bless the man! He's the answer to all our troubles. God bless him!' She paused. 'Listen, Ruth,' she said quietly. 'This Boaz is a relative of ours, from the same clan as Elimelech and Mahlon. He's one of those who can redeem us.'

'What do you mean, "redeem us"?' asked Ruth.

'When someone in your clan is in trouble, you've got to help them, make sure they're all right. Well, we're in trouble, aren't we? No man to look after us, me too old to marry again and you a foreigner. But Boaz might just…'

'"You can glean in my fields till the harvests are in, the wheat as well as the barley,"' interrupted Ruth. 'That's what Boaz said to me. "And stay close to my young men." He said that too.' She giggled.

'Young men!' said Naomi. 'Stay close to his young *women*, Ruth! The men aren't safe to work with. You never know what they might get up to! But that's good about the gleaning.'

Ruth smiled. Naomi hadn't heard her giggle. She hadn't realized Ruth was being mischievous. But there was another reason why Ruth was smiling. Naomi had stopped staring at the wall. She was climbing out of her despair. But what did her mother-in-law mean when she said that Boaz was the answer to all their troubles? Ruth didn't understand that bit. And what was Naomi about to say just then, when she interrupted her? Now she wished she'd let her finish. She could see Naomi thinking. She was plotting something. What could it be?

Ruth soon found out.

The barley and the wheat had been cut. The sheaves had been taken down to the threshing floor so they could be beaten to separate the grain from the chaff. It was tiring work, but once it was done the harvest was over. Threshing floors were places where lots of eating and drinking went on, particularly when the harvest was a good one. That year the harvest was very good indeed. The heaps of grain were unusually high. Until all the threshing was done, some of the men would sleep beside the grain, so it didn't get stolen in the night. Boaz always slept there to guard the grain from his fields.

Naomi knew that. She came up with a plan. It was a desperate one, but it was the only one she could think of. Ruth had come home each day with piles of grain and food from the midday meal. But that wouldn't last for ever. They needed a man in the house. Or rather, they needed a man to marry Ruth and take her and Naomi under his wing. Then they would be secure. Ruth might have a child – a son who could take over the land that had been in their family for so long. That way Elimelech and Mahlon's names, and Chilion's too, would not be forgotten. The family would live on.

The plan was a very risky one, but Naomi and Ruth were two desperate women – or would be if nothing was done.

Early one evening, before it got dark, Naomi turned to Ruth.

'Ruth dear,' she said. 'I've got an idea. You know I want the best for you. Well, I think I know how you might get it. That Boaz, he's a relative of ours, as I said. As I told you, he's a member of Elimelech's clan. Well, he'll be down at the threshing floor, dealing with the barley, and he'll be sleeping there all night. Now this is what you must do. Wash yourself, dress up in your best clothes, put on some perfume, and when it's getting dark, go down to the threshing floor. Don't let anyone see you. Wait till they've all finished eating and drinking, and watch where Boaz goes to lie down. Then after a bit, when he's had time to get to sleep, go to where he's lying, take your clothes off and lie down at his feet. He'll tell you what to do, when he wakes up.'

Ruth understood what Naomi was thinking. The only way she and her mother-in-law could survive in Bethlehem was if Boaz married her. The trouble was she was a foreigner. She suspected Boaz was in love with her, but he was a respectable man, one of the most distinguished men in the town. There was no way he could marry a Moabite woman... unless, of course, he was tricked into it. Naomi's plan might work, it just might.

'I'll do as you say,' she said to Naomi.

No one saw her as she walked down the path to the threshing floor. She watched Boaz as he finished his meal with the other men and went to lie down beside his grain. It was not long before he was fast asleep. Ruth could hear him snoring. She tiptoed up to him, took off her clothes and lay down at his feet.

She looked up at the stars and waited. It was cold, and she began to shiver. She shivered a particularly violent shiver and touched Boaz's feet by mistake. He sat up, his eyes wide open. He thought someone must be stealing his grain. Then he looked down at his feet. There was a woman there! He couldn't see who she was in the dark.

'Who are you?' he asked.

'I'm Ruth, sir,' Ruth replied. 'And I'm cold. Spread your cloak over me, sir. That way you can be our redeemer, the answer to all our troubles.'

Boaz was quite overcome. She was asking him to marry her! In those days, if a man spread his cloak over a woman in the way Ruth was asking, he made her his wife. It was a sign he would protect her as her husband. Boaz understood exactly what Ruth meant, and he was amazed, flattered and overjoyed all at the same time.

'God bless you!' he cried. 'This is the best thing you've ever done. Even better than all the kindness you've shown to Naomi. You've chosen *me* as your husband. Me! I'm getting on a bit, as you know. More than a bit, if I'm honest. But you haven't gone after the young men. You've chosen *me*! We're just right for one another, you and me, Ruth. All the men of the town admire you. We've got a lot in common, you and me. Because they admire me too, you see.

'However,' he continued, 'I'm afraid it's not quite so simple. There's a man in the town, another member of Elimelech's clan, who's a closer relative of yours than me. He comes ahead of me and must be given first choice. But don't worry. I think I can fix things when morning comes. Meanwhile, put your clothes back on, and stay here until the morning. If the other man doesn't marry you, I promise you I will myself. I swear it.'

So Ruth got dressed and lay down to sleep. Just before dawn, when it was still dark, Boaz nudged her awake.

'Quick!' he said. 'The sun will be up soon. You must get home before anyone sees you. Hold out your shawl.'

He poured some grain into it, so much she could scarcely carry it all. They tied up the shawl, and Boaz lifted it onto her head.

Naomi was awake when Ruth got home. She hadn't been able to sleep all night.

'Did it work?' she said urgently. 'Are you all right? Are you Boaz's wife yet?'

Ruth told her what had happened, and what Boaz had said about the other relative. 'And he gave me this present for you,' she said, plonking the sack of grain down on the floor. 'He said I mustn't go back to you empty-handed.'

Naomi clapped her hands. She looked down at the huge pile of grain. 'Just wait and see,' she said. 'Boaz will sort it all out. He'll do it this very morning.' And she took Ruth's hands and danced around the room as the sun came up and turned the fields to gold.

Boaz left the threshing floor and climbed the track towards the gate of the town. He still could hardly believe Ruth wanted to marry him. Inside the gate was a square. The men of the town had to pass through the square on their way to the fields. It was the place where they met one another, shared news with one another and did business with one another. It was also the place where they could get the elders of the place together, to decide complicated matters.

Boaz walked through the gate, sat down in the square and waited. It was still very early, but soon the men would be coming through. One of the first to arrive was the relative of Naomi and Ruth he'd mentioned to Ruth earlier that night, a Mr Thingummyjig.

Boaz called to him. 'Come over here, Mr Thingummyjig!' he

said. 'Come and sit down. I've got an important matter to raise with you.'

Mr Thingummyjig did as he was told. Soon the other men began to come through the square. Boaz called over some of the elders of the town, all men who were the heads of their families. They sat down too. In the end there were ten elders gathered, enough to decide upon the matter Boaz wanted to raise. He started to explain what it was all about. Lots of people stopped to listen and sat down themselves behind the circle of elders.

Boaz addressed Mr Thingummyjig. 'There's a plot of land Elimelech used to farm before he left for Moab. It's been in his family for as long as anyone can remember, but it's been untouched for years. Naomi can't look after it herself, so she's planning to sell it. Now, it can't be sold to someone outside the clan, can it? We must keep it within the clan, to keep the memory of Elimelech and his sons alive. You belong to the clan, and so do I. But you come before me. So if you're willing to buy the land from Naomi, then say so in front of the elders here and all the other witnesses. If you don't want to buy it, I'll purchase it myself.'

Mr Thingummyjig thought about it for a while. He knew the laws of the day. If he purchased the land, he would have to marry Naomi. If Naomi then had a son, the boy would inherit the land when he was old enough. That was the law too. But that was all right. Naomi was too old to have any more children, so he could marry her without taking any risks. He would have some more land, and his own sons would inherit it when he died.

'All right,' he said. 'I agree. I'll purchase the land, to keep it in the family.'

But Boaz had a surprise up his sleeve for Mr Thingummyjig. He had a surprise for everybody. 'You realize,' he said to Mr

Thingummyjig, 'that on the day you get the land, you also get Ruth, the Moabite woman, Mahlon's widow. Mahlon was Elimelech's eldest son, and would normally have inherited the land when his father died. But Mahlon is dead too, of course. So if you buy the land, you'll have to marry Mahlon's widow.'

Oh no! Mr Thingummyjig said to himself. The wrong widow! I thought I'd have to marry Naomi. Ruth's another matter altogether. She's still young. She could easily have a son, and then *he* would inherit the land, and my children would get nothing. I would have spent all that money on the land for nothing. And I'll have Ruth and Naomi to support as well. No, it's all too much. It's not fair on my children either. And another thing: Ruth's a Moabitess. She's an outsider. She's different. She's not one of us.

He coughed. 'I've changed my mind,' he said out loud. 'I'm sorry, but I can't buy the land and marry Ruth. It would ruin my children's inheritance.' He turned to Boaz. 'You buy the land,' he said. 'You marry Ruth.' He took off his sandal and handed it to Boaz, a sign that the deal was done.

Boaz took the sandal and turned to the elders and the rest of the men sitting in the square. 'You are witnesses today,' he said solemnly. 'I am buying the land from Naomi, and I am marrying Ruth. That way I will keep Elimelech's name alive, and Mahlon's and Chilion's names too.'

'We are witnesses,' the men said. 'May God bless you and Ruth! May God give you lots of children!'

It was all over. Mr Thingummyjig, the elders and the other men went off to their work. As soon as they had gone, Boaz went running off to find Ruth and Naomi. He burst into their house. 'I can be your redeemer!' he cried. 'I can keep your land in the family, Naomi, and you and I, Ruth, can get married.'

The three of them danced together for joy. Their troubles were over at last. Naomi wouldn't be poor any more and would have a man to look after her in her old age. Ruth would have a husband again and wouldn't be a foreigner in Bethlehem. And Boaz would have a wife – a wife he loved, a wife who loved him.

So Boaz and Ruth were married, and God did give them a child, a son. The women of Bethlehem danced and sang when the child was born. They remembered what Naomi had been like when she came back from Moab, how bitter she had been, how empty she had felt. Now her old age would be full to the brim and overflowing. She had a baby to help look after now. And the baby would grow into a boy, and the boy into a man, and the man would help look after her in her last years. The child was truly an answer to all Naomi's troubles. So was Boaz, of course, who had come to her rescue. So was Ruth, who'd risked everything to come to Bethlehem with her. Without Ruth, Naomi would probably have died. Ruth's love for her had made all the difference.

'That Ruth of yours,' the women said to Naomi, 'she's more of a blessing for you than seven sons!' In those days you couldn't pay anyone a higher compliment than that.

The women named Ruth's son Obed. When he grew up, Obed had a son called Jesse, and Jesse had eight sons, the youngest of whom was called David, the man who became king over Israel. So Ruth, the Moabitess, was king David's great-grandmother.

Jonah, a Big Fish, a Great City and the Forgiveness of God

The story of Jonah is the story of a prophet, a ship, some foreign sailors, a big storm, a big fish, a big city, its people, its king and its animals, a plant, a scorching wind, the sun, a nasty bug and God. Mostly it's a story about a prophet and God.

There's nothing else in the Bible quite like it. The other stories about prophets, such as the ones about Elijah we came across in chapter four, or the Amos and Jeremiah stories we covered in chapter five, tend to portray them as great heroes. They are courageous men and women – people who see things as God sees them, and who speak the truth even when that puts their own lives at risk. Their task is to challenge the people of God to live like the people of God, to be loyal to God and to be just and kind in their dealings with one another.

Jonah, however, gives God a very hard time. God tells him to speak not to the people of Israel or Judah, as we would expect, but to the inhabitants of the foreign city of Nineveh. Jonah does everything he can to get out of going to Nineveh. And when finally he gets there and opens his mouth, he says very little, and it's not clear that it's what God wanted him to say either. In the stories about the great prophets such as Elijah, Amos or Jeremiah, people often take little heed of what they say. The people of Nineveh, however, immediately take notice of Jonah's few words and act upon them. And when God forgives them, that drives Jonah mad!

We don't know anything about the author of the story, nor when he wrote it. On one level it's an amusing, sometimes hilarious story, full of all sorts of wonderful and impossible things. Yet in the end it's a story about the forgiveness of God, and how far that goes. It's only short, but it's one of the most profound and challenging stories in the Bible.

ONE DAY A PROPHET named Jonah was praying. As he prayed he heard God speaking to him. 'Get up,' said God. 'I want you to go to Nineveh, that great city, and cry aloud in her streets to warn the people. I've had enough of their wickedness.'

What might Jonah have said to that? This perhaps: 'Nineveh? I can't go there. It's the most wicked place on earth! It's the capital of the dreadful Assyrians – the most terrifying people on earth! Look what they did to the kingdom of Israel! They smashed it to pieces and deported great numbers of its people to other parts of their empire. And do you know what they did to the little kingdom of

Judah? Let me remind you, God. They invaded and captured *forty-six* of its towns and countless villages, and laid siege to Jerusalem. The king had to surrender to them, and they went back to Nineveh with cart-loads of treasure. They're ruthless and arrogant. They just trample over anyone who gets in their way. If I go to Nineveh, I won't survive more than five minutes. Send me somewhere else. Bethlehem, perhaps? Nice people in Bethlehem, so I've heard. Send me *anywhere*, God, but not Nineveh, not Nineveh!'

Well, if Jonah had said that, God could have had a proper conversation with him and tried to calm his fears. But Jonah didn't say that – he didn't say anything. Jonah went down to the coast of the Great Sea, the Mediterranean, to a port called Joppa, and got on a ship bound for Tarshish. God had told him to go to Nineveh. Nineveh was as far east as Jonah could imagine. Jonah thought he would go west, to Tarshish, which was as far west as he knew.

Jonah was running away from Nineveh, but mostly he was running away from God. The trouble is, running away from God is rather difficult. When the ship left port, Jonah imagined he was leaving God behind, but, of course, he wasn't. He bumped into God in the shape of a great storm, an astonishingly wild and ferocious tempest.

The foreign sailors of the ship were terrified. It was creaking terribly. Surely it was going to break up. They cried to their gods and threw the cargo into the sea to lighten the ship and help it sit higher on the waves, but it didn't do any good.

Jonah looked at the waves hurling themselves over the boat, and the sailors rushing about and praying to their gods. He turned his back on it all, went down to the deepest part of the hold, lay down and went into a deep sleep.

'What do you think you're playing at? Get up, you idiot!' It was the ship's captain. He was shaking Jonah to wake him up, and shouting above the noise of the crashing waves and the cracking timbers of the boat. 'Get up and pray to your god! Perhaps he will take notice of us and save us, so we don't all die.'

Jonah turned over and put his face against the side of the boat.

The sailors were at their wits' end. This was no ordinary storm. It was sent by the gods, they were sure of it. Their gods could punish wicked people by catching them in storms like this. So there must be someone on the boat who'd done something terrible to make the gods angry. They cast lots to find out who it was. It was Jonah, that passenger down in the hold! They went to get him.

'Now then, Mister,' they said. 'Tell us what's going on! You're the one who's caused all this trouble. We know that. But who are you working for and where do you come from? What people do you belong to?'

Jonah got up and steadied himself against the side of the ship. He stood on a coil of rope and looked down on the sailors. 'I'm what you foreign people call a Hebrew,' he said in a smooth, proud sort of voice. 'I work for God, if that's how you want to put it, the proper God, who is Lord of the sea and the land.'

'You're running away from him, aren't you?' the sailors cried. 'You stupid idiot! You can't run away from God. So what do we do next? Tell us that, Mr God-runner!'

'Throw me into the sea,' said Jonah. 'It'll calm down then.'

He sighed. If I drown, then at least I'll get away from God, and I won't have to go to Nineveh. Jonah didn't say that bit. But that's what he thought.

The sailors were good men. They didn't want Jonah to drown, so they picked up their oars and tried to row for the shore. But it was no good – the storm was getting worse and worse. In a few minutes it would turn the ship over, and then they would all drown. There was nothing for it. They would have to throw Jonah overboard after all.

'God, dear God,' they prayed. 'Don't hold this against us! We don't want to kill him. But this is your storm, and you've left us with no other option.' So saying, they threw Jonah into the sea. The wind dropped immediately, the waves subsided, and a nice little breeze blew the ship on its way.

The sailors were overcome with awe. They turned at once to God and offered up sacrifices to thank him for saving them. 'And when we get back from our voyage, we'll go to your temple in Jerusalem and offer you more sacrifices, God, we promise. Thank you, God. Thank you!'

Jonah sank down deeper and deeper in the water. 'Goodbye God, goodbye Nineveh,' he said among the bubbles.

But God hadn't finished with Jonah yet. He sent a great big fish to swallow him. Jonah was in that fish's stomach for three days and three nights.

To pass the time Jonah made up a song, a special kind of song addressed to God, called a psalm. Psalms are supposed to be mainly about God; Jonah's psalm was all about Jonah. This is how it went:

> 'It's all your fault, God!
> You cast me into the deep,
> into the heart of the sea,
> with waves crashing all around me.
> Deeper and deeper I sank,
> and then deeper still,
> with seaweed wrapped around me
> like a funeral shroud.
> I sank so deep
> I could see the roots of the mountains above me.
> Then, when the gates of death were about to clang shut
>   behind me,
> you sent this fish to snatch me away.
> As my life was ebbing away,
> I remembered you, my God.
> I prayed,
> and my prayer reached you,
> enthroned in comfort in your holy temple.
> People who worship other gods
> have turned themselves away from you,
> but I, I will not turn away.
> I will come to your temple
> to offer sacrifices to you.
> All I owe you I will pay.
> You are the only God who can come to the rescue.'

The psalm made God sick, it was so self-centred. It made the fish sick too. God made it vomit Jonah out onto the shore.

So, thought God to himself. Jonah's going to go to Jerusalem to offer sacrifices in my temple, is he? Oh no, he's not! He's going to Nineveh. He spoke to him once more.

'Get up,' God said. 'I want you to go to Nineveh, that great city, and cry aloud in her streets. Cry the words that I will give you.'

So Jonah got up, and this time he did go to Nineveh. It was no use running away any more.

It was a long way to walk, hundreds of miles, but eventually he reached the city. It was huge. It would have taken three days to walk all round it. Jonah walked for one day.

'Forty days more,' he cried, 'and Nineveh will be destroyed!'

That was all. No, 'This is the word of the Lord God,' the way

prophets usually began. No, 'Listen everyone, I'm Jonah, and I'm the prophet of God, who is Lord of the sea and the land.' No, 'God's had enough of your wickedness.' No call to the people to mend their ways. No hint of God's mercy, no word of his forgiveness and pity, just, 'Forty days and Nineveh will be destroyed.' Was that really what God meant him to say?

Whether it was or not, it certainly had an effect! Those wicked Ninevites immediately turned to God. The great king left his throne, threw aside his royal robes, put on sackcloth and went and sat on the city rubbish heap. He sent out his heralds to proclaim a solemn declaration in every part of the city.

'By decree of the great king and his councillors,' it began. 'O all you men, women and children; O all you cows, donkeys, sheep and goats, hear this! There will be a solemn fast. Not one of you is to eat or drink anything, to nibble a leaf or take a sip of water. You must all put on sackcloth and cry to God with all your strength. You must leave behind your wicked ways – put your violence behind you. You never know, perhaps God will change his mind and not be angry with us any more, so we won't all die.'

The people and the animals did exactly as they were told. And God did change his mind. He wasn't angry with them any more. He forgave them all, every one of them.

And that made Jonah mad!

'I knew you'd do that, God,' Jonah said. 'When you first told me to go to Nineveh, I knew you'd forgive them. That's why I tried to run away to Tarshish. You're soft, you are, God! So dreadfully compassionate. So slow to get angry. So kind and ready to forgive people. Have you forgotten what these Ninevites have done, God? They deserve destruction! So, if you're not going to destroy them, then destroy me instead! I'd rather die than live in this soft, forgiving world of yours, where people don't get what they deserve.'

'Dear, oh dear,' God replied. 'You really are upset, aren't you? Do you think you're right to be so angry, Jonah?'

Jonah didn't say anything more. He turned his back on God, and went and sat down on the eastern side of the city, outside the walls. He built himself a shelter. He was determined to sit there till the forty days were up. 'Forty days more, and Nineveh will be destroyed.' That's what he'd said. And he was a prophet, called to speak the word of God. Well, thought Jonah, let's see if God keeps his word!

The shelter he'd built wasn't very good, and it was extremely hot out there. Jonah wasn't sure he could stand forty days of such heat. Then God made a plant grow up overnight. When Jonah woke up in the morning, he found himself under a canopy of broad, fresh green leaves. The shade was delicious! The sun rose high in the sky, but Jonah was lovely and cool. He was overjoyed! It was wonderful, marvellous, like being in the Garden of Eden. But when the next day dawned, God sent a nasty little bug to attack the plant. The leaves shrivelled up and fell off onto Jonah's head. Next God brought in a hot east wind from the desert. It blew the leaves away, and the sun attacked his head until he thought it would burst.

'I'd rather die than live,' he moaned.

'Dear, oh dear,' God replied. 'You really are upset, aren't you? Do you think you're right to be so angry about the plant, Jonah?'

'Yes,' said Jonah pitifully. 'I'm angry enough to die!'

'Jonah, my old friend,' God said. 'You feel sorry for that plant, although you didn't plant it in the ground, nor water it to make it grow. It came up in a night and died in a day, and yet you feel such pity for it! And I, who made this world, who made the animals and the people upon it, should I feel no pity for Nineveh? Should I not weep over the people within its walls, all one hundred and twenty thousand of them? Look at them! They're my people, yet they're like helpless little children, not knowing their right hand from their left. And what about all their animals, their cows and donkeys, their sheep and goats? They're my animals too. I made them after all. Should I not have pity upon them?

'You're trying to put boundaries round my love, Jonah. But you can't do that. You can't stop me, Jonah. You can't stop the compassion welling up in my heart. You can't stop my pity, my mercy, my forgiveness. They will go anywhere – even to the darkest places of the world.'

The Book of Job: Shaking a Fist at Heaven

We want life to be fair. We want life to make sense.
But sometimes things happen we cannot understand.
Sometimes good things happen we know we don't
deserve. Sometimes bad things happen we know we
don't deserve either, and that can make us angry as
well as sad.

The book of Job is about some terrible things that
happen to a man called Job. He doesn't deserve them,
and he knows it. He believes everything comes from
God, so he believes his suffering must come from God
too, but he can't make any sense of it. He is a good
man. In his village he has been like eyes to the blind,
he tells us, like feet to the lame, a father to those in

261

need. If his own slaves have ever made complaints against him, he has upheld their cause. He has made sure strangers and foreigners are treated fairly. He has put a stop to bullying. He has rescued the poor and looked after children who have had no one to care for them. He has been like refreshing rain, he says, like warm sunshine. He has been like a king, the wisest and most loving of kings.

What, then, is God playing at, to make life so terrible for him? It's not fair. It's not right. It makes no sense. The world seems to Job all upside down. If this is the sort of thing God does, then God must be a thug. That is what his suffering makes him think and say.

Three friends come a long way to see him and spend time with him. At first they keep quiet, but when he starts railing against God, they get very cross and leap to God's defence. God is always fair, they say, so Job must have done something dreadful to deserve what has happened to him. They try over and over again to convince him, but Job knows they are wrong and becomes more and more enraged, both with them and with God.

Finally, after an agonizingly long wait, God appears to Job and shows him the kind of God he really is. That great vision transforms Job and gives him back his dignity. As for the friends, God tells them they have been speaking nonsense and is very angry with them.

The book of Job is set in the remote past, during, or even before, the days of people like Abraham and Sarah, the ancestors of the Jews. That does not mean it is one of the earliest works in the Bible. Writers often set their stories or poems in the past. It is, in fact, one of the most difficult works in the Bible to date, and could have been composed at almost any time between the seventh and the second century BC. We can be almost certain it was written by a man, probably a man who was rich and powerful, but we don't know his name, although he was one of the greatest poets the Jews before Jesus ever produced.

The work starts with a folk tale, which sets the scene for the poetry that follows. It's in the poetry that the poet says what he really wants to say.

ONCE UPON A TIME there was a good man called Job. He was not a Jew. He didn't come from the land of Israel; he came from the land of Uz. He was the richest sheikh in all the world: he had everything. But then, out of the blue, disaster struck – disaster upon disaster upon disaster upon disaster. First, raiders came and took all his oxen and donkeys, and killed the slaves who'd been looking after them. The same day all his sheep and shepherds were struck by lightning in a terrible storm and killed. Then more raiders came and stole all his camels and slaughtered the slaves who were with them. Finally, and worst of all, a tornado came whirling across the desert and struck the house where his ten children were eating and drinking together. It picked up the house as if it were a bag of sticks and hurled it to the ground. All the children were killed.

Job had had everything; now he had almost nothing. To make matters even worse, he fell ill with a terrible disease. His whole body was covered in burning sores. They itched unbearably, kept him awake at night and made him weep with the pain. No one could offer any cure.

He'd lost everything, except his wife, but he wasn't able to take any comfort from her. Life wasn't worth living any more. His animals were gone. His slaves were gone. His children were gone, every one of them. His dignity was gone also. He'd been the leader in his village, the one everyone looked up to, the one everyone respected. Now all that was over. He went outside the village and sat on the large rubbish heap, where everyone threw their garbage and their waste. He sat scratching his sores with a broken piece of pottery.

Three of his friends came to see him. They were sheikhs too. They came a long way to say how sorry they were and spend time with him before he died. When they first saw him sitting on the rubbish heap, they didn't recognize him. Then they looked harder and saw it was their friend. They howled their eyes out, tore their fine clothes, covered their heads with dust and sat on the ground with him, round the rubbish dump, for seven days and nights, not saying a word.

Then Job opened his mouth and cried:

'Perish the day I was born!
Perish the night I was conceived!
At creation God said,
"Let there be light!"
I say, "Would there had been darkness!"
Would that darkness had swallowed up the day of my birth!
Would that deep darkness,
the darkness of empty grief and death,
had carried off the night I was conceived!
Would that magicians had put a spell upon it,
so that it had lain barren, joyless,
with no pregnancy begun!

'Why did I not die newborn,
perish as I left my mother's womb?
Then I would have slept in peace in the land of death;
then I would have had rest with kings and princes;
then I would have been at ease,
where slaves no longer hear the slave-drivers' shouts,
where all are alike, both small and great,
where all are free.'

The three friends were shocked to hear such anger from Job, and the pain in his words was more than they could bear. They found it even worse when Job started blaming God.

What had he done to deserve all the terrible things that had happened to him? What had he done to deserve all his animals and slaves and all his children, every one of them, being taken away from him? What had he done to deserve the fearful itching of his sores? It seemed to Job he would never recover. He would die on the stinking village rubbish heap. What was God up to?

Job shook his fist and cried:

'God has torn me apart!
Like a lion he has torn me limb from limb.

Everyone laughs at me;
they strike me on the cheek to insult me.
God has abandoned me,
left me to their cruel, unceasing mockery.

'Once I lived in peace.
Then God came and shattered me,
seized me by the neck and smashed me to pieces.
He attacked me with his army,
put me up against a wall,
ordered his archers to shoot their arrows into me.
He told them to have no pity
but pierce me through till I was full of holes.
He besieged me like a city
and sent his battering rams against me,
till finally he breached my walls
and overthrew my defences.

Then he leaped through the breach
to destroy me and lay me waste.

'I can scarcely see for tears.
I am wasted away to a shadow.'

'How dreadful to speak about God like that!'
the friends said.
'You cannot blame God.
It is we humans who are to blame.
God rewards those who are good
and punishes those who are bad.
We bring calamities upon ourselves.
It is as simple as that, Job.'

'God is trying to teach you something,'
said the first.
'All this is God's good discipline.
He is like a father to you,
and you are his child.
He disciplines you
that your goodness may grow as strong as iron.'

'Your children must have sinned,'
said the second.
'That is why they died.
There can be no other reason.'

'How dare you speak with such certainty of the mystery of God!'
cried the third.

'You think you know all the secrets of heaven, do you?
You are a fool, and a wicked one too.
Turn to God,
confess your sin,
then you will have nothing to fear,
then your suffering will be like water that has flowed away
    and gone.'

All that only put Job into a greater rage.

'How long will you torment me?'
he answered.
'How long will you seek to crush me with your words?'

The friends were not really concerned about him any more. Their only concern was what they believed. They didn't notice Job any more or see his pain. They held their holy books in front of their faces and could only see the words that were written there. Their books said that everything came from God, so Job's suffering must come from God. That was what Job himself believed, of course. Their books said God was just and fair. Job had thought so too when all was well. Their books said God rewarded good people and punished bad people, and Job had once believed that was true also. Job was being punished, so Job must be bad, concluded the friends. And that's where Job disagreed. He knew he was innocent. He knew he didn't deserve all that had happened, all he was going through. He didn't deserve any of it, not a breath, not a whisper of it!

The friends stuck to their books, and Job stuck to his anger and his accusations against God. In the end the friends became quite distraught. Again the first one spoke:

'Such a goody-goody, were you?'
he shouted.
'I will tell you what you were.
You believed that might was right.
You had no pity for the poor.
You left them naked,
shivering in the night's bitter cold.
When women who had none to care for them
appealed to you for help,
you sent them away empty-handed.
And as for the orphans,
the children who had nothing,
you broke their arms.
Such was your brutality!'

None of that was true, but the friend thought the only way he could defend God was by attacking Job and making up lies about him. He actually believed the lies he invented. But Job didn't, not for one moment.

'Don't just look at me!'
cried Job.
'Look around you!
Look at all the suffering,
all the injustice in the world.
God goes round like a rampaging monster,
like a vicious tyrant with no pity in his heart.
He brings drought and flood,
shakes cities to pieces,
casts us in prisons of despair.

If plague strikes and thousands die,
God laughs with glee!
If a wicked man seizes power in a land,
God blindfolds the judges
so they cannot see the plight of the poor
or the bodies that lie in the streets!

'If you do not believe me,
then ask the animals and the birds,
speak to the fish in the sea,
turn to the earth herself.
They know enough of God's cruelty.
They know it lurks in every field,
in every wave,
in every inch of ground,
in every breath of the tall air.'

If only God would reply! Job thought. Yet beyond his accusations and the cruel words of his friends there was only silence. It was as if God was not listening, as if God did not care. If only God would appear, to answer the charges Job had brought against him! But Job's court was empty, except for himself and the three friends who had become his accusers. Well then, he said to himself. I will have to proceed with the case without him.

He swore a long oath of innocence, submitted a formal, written, signed testimony. He put it beside the pile of accusations against God. We human beings would make a much better job of looking after the world, than you, God, he said to himself. Then he waited. Would God appear? Probably not, he thought. I'll probably die first. And even if he does come, what hope have I got? He'll twist things just the way he wants. What hope have I of justice, when the one I accuse is also the judge?

Suddenly, just when Job had given up all hope, a mighty rushing sound filled his ears. It came nearer and nearer. It was like a whirlwind racing across the desert. It seemed to pick him up and lift him high above the earth.

    'Prepare yourself, Job!'
a voice said.
'Be a hero once more.
I wish to show you the world in which you live,
the world in which I work.
Come, my friend, give me your hand.'

Job knew the voice at once. It was the voice of God, the voice he'd been waiting to hear for so long. But this was not the voice of a merciless tyrant. It was soft and enquiring – full of delight and laughter.

The wild, whirling God took Job all over the world, to the foundations of the earth, to the springs of the sea, to the dwelling place of light and darkness, to the storehouses of the snow, to the gates of death. God took him back to the time the world was made. 'Look!' God cried, 'Look!'

Job saw God laying the foundations of the earth,
stretching a line upon them
to make sure they were level
and all in good order.
He heard the stars of the morning crying out for joy,
and all the sons of God shouting in triumph.

He saw the waters of the ancient sea
issuing from God's womb.
He watched as God wrapped it tight in clouds
and put it to bed,
saw the sea grow to a child,
listened as God told the waves
where they could play
and where they could not.

He saw God giving orders to the dawn,
as if to a servant.
'Take the corners of the earth, like a cloth,' God said,
'and shake the wicked out of it.
We will bring an end to their night of mischief,
you and I!'

Job watched in time of war,
when men were fighting one another
and strewing the earth with their dead,
as God went to the storehouses of the snow.
He saw God pulling out great heaps of snow
and throwing them down upon the battling armies.
'That should stop them fighting for a spell,' God said.

From the height of the whirlwind
Job watched as God dug channels
from the rivers of heaven
to bring water to the desert
and flowers to the dry ground.

He saw God untying the ropes of the stars
and letting them out to pasture in the fields of night.
He saw God counting the clouds,
tilting the waterskins of heaven to make it rain.

He saw the lion cubs crouching in their dens,
curled in the thicket,
waiting for food.
And there was God hunting,
catching game to fill their stomachs
and drive away their hunger.

There was God feeding the young ravens,
poking his bill down their noisy throats.

There was God keeping watch over the goats of the wild crags

and the pregnant deer roaming the desert hills.
See how God helped them with the birth,
stood by them in their labour,
like a midwife,
hidden in the desert,
far from human eyes,
far from human care.

See how God set the wild ass free
to roam the desert at his pleasure!
How God laughed at the ostrich
outrunning the horse and rider!

How proud God was of the warhorse,
flying into battle,
eating up the ground,
the flashing spear and the quiver full of arrows
rattling upon its flank!

Job watched the migrating eagle,
soaring, gliding towards the south on its great wings,
guided by God in every turn.
He saw God caring for the vulture,
providing shelter for its nest on the sharp crag,
where no human being could climb.

'Do you see? said God, 'Do you see?
How could you human beings
care for all these?
How could you look after the whole earth?

I am not the monster you thought I was, Job, my friend.
I do not rampage around
bringing chaos wherever I go.
Ask the animals and the birds,
speak to the fish in the sea,
turn to the earth herself.
They know enough of my compassion and delight,
that play in every field,
in every wave,
in every inch of ground,
in every breath of the tall air!'

Job was overwhelmed. God was right, of course. Human beings couldn't look after the world as God did. They were far too small for the job. They were not imaginative enough, nor creative enough, nor compassionate enough. And God was not a monster – just the opposite. And yet God had shown him a world which was not his world. The village ash heap was very different. Where was the care, the delight, the laughter of God there? That was what Job really wanted to ask, but instead he answered God and said:

'How small I am!
How can I answer you?
I put my hand over my mouth.

Once I have spoken,
but now I cannot reply.
Twice I have spoken,
but now I have nothing to add.'

God looked at Job. He saw the look in his eye and knew the question he was wanting to put. Once more he took his hand and whisked him off in the whirlwind. 'I have something more to show you, Job,' he said. 'It is terrifying, but I will keep you safe. Hold tight!'

The whirlwind sent them hurtling across the desert and put them down beside a huge river. God still had hold of Job's hand. Suddenly his grip tightened. 'There!' God said. 'Look!'

Job looked across to where God was pointing. What looked at first like a huge hippopotamus lay wallowing in the shallows, and something the shape of a vast crocodile lay sleeping on the muddy bank. Yet these were no ordinary beasts. They had no fear of anyone or anything. Even God hardly dared approach them. The crocodile was breathing fire; smoke issued from his nostrils. They seemed invincible, beyond anyone's control.

'These are the Great Beast and the Dragon,' said God. 'These are the Dark Forces that threaten the good order of my world and challenge my care. When they go on the rampage, the gods are terrified, and even I have a job bringing them to heel. They are the ones who cause all the suffering, the chaos and injustice in the world. You have been living in their shadow for too long, my friend.'

'Take me away,' said Job. 'I have seen enough.'

The whirlwind picked him up for the last time and returned him to his village.

Job had seen the truth. He had heard the morning stars cry out their joy. He had smelled the breath of the Dragon. Above all he had seen God – and heard him too!

> 'Before your whirlwind came
> I was speaking nonsense,'
> he said to God.
> 'I spoke then of things far beyond my understanding.
> All those accusations,
> all those angry words!
> I renounce them all,
> I withdraw my case.
> I had heard of you, my God,
> by the hearing of the ear.
> Now my eyes have seen you.
> I put this dust and ashes behind me.'

So saying, Job got up from the rubbish heap. His skin was not itching any more. He dusted himself down and pulled himself up to his full height. He had found a new humility. He had found a new dignity also. God had done him a great honour. God had remade him. It was time to resume his place in the village.

'I am very angry with you lot,' God said to Job's three friends. 'What did you think you were doing, saying all that fearful stuff to Job? When Job was angry with me, he spoke from the heart. He came to me as he was. He did not pretend. You spoke from your books. You tried to bend Job to your ways of thinking, your ways of talking and believing. You tried to break him. Well, you have not succeeded. He has more goodness and wisdom than ever you imagined. Go and offer sacrifices and ask Job to pray for you.'

The friends did as God told them. And Job did pray for them, despite all the cruel things they had said.

Then he went home.

Songs of Light

The Old Testament, or *Tanakh*, contains a collection of poems called the book of Psalms. The poems are sacred songs or prayers composed over many, many centuries, from the time of the kings in Jerusalem, through the exile in Babylon and well into the period after that.

Some of them were written for important national occasions, such as the coronation or wedding of a king, for the annual pilgrim festivals, or for when disaster overtook the country. Others seem to have been composed originally for families or individuals to use in their own prayers.

The psalms are very honest in the way they speak to God, like the rest of the prayers in the Old Testament.

Some are happy songs, which praise God to the skies. Others are full of pain and bewilderment, and get angry with God and accuse him of not doing anything to help. Whatever feelings we have, we can find them expressed somewhere in the psalms. No wonder they have played such an important part in Jewish and Christian worship over the centuries.

Some of the psalms have instructions attached to them, such as, 'To the leader: according to The Deer of the Dawn', or, 'To the leader: according to Lilies'. Presumably in those cases the leader was the person leading the music in the act of worship, and 'The Deer of the Dawn' and 'Lilies' were the tunes. Unfortunately the music has not survived, and we shall never know how the tunes went.

The titles of many of the psalms also mention particular people. One says it is 'A Prayer of Moses', and lots of them are introduced with the words, 'A Psalm of David'. That has made many people believe King David actually wrote most of the psalms himself. However, the titles were added after the psalms were first composed and cannot always be trusted. Sometimes they clearly don't fit. It is possible that David, or poets in his court, did write some of the psalms, but we cannot be sure.

In the end who wrote any particular psalm and for what occasion is not so important. What matters is that over so many centuries they have helped countless people, in all kinds of situations, to be more honest with God and to feel closer to him.

The most famous of all the psalms is Psalm 23. It is
written by or for those who have suffered from people
bullying them, perhaps, or abusing them, or attacking
them, or telling lies about them. We can tell that
because they mention their 'enemies' near the end.
The poem also makes clear those enemies have not got
the better of them. They still have them around, but
they don't feel threatened by them any more. This is
because God is protecting them, as a shepherd protects
his flock, and because in the temple, where they have
come to seek help, it feels as though God is welcoming
them as his guests of honour, or even waiting on their
table as their servant. He's treating them like kings and
queens. In the middle of the song they speak directly
to him. This is how it goes:

'THE LORD GOD is my shepherd;
I lack nothing,
he fills my every need.
He leads me through the dry hills
down to lush pastures,
where I can eat my fill,
lie down and rest.
When the sun is hot, and I am weary,
he takes me down to still, calm waters,
where I can drink and quench my thirst.
He gives me back my strength, my life.
He leads me along the right paths,
the paths where all is well.

This is how God always shows his care.
This is the kind of God he is!

'Even when I find myself in the valley of the shadow of death,
in the bottom of the deepest, darkest gorge,
where the sun cannot reach,
where lions and bears might attack,
even there I fear no harm.
For you, my God, are with me,
carrying your shepherd's club and your crook.
They make me feel safe, secure,
beyond all danger.

'You prepare a table before me.
You, the God of all the earth
wait upon me,
as if you are my servant.
You anoint my head with oil,
making me smell sweet to high heaven,
making my hair glisten and my skin shine.
You treat me, my God, like a king or a queen.
You pour fine wine into my cup,
more and more, till it overflows.
And all this in front of my enemies!
They cannot touch me now.

'Surely, God's goodness and love
will pursue me all the days of my life.
I will come back again and again to this place
for the length of all my days.'

The second psalm, Psalm 121, is a pilgrim song, sung by and for pilgrims who'd walked to Jerusalem to take part in one of the festivals at the temple. Perhaps it was sung as they prepared to set out for the journey home. They looked at the hills of the desert around the city and thought of all the places they would have to go through on the way. The journey would be a long one and dangerous too. 'Will we get home safely?' they ask at the beginning of the psalm. Then they remember the protection God will give them. 'Yes, we will,' they say, 'for God will protect us.' At this point one of the priests of the temple speaks and adds to what they have just said. The rest of the poem is his words, a farewell blessing for them to take home with them, a reminder of their time in Jerusalem.

'I LIFT UP my eyes to the hills
and think of the dangers hiding there.
From where will my help come?
My help comes from the Lord God,
the God who made heaven and earth.'

'The hills and all their paths are in his hands.
He will not let you stumble or fall.
He is your protector;
he never sleeps.
The God who protects the people of Israel
never sleeps, never slumbers.
Day and night he stands guard over you,
to keep you safe.

The Lord God is your protector;
he is your shade against the burning sun,
he is always beside you to guard you.
The hot sun will not strike you down by day,
nor will the dark forces of the night attack you.
The Lord God will protect you from all disaster,
he will protect your very life.
The Lord God will protect your going out
and your coming in,
wherever you go,
whatever you do,
now and always.'

INTRODUCTION TO THE NEW TESTAMENT

So far The Book of Books *has covered stories and poems from what Jews call* Tanakh *and Christians call the Old Testament. For Jews, the books of* Tanakh *make up their Holy Scriptures. They are their Bible. For Christians the Old Testament forms the larger part of their Bible, but there is a second part to it, which they call the New Testament. The remaining chapters of* The Book of Books *will be on that.*

The books of the New Testament are about Jesus, who Christians also refer to as Christ. Jesus was a Jew, and his first followers were Jews. He did nothing to suggest that he wished to found a new religion; he was born a Jew and died a Jew. At first his followers stayed within the boundaries of the Jewish faith, though people who weren't Jews quickly began to join them.

Jesus' followers believed he showed them what being a Jew meant. They believed he showed them what being a human being meant. Above all, they believed he showed them God.

He was so important to them, they wrote down his story. The saw it as following on from the Old Testament, or Tanakh. *They had come to read* Tanakh *with fresh eyes. When they thought of Jesus, it all made sense to them, as if they were reading it properly for the first time. It was as if he fulfilled all the good things that it had promised.*

Their story of Jesus was not meant to tell people everything about him. It was not a biography, a careful account of the whole of his life. They never even said what he looked like, or how tall or thin or fat he was. Almost the whole of their story was about the last year or so of his life, and in particular about his death and what happened after he died. They wanted to show what his life meant, to declare how significant he was and to encourage his followers to remain loyal to him, even if lots of people were against them. That story is in the New Testament.

But it doesn't appear there in just one version. It is told four times over, in what we call the four Gospels: Matthew, Mark, Luke and John. Christians regard the Gospels as the most important books in the entire Bible, and our next four chapters will be devoted to them. Sometimes in Matthew, Mark or Luke we have to work out for ourselves what they are trying to say about Jesus. This book adds its own slant to try to help our understanding. John, however, in his Gospel, tends to tell us directly what he wants us to understand.

Luke added a second volume to his Gospel, called the book of Acts. It continues the story of what happened after Jesus' death, telling how the numbers of his followers quickly grew and how Christian communities were founded in the cities of the eastern Mediterranean. Acts is mainly about two followers of Jesus: Peter, who had been with him during his lifetime, and Paul, who had a vision of Jesus a few years after his death. Chapter eleven of The Book of Books *will cover Acts.*

Virtually everything in the whole Bible up to the end of Acts is either storytelling or poetry. But most of the rest of the New Testament after Acts is made up of a collection of letters. The earliest of these were written by Paul – not to members of his family or personal friends, but to churches. These new Christian communities were struggling to work out what the Christian faith meant, what they should believe and what they should do. Our final chapter will offer a small collection of some of the finest passages from Paul's letters, as well as two passages from the last book in the Bible, Revelation, which contains visions of the time when God's reign will be complete and all things will be well.

7

THE NEW BEGINNING: JESUS IS BORN

Each of the Gospels in the New Testament is different from the rest.
Mark was written first, probably in the late AD 60s. Matthew and
Luke used Mark as their main source, so a lot in those three Gospels
is similar. But Matthew and Luke often changed Mark a bit, and
they also had stories to tell which weren't in Mark, and lots of Jesus'
teaching too, which Mark didn't know about, or, at least, didn't
include. The last Gospel to be written was John's, probably near the
end of the first century AD or soon after the beginning of the second
century, and he probably didn't know the other three Gospels. In some
respects his Gospel is very different from the others. For instance, he
thought the really important bit of Jesus' life lasted three years, not
just one, and the style of Jesus' teaching is not the same as in the others
either. But he too concentrated on the end of Jesus' life and spent a
lot of time telling the story of his death and what came afterwards.
And, like the others, he was trying to answer the questions: 'Who
was Jesus?', 'Who is Jesus?', 'What does his life mean?', 'What is
his significance?'

If there was room, it would be best to tell Mark's story of Jesus,
then Matthew's story of Jesus, then Luke's, then John's, but that would

make this book too long. So it will tell the story just once, picking pieces from each of the four Gospels.

At least it can start by telling Matthew's account of Jesus' birth, and then tell Luke's version. As you will see, they are quite different from one another. (Mark's and John's Gospels don't have any stories about his birth at all. Their first stories speak of him when he was already grown up and near the end of his life.)

Matthew and Luke's stories of the birth of Jesus are among the most famous in the Bible, and Christians retell them every year at Christmas.

Disgrace Turned Quite All to Grace
Matthew

IN A TOWN called Bethlehem, a few miles from Jerusalem, there lived a young couple called Mary and Joseph. Although it was only a small place, Bethlehem was famous among the Jews. It was where Ruth and Naomi and Boaz had once lived, and where king David had been born. As it happened, Joseph was descended from David.

Mary and Joseph were betrothed. When people got married in those days, they went through two stages and two ceremonies, and betrothal was the first of them. Mary was twelve when she was betrothed, and that meant she was Joseph's wife, and he was her husband, although she still lived with her mother and father. Soon the second marriage ceremony would be held, and she would go and live with Joseph.

But before that happened, Mary became pregnant. It wasn't Joseph's child, he knew that. She knew that too.

Joseph was heartbroken. It was a disaster – a terrible disgrace for Mary, her mother and father and the rest of her family, and for him, his parents and the rest of his family. He and Mary couldn't complete their marriage now. He could accuse her publicly of adultery. That way he could save face perhaps. Mary had made him look a fool after all, and feel a fool too. She'd hurt him terribly, and he could hardly bear the pain. If he made the matter public, he would at least be able to recover some of his pride, because everyone would know it was all Mary's fault.

That's what first went through Joseph's mind. But he was a good man, and he loved Mary. He couldn't expose her to such public shame. He decided he would divorce her quietly. He would pay back the bride-price he'd given her father. They wouldn't complete their marriage. Mary would stay at her parents' house. She would have a job explaining the baby when it arrived, but that would be her problem and her family's. There was nothing he could do about that.

Joseph went to bed and cried himself to sleep.

It was very dark that night. The clouds hung thick over Bethlehem. The moon and stars were invisible. Yet in the middle of the darkest hour Joseph's room became full of the light of heaven. There was an angel in his room; heaven had come to earth! And heaven spoke too!

'Joseph, son of David,' the angel said, 'do not be afraid! The Holy Spirit of God has turned this disgrace all to grace. It is a miracle! This child in Mary's womb you thought spelled such ruin will save your people from all that harms them, all that separates them from God. When this child is grown up, all the ancient hopes of your people will be fulfilled. "God is with us!" people will cry. "God is with us!" This child is beyond your wildest dreams, Joseph, and beyond Mary's most dazzling joy. Yes, Mary will have a son, and you must name him Jesus, for Jesus means Saviour, One who Saves. Complete your marriage, take Mary to live with you and be a father to her child. Do not be afraid! There is no cause for fear.'

Joseph woke up, his head still full of the angel's light. He did as the angel said. He completed his marriage to Mary, and they lived together in his house in Bethlehem.

Mary safely had her child. It was a boy, just as the angel said it would be. Joseph named him Jesus, just as the angel told him to.

Gifts Fit for a King
Matthew

At the time of Jesus the land of the Jews was occupied territory. It was part of the Roman empire. The man ruling the land was called Herod. He was not even a full Jew, and he was a friend of the Romans. The Romans had declared him 'King of the Jews'. Many Jews longed for someone who would give the Land its freedom again, someone who would restore their pride, someone who wasn't a friend of the Romans but a friend of God. Some of them hoped for someone who would be a king like David. They called the one they hoped for 'the Messiah'. 'Messiah' means 'Anointed One' or 'King'.

When he grew up, Jesus' followers claimed that he was that Messiah. But in Matthew's story of Jesus a few people, beyond Mary and Joseph, recognize who he is as soon as he is born. They are not Jews, they don't worship the God of the Jews, and they don't follow Jewish teaching or customs. They live hundreds of miles from Bethlehem, in a country far to the east, called Persia. And yet they travel all the way to Mary and Joseph's town just to see Jesus, to pay him homage and bring him gifts.

Matthew calls them 'magi'. Magi were clever men, skilled at reading the stars, wise men, who could interpret dreams and see into the future. Many people believed they had magical powers.

ONE DAY HEROD was in his palace in Jerusalem, feeling rather bored, wondering what to do, when a slave came into the room with

a message for him. The slave bowed low, 'Your Majesty,' he announced, 'two of your...' he coughed quietly, 'you know, sir, your special... er... your secret... They're outside. They've got something rather important to tell you, sir.'

The rest of Jerusalem knew what that was. The magi were going round the streets, asking the same question of everyone they met: 'Where is the child who has been born king of the Jews?' People would look at them in amazement. 'We saw his star rise into the night sky back in Persia,' the magi would explain. 'It took us a little time to work out what it meant, but we set out to follow it, and here we are.'

'We've been travelling by night, by the light of his star,' one would say.

'Not knowing where it would take us next,' another would add.

'It's brought us to Jerusalem, but we don't know where to go from here,' a third would explain.

Their words terrified the people of Jerusalem. 'King of the Jews?' they said to one another. 'A child, born king of the Jews? Herod's not going to like this. Herod is king of the Jews, and he doesn't plan to retire just yet. Two kings of the Jews is one too many. If the magi are right, and magi usually are, we're in for trouble and plenty of it.'

Herod had his secret agents out on the streets of the city. One of them heard what people were saying. Another bumped into the magi themselves, and they put their question to him, not realizing who he was.

The agents went straight to the palace. At that moment they were waiting impatiently outside Herod's door.

'Tell them to come in,' Herod said to his slave.

They came in and told Herod everything they had heard. Now it was Herod's turn to be frightened. Magi had to be taken seriously. What they said must be true. So, there's another king of the Jews around somewhere, is there? Herod said to himself. The Messiah must have been born!

When his agents had finished their report, Herod said to them quietly, 'Wait outside the door until I tell you to come in again.' Then he sent some more slaves through the streets of the city to summon the chief priests and the religious experts called scribes to come to his palace at once. Twenty minutes later they were gathered in front of him.

Herod got straight to the point. 'When the Messiah arrives,' he asked them, 'where is he going to be born?'

The chief priests and scribes were out of breath. The slaves had had them running all the way there. But it wasn't a difficult question. A prophet called Micah had already given the answer centuries before.

'Bethlehem,' they said. Panting hard they started to recite the relevant passage from Micah.

'Thank you, thank you,' Herod said quickly. 'You can go now. You've told me what I needed to know. On your way out, send in those two men waiting outside the door. Tell them I want to see them.'

The secret agents came in. 'Go and fetch those magi,' Herod ordered, 'and bring them here as quick as you can! Hurry!'

He didn't have long to wait.

'Ah, how nice of you to come all this way to see me,' Herod said, when the magi arrived.

'We haven't come to see you,' they replied. 'We've come to see the child who's been born king of the Jews. We've been following his star.'

Herod smiled. 'Of course, of course,' he said in his most oily voice. 'A slip of the tongue, I do apologize. Now tell me about this star of yours, I mean this star of *his*.'

The magi told Herod what they knew. Then Herod told the magi what he knew. 'You'll find the child in Bethlehem,' he said. 'It's not far at all – about six miles. I'll send a slave to put you on the right road. When you've found him, come back and tell me. Then I can go and bow down before him myself.' He smiled his oiliest smile.

The magi set out on the last short part of their journey. The sun had already set, and when they looked ahead, there was the strange star shining right above the middle of the road.

When they reached Bethlehem, they didn't need to ask anybody where the child was. There was a house just inside the walls of the town, and the star seemed stuck in the sky right over it. It was Joseph's house. A strange joy overcame them.

Their camels stopped and folded themselves down upon their knees. The magi slipped to the ground and carefully unpacked some things from their saddlebags. Carrying their gifts, they quietly entered the house.

As soon as they saw Mary and her baby, they knelt down on the floor. They were not in a fine palace, but that didn't matter. Mary was not a princess either, just a peasant girl, but that didn't make any difference. The baby looked like an ordinary baby, but the magi knew he wasn't. They were wise men and saw what others couldn't see. There was the air of heaven about this child. He was still only a small baby. He couldn't talk yet, or walk, or even smile properly. But being with him was like being in the presence of God. They bowed themselves low before him and presented him with gifts: gold, frankincense and myrrh. They were rare and expensive presents, presents meant for a king, gifts of love for a God.

Later that night they had a dream. It came as a warning: a warning not to go back to Herod. It showed them what kind of man Herod was. So they went back to Persia by a different route, avoiding Jerusalem altogether.

After they'd gone, it was Joseph's turn to have a dream. The angel who had appeared to him before, when Mary was pregnant, came to him again.

'Quick!' the angel said. 'There's no time to lose. Take Jesus and Mary and escape to Egypt. Hurry! Herod wants to search Bethlehem for the child and kill him. Stay in Egypt till I tell you it's safe to come back.'

So Mary, Joseph and Jesus became refugees. They travelled all the way south to Egypt. It was a hard journey, an exhausting one and a frightening one too. Lots of babies died in those days. It was hard enough looking after them at the best of times, and this was certainly not the best of times. Mary and Joseph wondered how they would all survive in Egypt.

But it was worse, much worse for the other mothers and fathers in Bethlehem and their babies.

When the magi did not return to Herod, he was furious. 'I was going to send my soldiers into Bethlehem to kill that so-called king of the Jews,' he shouted, 'Now I don't know which baby he is. I'll have to kill every baby in the village! I'll have to kill every one of them that's two years old or under, just to be safe.'

So he sent his soldiers to the village, and they searched every home. There was a terrible slaughter. The wailing of the mothers and fathers filled the place. Herod stood at the window of one of the rooms in his palace in Jerusalem and thought he could hear it, even from there. It made him smile. I'm safe now, he said to himself.

But soon he was dead.

For a third time the angel appeared to Joseph, this time in Egypt, and told him it was safe to return home. Relieved, they set out once more, but when they reached the borders of the country, they learned that Herod's son Archelaus was ruling in his father's place. People said Archelaus was as bad as his father, if not worse. They didn't dare go back to Bethlehem. Instead they travelled far to the north, beyond Lake Galilee, to a village called Nazareth. Nazareth was a tiny place – only a few hundred people lived there. It wasn't famous; most people in the country didn't know it existed. They could disappear there, and Archelaus would never find them. In any case, his rule didn't stretch that far north.

So it was in the region called Galilee, in the tiny, obscure village of Nazareth, that Jesus grew up. Joseph had no land he could farm, so he made as much of a living as he could by hiring himself out as a carpenter. You couldn't get much poorer than a carpenter in those days.

Mary Meets an Angel
Luke

Luke also tells us that Jesus was born in Bethlehem, but in his version Mary and Joseph come from Nazareth and go back there after Jesus is born. In his Gospel an angel appears not to Joseph but to Mary, and the first people to visit them after Jesus is born are not foreign magi but Jewish shepherds from the hills around Bethlehem. Herod plays no part in Luke's stories either. There are no soldiers, nor any babies killed, and Mary, Joseph and Jesus do not have to flee to Egypt. Matthew's stories of Jesus' birth are quite dark. True, Jesus brings the light of God into the world, but his birth is surrounded by fear, threat of disgrace, slaughter and flight. Luke does not focus on the darkness of the world nearly so much. Although the circumstances of Jesus' actual birth are more difficult in his story than they are in Matthew's, overall Luke prefers to emphasize the great joy that the birth of Jesus brings.

Luke's Gospel contains a further story about something Jesus did when he was twelve. It is the only story in any of the Gospels about Jesus when he was a boy, and we have included it here.

ONE DAY GOD SENT an angel to Nazareth. The angel was called Gabriel, and Gabriel knew exactly which house to go to.

Mary was on her own in her parents' house. She was betrothed to Joseph, but their marriage was not yet complete, and she was still living with her mother and father. She was looking forward to the day when she and Joseph would live together. Her family was pleased about the marriage too, for Joseph was descended from king David.

Suddenly the house became a holy place. Heaven had come to earth! The room was filled with an angel.

'Greetings!' Gabriel said to Mary. 'You are someone very special to God, covered from head to foot in his grace. God is with you.'

Mary was not expecting an angel. She was not expecting what he had just said either. She was bewildered, alarmed even. What did it all mean?

The angel saw her fear. 'Don't be afraid, Mary. God has given you something very special to do. Very soon you will conceive a child in your womb. You will have a son, and you will name him Jesus. He will be a great man. He will be called the Son of the Most High God, and God will give him the throne of David. He will be king of the Jews for ever. His kingdom will never come to an end.'

Mary hardly heard most of that. After the words, 'Very soon you will conceive a child,' her mind went into a spin.

'How will this be?' she cried. 'I'm a virgin, and Joseph and I are not yet living together!'

'The Holy Spirit will protect you and will surround you with the power of God,' the angel replied. 'The Spirit will turn all to grace and make your child holy. He will be called the Son of God. You know your old cousin Elizabeth, the one who has no children? She and her husband have been trying for a child for years and years, haven't they? Well, God has taken away all the disgrace she has felt, all her hopelessness, all her blaming herself. Elizabeth is expecting a son. She is already six months pregnant. Now you see what God can do!'

Elizabeth expecting a child! Mary could hardly believe it. 'Then I will be God's servant,' she said. 'Let it happen to me as you say.'

The servant of God, that's what she'd said! Abraham was called God's servant. So was Moses, King David and the prophets. So was Hannah, Samuel's mother. Abraham, Moses, Hannah, David, the prophets – and now Mary of Nazareth! She felt like the proudest woman on earth. She was a member of God's household. Where God went, she would go.

Gabriel saw her pride and smiled. Then he left, and Mary was once more alone in the house.

Mary's Song
Luke

SOON AFTER GABRIEL APPEARED to her Mary travelled south, to the town in the hills of Judea where her cousin Elizabeth lived. By this time she herself was pregnant.

The two women embraced one another, and the child in Elizabeth's womb seemed to jump for joy.

'So you're expecting a baby too!' Elizabeth exclaimed. 'And I know who your child will be as well. The Spirit of God has shown me that. Everyone will call him Lord. Well, well. I'm expecting a baby at long last, and now this! Now you – and the special child that you will have!'

The women laughed, and Mary broke into song.

'God is great!'
she sang.
'God is my saviour
and my warm delight.
For he has come to my rescue,
taken me from nowhere,
from nothing,
put me on his pedestal,
lifted me as high as heaven.

'This is the way of God.
He turns the world quite upside down.
The high and mighty fly scattered to the winds,
the weak and the poor are raised to the heights.
The rich go empty away;
the hungry are filled with good things.

'This is how our God has always been,
since Abraham so long ago
and the promises he received.
This is the mercy we have always known.
This is God's strength to turn tables over
and set free those who are oppressed.

300

'From now on
everyone will remember me
and call me blessed by God.
God is great, God is great!'

Mary stayed with Elizabeth for about three months and then went home to Nazareth. Very soon after that, Elizabeth had her child, a son. She called him John. Her husband agreed that that should be his name, because an angel of God had told him what the name should be even before the child was conceived.

One day Jesus and John would meet each other, down by the river Jordan.

Jesus is Born
Luke

FAR AWAY FROM NAZARETH, across the Mediterranean Sea, in the great city of Rome, Emperor Augustus decided he would hold a census throughout the whole empire. That meant everyone had to go and report to the Roman authorities and have their names put on an official list.

'Where do we have to go?' Mary asked Joseph. Although they

were only betrothed, they counted as husband and wife and would have to go together.

'Bethlehem,' answered Joseph.

'Bethlehem!' Mary exclaimed. 'Why Bethlehem?'

'That's where my family came from originally, before they moved up here to Galilee. The Romans say everyone has to go back to where they first came from.'

'Just to get their names on a list?'

'Yes.'

'But that's ridiculous!' cried Mary. 'Bethlehem's miles away! We'll have to walk all the way, and I'm already nearly nine months gone. The baby could come any day. What if it arrives on the way?' She burst into tears.

There was nothing Joseph could say, nothing he could do except hold her till she'd stopped crying.

So off they went. They walked one hundred and fifty miles, all the way to Bethlehem. By the time they arrived, there was nowhere for them to stay. The lodging for visitors and travellers was already full. There was no room for them. To make matters worse, Mary went into labour.

They did as best they could. The baby was safely born, and Mary swaddled him tight in bands of cloth to keep out the cold of the night. She laid him down to sleep in an animals' feeding trough; there was nowhere else to put him.

In the fields below the town a group of shepherds were gathered round a fire, watching over their flocks, guarding them from any thieves or lions or bears that might happen to come along. They were talking and laughing together, when suddenly the light of their fire became part of a greater light, a light that stretched from earth to heaven, a light that shone with the glory of God. In the middle of the light an angel stood. The shepherds were overcome with awe.

'Do not be afraid,' the angel said. 'I am the bearer of good news, news of great joy for all your people. A Saviour has been born this night, the Messiah, the Lord himself! If you go up to Bethlehem, you will see him. You will find him swaddled tight, laid to sleep in a feeding trough.'

As soon as the angel had finished speaking, the whole sky and the fields and hills around seemed to be dancing with angels, all of them praising God and singing,

'Glory to God in the highest heaven,
and on earth peace for all
on whom God's grace is poured!'

Then there was silence: only the crackling of the fire and the bleating of the sheep and goats.

'Let's go to Bethlehem!' the shepherds cried.

They ran all the way. It was uphill to the town, but they didn't mind, they were so excited. It didn't take them long to find what they were looking for. There was only one newborn baby in Bethlehem lying in a feeding trough!

So they found Mary and Joseph. They found the baby. And when they knelt down to look into Jesus' face, it was like looking into the face of God.

They went and told everyone all about it: about the strange light and the angel; what the angel had said; how the angels had danced and sung; how they'd run all the way to Bethlehem; and all about Mary and Joseph, the baby in the feeding trough and the face of God.

Everyone was amazed by it all. Then the shepherds went back

to their flocks, singing the angels' song all the way.

Mary kept the memory of the shepherds' visit locked away safely in the corner of her heart. She would never forget it.

Jesus' Real Home
Luke

MARY AND JOSEPH were devout Jews. When Jesus was still a baby, before they returned to Nazareth, they took him to the temple in Jerusalem, just a few miles from Bethlehem.

Twelve years later Jesus went to Jerusalem again.

Every year Mary and Joseph travelled as pilgrims from Nazareth to Jerusalem for the great festival of the Passover. When Jesus reached the age of twelve, they took him with them.

The city was packed with pilgrims. Many of them had travelled a long way to be there. In the festival they looked back to their beginnings as a people and celebrated the time when God rescued them from the grip of a terrible pharaoh in Egypt and brought them safely across the Red Sea. That was the time when they ceased to be slaves and moved on towards freedom and dignity and a land of their own.

Mary had already taught Jesus the story of his ancestors coming out of Egypt. Now he found himself among thousands and thousands and thousands of people all remembering that story, all hearing it again, all dreaming the same dreams of freedom and discussing how they could really live as friends of God in the land.

Jesus was fascinated by it all; he wanted to learn more. There were lots of questions he wanted to ask, and there were clever men

in the temple he wanted to listen to. They would be able to answer his questions.

So when the festival came to an end and Mary and Joseph started out on the journey back to Galilee, Jesus stayed behind.

The trouble was, he didn't tell them. They thought he must be walking with some of their relatives and friends. They went a whole day's journey. Then they realized Jesus wasn't there. They didn't get any sleep that night. The next day, as soon as it was light, they set off back to Jerusalem. By the time they got there, it was dark, and there was little chance of finding him in the dark. Another sleepless night. Then, finally, the next day, in the temple, they found him. He was sitting there as calm as could be, listening to the Jewish teachers. The teachers were talking about God and how people should live, and discussing details of the great story of the Jewish people. All of them had been amazed by the questions Jesus had been asking, and by the answers he'd given when they'd asked him questions of their own.

When they caught sight of him, Mary and Joseph rushed over.

'Jesus, what have you been doing?' Mary said. 'We've been worried sick, your father and I! How could you do this to us?'

Jesus turned to them and replied, 'But why were you looking for me? Didn't you know that this is where I belong? This is God's house. God is my Father and I am his Son. This is where I must be.'

Mary and Joseph didn't understand what he was saying. Jesus belonged with them back home in Nazareth. That was all they understood.

Jesus did as he was told and left Jerusalem with his parents. Their relatives and friends had waited for them, so they joined up with them again and walked back to Galilee.

Mary had another memory to keep safe in the corner of her heart. One day she would understand.

8

Who was Jesus?

If we want to understand the way the story of Jesus is told in the Gospels, we have to jump to the time after his death. Very soon after he died, Jesus' friends had some extraordinary experiences. On a number of occasions they felt that Jesus was as close to them as he had been during his lifetime. It was as if he was in the same room as they were, as if they could hear his voice, touch him even, as if they could share a meal with him, as they had so often before. They said he was risen from the dead. But there was something else which made their experiences more remarkable still, much more remarkable. It was not as if Jesus was some kind of ghost, or had simply come back to life. Meeting him now was like meeting God. When they felt Jesus was in the room with them, or sitting with them on the shore of Lake Galilee, it was like having God in the room, like having God sitting beside them.

These experiences changed them and took their lives in a new direction. They thought about God in a new way, and their understanding of Jesus was radically altered too. They looked back over his life and saw it in a new light. Suddenly they saw what it all meant. They realized Jesus wasn't just a peasant from Nazareth who had told marvellous stories and healed people from their troubles and illnesses. Jesus had brought God down to earth; they could see that now. Jesus himself had talked a great deal about the kingdom of God. Now they realized he had set up that kingdom on earth and given God the freedom to show what he could do. Wherever Jesus had gone the dark forces of evil had been beaten, and God's light and love had been allowed to reign supreme.

Almost certainly none of the writers of the four Gospels knew Jesus during his lifetime. But they too met him once he was risen from the dead. They also knew what it was like to be close to him, and they felt he showed them God. They were all members of Christian communities, where many stories about Jesus were told week by week. In their Gospels they retold some of those stories, or composed stories of their own designed to express the astounding truths they had discovered. Though each of the four Gospels is different from the other three, they all share that same urgent purpose.

The previous chapter of The Book of Books *was on Jesus' birth and his boyhood. It covered only the Gospels of Matthew and Luke, because they are the only ones to include any stories about the beginnings of Jesus' life. This chapter moves on to the last part of Jesus' life, the time when he emerged from the obscurity of Nazareth, started travelling through the villages of Galilee and built up a following. Each of the four Gospels covers that part, and this chapter will retell stories from all of them. Sometimes it will be dealing with a story found in three of the Gospels, or in all four of them; sometimes a story will be from just one of them. We will make clear at the beginning of each story in which Gospel or Gospels the story can be found, and indicate in the references at the back of the book which Gospel was the main source used for retelling the story.*

John Baptizes Jesus
Matthew, Mark and Luke

IN THE WILDERNESS, down in the Jordan valley, away from Jerusalem and the temple, away from the centres of power, John appeared, Elizabeth's son. He was grown up now, and people called him John the Baptist, or John the Baptizer. Crowds of people went to hear what he was saying and to be baptized by him in the river Jordan.

'It is time for the people of God to begin again,' John told them. 'It is time for a new start, time for those of you who have turned your backs on God to turn round and face him again. Then you will see his forgiveness. It is time for a new Israel – a people who will no longer go their own way but will follow God's way instead.'

People came from Jerusalem and all the towns and villages of Judea to hear John. He was dressed in camel skin, with a leather belt around his waist. It was how prophets used to dress. The people knew that from their old stories, particularly the ones about Elijah. John ate locusts and wild honey, the food of the desert, to remind the people of the time when their ancestors had escaped from Egypt and met God in the middle of the Sinai desert. He wanted them to remember how their ancestors had gone through the waters of the Red Sea when they were escaping the cruel pharaoh and his Egyptian soldiers, and how they had later crossed the Jordan river to enter the land promised to them by God. So he baptized them in the Jordan and plunged their heads deep into the water. He brought their heads up again, up into the light of the sun, ready to claim the new freedom of the people of God.

But who would lead them? 'Will you be our leader?' the people asked.

'Not me,' said John. 'There is one coming who is mightier than I. I am not worthy even to kneel at his feet to undo the thong of his sandals. I have poured the water of the Jordan over you; he will pour the Spirit of God over you! You will all be kings and queens in God's fair Land.'

One day Jesus came to where John was baptizing. He had come all the way from Nazareth in Galilee, and he joined the line of people waiting on the river bank. Eventually it was his turn. John plunged his head under the water. For a moment all creation held its breath. Then Jesus' head broke the surface again and disturbed its calm.

Jesus climbed the bank of the river, and as he did so, it seemed as though the heavens were torn apart. God was out of hiding! God had come again to walk the earth, as once he had walked the paths of Eden! The Spirit of God flew to Jesus like a bird, and a voice came from heaven, saying, 'You are my Son, the one I love. You are my delight. In you I am well pleased.' It was the voice of God.

A Reading in the Synagogue
Matthew, Mark and Luke

THE SABBATH WAS the Jews' holy day, and whenever Jesus was in Nazareth he went to the synagogue with the other villagers.

One sabbath the ruler of the synagogue asked him to read from one of the books of the ancient Jewish prophets and to speak about the passage afterwards.

The service began. They all sang a psalm and recited ancient, holy words their mothers had taught them when they were small: 'Love God with all your heart, with all your soul and with all your strength.' Next there were prayers, and readings from the books about Abraham and Moses. Then it came to the reading from one of the prophets. Jesus got up from his place and stepped onto the dais in the middle of the room. The scroll was already on the stand – the scroll of Isaiah. Jesus unrolled it until he reached the place he wanted.

'The Spirit of the Lord God is upon me,'
he read.
'He has anointed me to bring good news to the poor.
He has sent me to proclaim release to those in prison,
freedom to those trapped in debt,
to tell the blind they will see again,
to give freedom and honour
to those broken by calamity and oppression,
to proclaim that the time of God's generosity is come.'

He rolled up the scroll, handed it back to the attendant and sat down. There was silence in the synagogue. It was the way he'd read those words. They'd all heard them before, but not read like that. All eyes were fixed on him.

'Today,' he said, 'in this very place, in this poor synagogue, these words of Isaiah have found their meaning. They have come true in this small village of ours. I am the one Isaiah was talking about.'

'But you can't be!' they cried. 'You're Joseph's son. We know you. Nothing ever happens in Nazareth. Nobody important has ever lived here. Don't be ridiculous.'

Jesus shook his head sadly. 'No prophet is accepted in his home village. I won't be able to do anything here. Your minds are closed; I will have to find the poor somewhere else. Plenty of you are poor here. Plenty of you are broken by calamity or oppression. I know what you have to put up with. I live here and have had to put up with it myself. But you won't let me help you. I will have to go elsewhere.'

The synagogue fell into an uproar. People were yelling and shouting. 'We're not good enough for you then, Jesus, eh? Call yourself a prophet, do you? Think again, Joseph's son! Remember where you belong!'

Soon they became a violent mob, and they drove Jesus out of the synagogue and out of the village. They nearly drove him over a cliff.

The sabbath service should have finished with these ancient, holy words of blessing:

'The Lord God bless you and keep you.
The Lord God make his face to shine upon you
and be gracious to you.
The Lord God lift up his face towards you
and give you peace.'

The people should have gone back to their homes with those words ringing in their ears. But it was too late. The service was over. Bewilderment, violence and fear had brought it to an untimely end. The blessing had never been pronounced.

Peter, James and John
all four Gospels

In all the Gospels, Peter plays an important role as one of Jesus' very closest friends, and in Mark, Matthew and Luke, two brothers, James and John, form with Peter an inner circle among Jesus' followers. They share a number of experiences with Jesus that others do not, and have several chances to see the deeper truth about Jesus and who he is.

Each of the Gospels has a story about how Peter, James and John first came to follow Jesus. Luke's is different from the rest and is the most colourful of the four. That is the one we will retell here.

THE PEOPLE OF NAZARETH threw Jesus out of the village, but it wasn't like that everywhere. In other places people flocked to see him and listen to him.

One day he was standing on the edge of Lake Galilee, telling some of his stories. There were some fishermen nearby. Their boats were moored by the shore, and they were standing near them in the shallow water, washing their nets. One of them was a man Jesus had already met. His name was Peter, and he had a house in

Capernaum, a fishing village at the northern end of the lake. Peter's mother-in-law had been very ill with a fever, and Peter had asked Jesus if he could heal her. Jesus had come to his house and driven her fever away. Now Peter was cleaning his nets, listening to Jesus while he was working. Two of Peter's friends were listening to him as well. They were called James and John. They were also fishermen, and like Peter were busy washing the nets. The morning sun sparkled on the water, and a kingfisher hovered a few yards out from the shore, suddenly folded its wings and dived to catch a fish.

As Jesus carried on with his stories, more and more people came down to the shore to hear him. Those at the back could hardly hear what he was saying, and they pushed forward hoping to get closer. The whole crowd lurched towards the lake, and Jesus was nearly knocked off balance into the water. He stopped and looked about him. He saw the boats and the fishermen and at once recognized Peter.

He called across to him. 'Peter, can I use your boat? The crowd is going to push me into the lake if I'm not careful!'

'Of course,' Peter said.

'Could you push it out a bit from the shore?'

'Certainly.'

Jesus climbed into the boat, and Peter, James and John threw in the nets and took the boat a little way out into the lake. It rocked gently on the water as Jesus continued teaching the people. His voice bounced off the surface, and even those at the very back of the crowd could hear what he was saying.

Eventually he came to an end, and the people turned and went their various ways.

Jesus sat down in the boat. 'Go further out into deeper water,' he said to Peter, 'and cast your nets for a catch.'

'The fish must have gone to a different part of the lake,' Peter answered. 'We were fishing out here all night and caught nothing.' He paused. Jesus caught his eye. 'All right,' said Peter, 'we'll give it one more try.'

They raised the sail and took the boat into the deep water. The threads of the nets shone in the sun as they threw them into the water, and they made a soft swishing noise as they hit the surface. Immediately the water inside the circle of nets started churning. The men looked over the side and saw a huge shoal of fish caught inside them. They started hauling the nets towards the side of the boat, but they were so heavy with fish, they looked as though they might tear.

Peter waved to his other fishermen friends on the shore to come and help. They brought another boat out, and between them they managed to get the nets in. The catch was so huge, there was not room for it all in Peter's boat. They had to put half of it in the other boat, but even then they were weighed down so much they were nearly sinking.

Peter was quite overwhelmed. He'd had good catches in his time, but nothing like this. He looked at Jesus. He'd seen him heal his mother-in-law. He'd listened to him telling the crowd his stories. But this man was not just a healer and a teacher – he was more than that. Peter got down on his knees in front of him. It was almost as if God was sitting there in his boat. He was not good enough to be with Jesus, surely, and he said so. James and John felt the same.

'There is nothing to be afraid of,' said Jesus. 'Come with me and help me in my work. I want you to catch people from now on, not fish. It is too much for me to do on my own.'

Peter got up from his knees. They turned the boats towards the shore, slowly brought them to land and emptied their catch.

Peter, James and John had always fished on that lake. Their fathers had fished there before them, and their grandfathers, and their great-grandfathers, as far back as their families could remember. Fishing was their business, their trade. Jesus was asking them to leave it all behind, to leave their boats, their nets, their

friends, their village, their families – their whole way of life. He was asking them to leave the world they knew for another which was entirely hidden from them. What would happen to them if they followed Jesus? They had no idea.

And yet they did go with him. They couldn't forget the feelings that had overcome them out on the lake after they'd caught all those fish. This man could show them God. He already had. They would keep him company, whatever happened.

'Yes, Jesus,' they said. 'We will follow you.'

Photina: the Woman at the Well
John

In this story Jesus and some of his close friends are travelling north from Judea back to Galilee through a region called Samaria. (Judea was once called Judah, and was the region where Jerusalem and Bethlehem were.)

Often, Jews would avoid going through Samaria, because Jews and Samaritans didn't get on. The hostility between them went back a long way, over seven hundred years, to when the Assyrians had turned Samaria into part of their empire. They had deported many of the local people and brought in a lot of foreigners to run the country and work on the farms. Those foreigners had brought their own customs and beliefs with them, and their own gods too. After that many of the Jews down south thought the people of Samaria weren't proper Jews at all. Then, to make matters worse, two hundred and fifty years later, when Jerusalem had been destroyed by the Babylonians and Nehemiah had come to rebuild its walls, the Samaritans had wanted to stop them. But by the time of Jesus, Jews and Samaritans hated one another even more. The Samaritans had built their own temple on a place called Mount Gerizim to rival the temple in Jerusalem, and just over one hundred years before Jesus was born, Jewish soldiers had attacked and destroyed it. Since then there had been a number of ugly incidents, and people had been killed on both sides.

So it is surprising, in this story from John's Gospel, to hear that Jesus and his friends are walking through Samaria to get to Galilee to the north. They have come to a small town near Mount Gerizim. Jacob's well is there – at least, everyone calls it Jacob's well. According to an old story, which the people of the town believe, Jacob dug it himself. The women of the town fetch their water from it every day. John's story is about how Jesus meets one of the women by the well as she comes to fetch her water. John does not give her a name, he simply calls her 'a Samaritan woman'. Later some Christians called her Photina. It is good for people in stories to have a name, so we will call her Photina too.

IT WAS THE MIDDLE of the day and very hot, without a cloud in the sky. Jesus' friends had gone into the town to buy food. Jesus sat near Jacob's well, facing the gate of the town. At that hour there were not many people about. But then he noticed a woman coming through the gate. She was carrying a large water jar on her head, and she held a bucket in her hand. She was obviously coming to the well to draw water.

The woman's name was Photina. She could see a man sitting on the edge of the well. What did he want? Better not say anything, she thought. It wasn't right for a woman to talk to a strange man.

'Give me a drink, please,' Jesus said. Photina was just lowering her bucket down into the well.

The man's a Jew! Photina said to herself. I can tell by the way he speaks. I know what Jews say about us Samaritans, especially us Samaritan women. Filthy scum, they call us. What's he doing, asking me for a drink? I wish he'd leave me alone.

Jesus was looking at her. She would have to give him an answer. 'You're a Jew,' she said out loud. 'What do you think you're doing, asking for a drink from me, a Samaritan, a filthy Samaritan woman, with her filthy Samaritan bucket?'

'If you knew how generous God is and who I am,' Jesus replied, 'then you'd be asking me for a drink, and I would give you living water, like a fresh running stream, that you didn't have to fetch and carry twice a day.'

'Don't be silly!' Photina said, starting to pull up her bucket. 'How could you give me a drink? You haven't got a bucket and this well is very deep. And where will you get this living water of yours from? Are you a greater man than our ancestor Jacob who dug this well?'

The bucket was at the top now, brimming with water.

'Those who drink this water,' said Jesus, 'will get thirsty again. But those who drink the water I give them will never be thirsty. It will be like a spring of fresh water bubbling up inside them, like water from the Garden of Eden. It will bring true life, the life of heaven, God's life. Those who drink the water I can give will be alive with the very life of God!'

For the first time Photina looked properly at Jesus. This man was serious. She didn't understand everything he said, but it sounded wonderful.

'Give me some of this water, please, sir,' she said. 'Then I won't have to tire myself out every day fetching and carrying.'

Jesus looked her straight in the eye. She was beginning to understand.

'Go and fetch your husband,' he said softly.

'I don't have a husband,' Photina replied.

'Quite right,' said Jesus. 'You've had five husbands, and the man you're living with now is not married to you. You've told the truth.'

Photina was overcome. The man seemed to know everything about her!

'My Lord,' she said, 'I can see you're a holy man, a real prophet. Tell me, there's something I want to know. It's important. We Samaritans worship God on this holy mountain here, Mount Gerizim, but you Jews say God should be worshipped at Jerusalem instead. What do you think?'

'A time is coming,' Jesus answered, 'when you will worship our Father, God, neither on this mountain nor in Jerusalem. Instead, you will worship him bathed in his Spirit and his Truth.'

'These are deep things,' said Photina. 'I know there's a Messiah coming. When he arrives, he will tell us about everything like that.'

'I am the Messiah,' said Jesus. 'The Messiah's speaking to you now.'

Just then Jesus' friends came through the gate of the town. They could see Jesus sitting on the edge of the well. There was a woman sitting beside him! They were talking together – completely lost in conversation by the look of it! What was Jesus doing, talking to a woman like that? Everyone knew you didn't talk to women in public – not women you didn't know, at least.

As they were approaching the well, the woman suddenly got up and ran past them, leaving her water jar behind. What was going on? They raised their eyebrows at one another and shook their heads. They didn't say anything to Jesus though.

Photina went rushing into the town. 'Come and see!' she shouted. 'Come and see! There's a man by the well. He told me everything I've ever done. I think he must be the Messiah!'

The Messiah? What *now*? Outside their town? By their well? The people went running off through the gate with Photina. Many of them began to believe Jesus was the Messiah straight away, just because of what Photina said and the way she said it. Then they saw him for themselves. Photina was right. They begged Jesus to stay with them, and he did, for two whole days. Many, many people believed in him then.

When at last he and his friends were gone, the people said to Photina, 'You were right. That man is the Saviour of the whole world. Fancy having him to stay in our little town, here in Samaria!'

So Photina, a Samaritan woman, was the first person to bring lots of people all at once to believe in Jesus.

Commander of the Dark Forces
Matthew, Mark and Luke

To understand this story properly it is necessary to go back to the Old Testament, or *Tanakh*, or rather to stories and poems that are even older, which the Jews heard when they settled in the land. Those stories and poems spoke of a battle between the gods and the sea.

The sea was fierce and dangerous. It could become angry and crash great waves on the shore. It could take small boats and toss them over and drown all those inside. It was like a great monster, like the Dark Forces of evil and chaos that threatened to overthrow creation. The ancient stories and poems spoke of how the gods defeated those dark forces and calmed their raging. The Jews themselves, in *Tanakh*, spoke of God trampling the waves of the sea, or being able to control its storming waves.

Mark, Matthew and Luke had all this in mind when they wrote their story about Jesus and his friends sailing across Lake Galilee. Lake Galilee is not particularly large. It's usually a calm and beautiful place, with cormorants and egrets flying low over its surface and kingfishers diving into its waters for their fish. But sometimes storms spring up all of a sudden, and the lake turns ugly and dangerous. The story from Mark, Matthew and Luke is about one of those times – only this storm is no ordinary storm.

JESUS WAS STANDING on the shore of Lake Galilee with his friends. All was calm. Soon the sun would set behind the hills on the western side of the lake and turn it all to gold. Some of the friends, such as Peter, James and John, were fishermen and had their boats there.

'Let's go across to the other side in one of your boats,' said Jesus.

They all got in, and Peter, James and John put up the sail. It wasn't far to the other side, just a few miles, but the boat looked awfully small out there on the water.

Suddenly the Dark Forces spied the boat and saw Jesus asleep on a cushion at the back. 'Now we've got him!' they cried.

They swept down over the hills and hit the lake from all sides at once with a mighty storm. They whipped up the water into huge waves and sent them crashing down on the boat. Jesus' friends had been in many a storm on the lake, but never one as terrifying as this. Frantically they started bailing out the water, but it was no good. They were going to sink – and Jesus was still asleep! How could he possibly sleep through it all? The winds were howling like demented wolves, the waves were smashing things to pieces, and the boat was bucking and kicking like a horse bitten by a hundred flies. It seemed the whole world was about to collapse about their ears, and there was Jesus sleeping like a baby!

'Wake up, Jesus!' they yelled. 'Wake up! We're sinking! We're going to be drowned! Don't you care about us? Wake up!'

Jesus opened his eyes. A wave as big as a cliff was coming towards the boat. It was curling over, ready to crash down upon them and snap the boat in two. He sprang up. 'Stop!' he shouted. 'Calm down! Be quiet!'

Immediately the wave folded back on itself and disappeared, and the whole lake sank down into a flat calm. The boat trembled slightly, pulled itself together and resumed its course.

The Dark Forces were beaten! They went back to their lair and hid in its darkest corner. One day they would have him. One day.

Jesus turned to his friends. 'Why were you so frightened?' he said. 'Don't you realize who I am?'

His friends were suddenly overcome with awe. They looked at one another. Who *was* Jesus? Who was he, if even the winds and the waves obeyed him?

A Madman Among the Tombs
Matthew, Mark and Luke

In each of those three Gospels, this next story follows
on straight after the one about the calming of the storm.

WHEN FINALLY JESUS and his friends got to the other side of Lake Galilee, it was almost dark. They were in Gentile territory now. They had left the Jews behind for a spell. Yet the Roman grip on this part of Palestine was just as strong. From time to time the people of some village or other would try to wriggle out of it, but the Romans would always be too strong for them. The people would be slaughtered, their houses looted and burned, their crops destroyed. There seemed to be no escape.

Some escaped into madness.

There was a graveyard near the place where Jesus and his friends landed. No sooner had Jesus stepped out of the boat than he was confronted by a madman. The poor man lived among the tombs and wandered among the hills above the lake. Night and day he howled like a pack of wolves and hit himself with stones. The local people were terrified of him. They'd tried to restrain him. They'd even tried to chain him up and put shackles on him. But his madness made him too strong for them. He broke the chains and shackles as if they were straw.

He'd seen Jesus coming. He'd danced and shrieked during the terrible storm, and then had watched with strange fear as Jesus had stood up in the boat, faced the wave and drawn out all its strength. He'd come running down to the shore to meet him.

Jesus stood still and called to him.

The man prostrated himself on the ground, as if he was worshipping him. 'Get away from me!' he yelled. 'What do you want with me? I know who you are. You're the Son of the Most High God! I know you. Leave me alone. Leave me alone!'

'What is your name?' Jesus asked.

'Legion!' the man replied. 'I am many men. I'm a whole legion of men, military men, soldiers. Roman soldiers. Marching feet, clank of armour, flashing swords, slaughter, burning, shouting, weeping, moaning, dying. That's me. I'm a legion of Roman soldiers, that's what I am!'

'Then I will drive you out and rid the land of your fearful oppression!' cried Jesus.

'No, don't do that,' answered Legion. 'Don't do that! We Romans do terrible things when you try to drive us out. Terrible things. I've seen them. I've seen them! My own village... my family... my wife... my children...' His voice tailed off into silence.

But Jesus gave his orders. 'Come out of him, you legion of soldiers!' he barked. 'Come on, come on now! Quick march! You're like a bunch of raw recruits. Call that marching? You waddle like a lot of pigs. Now… wait for it… wait for it… CHARGE!'

The black waters of Lake Galilee swallowed up the madman's legion of soldiers, and they sank down deep into its depths, just as the soldiers of the pharaoh had once drowned in the Red Sea.

The man wasn't mad any more.

The people of that region, however, were terrified. They saw the meaning of it all, or they thought they did. If this Jesus was going to stand up to the Romans and try to drive their armies into the sea, then they were in for trouble. They didn't want troublemakers. 'Get back into your boat,' they cried. 'Sail back across the lake and leave us alone.'

Jesus turned and started to climb back into the boat. The man who'd been healed ran forward. 'Let me come with you,' he said.

'No, my friend,' said Jesus. 'You must go home now. You must live once more among your people. That is where you belong. You must tell your friends what has happened this day, tell them you have found the freedom and mercy of God.'

The boat began to move away from the shore. 'Goodbye, my friend,' Jesus called.

The man turned and went home.

The Hungry are Filled
all four Gospels

The small boy in this story only appears in John's version, and John doesn't give him a name. We will call him Nathan.

THE PEOPLE OF NAZARETH, Jesus' home village, drove him away. Those who lived in the same part of the country as the madman who was healed begged him to leave. But lots and lots of people flocked around him. He had some disciples, close friends, men and women, who went round with him all the time, but many, many others walked miles to hear him teach, or brought him their troubles, or came to him hoping he would get rid of the Romans or release them from their poverty.

One day, when they were by Lake Galilee, so many people were coming to him, he and his disciples were getting worn out. They didn't even have time to eat.

'Let's get away in one of your fishing boats,' Jesus said to his friends. 'We can sail across the lake to a deserted place where no one lives. We can be quiet there, have a meal and take some rest.'

They did have a meal, but it was not as they expected. And as for peace and quiet, they had to wait for those.

It was peaceful while they were on the boat, certainly. The water was calm, and they let the boat drift for a time out in the middle of the lake before they put up the sail again and made for the far shore. But when they reached the shore, there was a great crowd waiting for them – about five thousand of them! The people had seen where the boat was heading and had run round the shore and got there first.

Jesus looked at them all. He saw the thin drawn faces, the fear and longing in their eyes. They were like sheep without a shepherd, he thought, just left to wander about and fend for themselves as best they could. They seemed to have no one looking after them. The rulers in the towns and cities didn't care – they themselves were all right, and that was all that mattered to them. It was the spring too, a particularly difficult time of year for these people. The new harvests were not in yet, and the food supplies they'd kept over the winter were very low.

Jesus began to teach them. Many of the stories he told, he made up himself. But he also told them some of the old stories, stories the Jews had been telling for longer than anyone could remember: the story of the Garden of Eden, where the trees were laden with delicious fruit and the rivers were full of water; and the story of God feeding his people in the desert, when they came out of Egypt.

Jesus forgot about himself and his friends needing some rest and some food. He carried on teaching, and after that he still carried on teaching, and after that he *still* carried on teaching! The stories were wonderful, but his friends' stomachs started rumbling. The sun was getting low in the sky. It was definitely supper time. The people would have to go and get some food, or they would be starving. And if the friends didn't eat soon themselves, they would be starving as well. They decided they would have to interrupt Jesus.

They waited until he'd reached the end of one of his stories, then they butted in before he could start the next one.

'Excuse us,' they said to Jesus, 'but it's getting very late, and these people have nothing to eat. They're starving! Send them away to the farms and villages over the hill, so they can buy themselves some food.'

'You give them some food,' Jesus replied.

'Don't be ridiculous!' the disciples answered. 'Where do you think we're going to get the money to buy enough food for all these people? There are thousands of them. It would cost a fortune!'

'How much food have you got?' Jesus asked. 'Go and see.'

They went through the crowd, asking the people if they had any food with them. They had nothing, nothing at all. Eventually, just as they were about to give up and go back to Jesus, they found a small boy. He had some food his mother had packed for him.

'What's your name?' they asked.

'Nathan,' the boy replied.

'Come with us, Nathan,' they said, 'and show Jesus what you've got in your bag.' He got up and followed them through the crowd.

'This is Nathan,' they said to Jesus. 'His mother's put five barley loaves and two dried fish in his bag. It's plenty for him, but it's hardly enough just for you and us, let alone all the rest of the people here.'

Jesus didn't answer. He smiled at Nathan. 'Thank you,' he said. 'This is very generous.' He told the people to sit down on the grass. When everyone was settled, he took Nathan's food, said a prayer of blessing over them, broke the loaves into pieces and then gave them to his friends, together with the fish, to give to the people.

His friends walked once more among the people, as they sat there with their bent backs and thin faces, and fed them all, every single one of them. No one went without food; everyone had enough. In the end they couldn't eat any more, and there was still food left over. The friends filled twelve baskets with it. For the first time in their lives those people had been given more food than they could eat.

This was how it was, being with Jesus. It was like being back in the desert with Moses, when God fed his people and kept them alive. It was like being in the Garden of Eden. It was like having all your best hopes fulfilled, all your wildest dreams come true.

These people from the villages of Galilee were used to handing over the best parts of their crops to the rich landowners in the towns and cities. They weren't used to being given food, not like this. They weren't like sheep without a shepherd any more. They had a leader now. A leader who would look after them.

But where would Jesus take them?

A Man Sees for the First Time
John

In this story Jesus cures a man who is blind. John doesn't give him a name, but we have called him Jonathan.

JESUS WAS WITH HIS FRIENDS in Jerusalem. They had gone there for one of the festivals in the temple. It was the sabbath, and they were close to a pool called Siloam.

As they were walking along, they saw a man begging. He was blind. He'd always been blind. That's why he was begging. He was a clever man, but no one would give him a job, because they thought he would be useless at it, not being able to see. So he had to beg on the streets. It was either that or starve to death.

To the people who passed him by he didn't have a name. Sometimes they called him lots of names, but that was different. His real name was Jonathan.

Jesus' friends stopped and looked across at him. 'What did that man do to deserve being blind?' they asked. 'Did he do something wrong, or was it his parents?'

'It's nobody's fault,' said Jesus firmly. 'Nobody's. He doesn't deserve it, nor did his parents. But now God's bright work can be done! I am the light of the world, my friends. Wherever I go, darkness is banished. You'll see.'

Jesus went up to Jonathan and knelt down in front of him. He spat in the dust, made a little mound of mud and smeared the mud over the man's sightless eyes. 'Go and wash your eyes in the pool of Siloam,' he said.

Jonathan went off to the pool. He couldn't see where he was going, but he knew exactly how to get there. He had a fantastic memory for that sort of thing. The mud on his eyes was beginning to dry in the heat. It pulled at the skin round his eyes. He would be only too glad to wash it off. When he got to the pool, he went down to the water and splashed great handfuls all over his eyes. The mud ran down his face. He bent down to get more handfuls of water to wash the last bits off... He could see his reflection! He'd never seen himself before. He'd never seen anything before. He could see. He could see!

When he got back to his house, his neighbours and the people who used to see him begging couldn't believe their eyes.

'It's Jonathan!' some of them cried.

'It can't be,' others said. 'Jonathan's blind. This man can see. It must be someone who looks like Jonathan.'

'It's me all right!' Jonathan said.

'But you can see!' they exclaimed. 'What happened?'

'Someone they call Jesus made some mud and smeared it on my eyes and told me to wash it off in the pool of Siloam. So I did, and here I am, able to see.'

'Where is this Jesus?' they asked.

'I don't know.'

They couldn't understand it, so they took Jonathan to the Pharisees. The Pharisees were religious experts. They would be able to explain everything.

They told the Pharisees everything, but the Pharisees wanted to hear the story straight from Jonathan himself.

'How did you get your sight?' they asked him.

'This man put mud on my eyes,' Jonathan said, 'and I went and washed it off, and I washed my blindness away too!'

The Pharisees fell into a huddle.

'But it's the sabbath,' some of them said. 'This beggar wasn't in danger of his life. The man who healed him should have waited until tomorrow or the next day or the day after that. It's not right to do work on the sabbath, and he made mud, put it on the beggar's eyes and healed him. That counts as work, and three lots of work too. So the man who did this is a sinner. He's got no respect for the teaching of God.'

'Hold on!' others of them said. 'You can't call someone a sinner, who's just given someone their sight.'

'What do *you* think about this man?' they asked Jonathan.

'He's a prophet,' Jonathan said. 'He must be!'

The Pharisees still weren't satisfied. Some of them began to think the beggar was making it up and hadn't really been blind at all. So they asked to see his parents.

When they arrived, the Pharisees pointed to Jonathan and said, 'Is this your son?'

'Yes,' they replied.

'Was he born blind?'

'Certainly.' Tears were running down their faces, they were so happy.

'In that case, how come he can see now?'

'We don't know,' they said. 'We don't know. Ask him. He's grown up, he can answer for himself.'

The Pharisees called Jonathan over for a second time.

'This is serious,' they said. 'We don't want any nonsense from you. We want the truth, that's all. The man who did this to you is a sinner. You need to know that.'

'I don't know whether he's a sinner or not,' said Jonathan. 'One thing I do know: I was blind; now I can see.'

'Tell us exactly what he did to you,' they said. 'How did he do it?'

'I've told you already!' Jonathan cried. 'Why do you want to hear the story all over again? Do you want to become his followers yourselves?'

'You're the one who's following that sinner!' they exclaimed angrily. 'As for us, we follow Moses and everything he taught. God spoke to Moses face to face. We know that. As for the fellow who put that mud on your eyes, we don't even know where he comes from.'

'Well, well,' said Jonathan. 'That's odd. Someone opens the eyes of a man like me, a man born blind, who's never seen anything before, and you don't know where he comes from! He comes from *God*, of course. He must do, otherwise he wouldn't have been able to do it.'

'How dare you!' they cried. 'You're a sinner too, always have been, always will be. And you dare to stand there and teach *us* what to think! How dare you! Get out!'

One of Jonathan's neighbours found Jesus and told him what had happened, and immediately Jesus went to look for Jonathan. When he found him, he asked, 'Do you believe in the Son of God?'

Jonathan thought the voice was familiar, but of course he hadn't been able to see Jesus the first time. He wasn't quite sure who this man was.

'Who is he, sir, this Son of God?' Jonathan said. 'I would like to believe in him, sir.'

'You're looking at him with your own eyes!' Jesus cried. 'He's speaking to you.'

Now Jonathan knew for certain who it was. 'I believe in you!' he cried, and he got down on his knees to worship him.

'I can make the blind see,' Jesus said to his friends, 'while those who think they can see everything properly, like those Pharisees, become blind to the truth when I'm around.'

A Woman and a Girl are Brought Back to Life
Matthew, Mark and Luke

Apart from Jesus there are three main characters in this story: a man called Jairus, his young daughter and a woman in a crowd. The woman and Jairus' daughter are not named in any of the three Gospels where this story appears. The woman we have called Miriam, and Jairus' daughter we have named Rachel.

ONE DAY JESUS and his friends sailed across Lake Galilee to a small fishing town. The people of the town saw them coming, and as soon as they landed, a great crowd gathered around Jesus. Among them was a man called Jairus. He was an important man in the town, one of the leaders of the local synagogue. He helped look after the building and arrange the services there.

Just at that moment, however, Jairus wasn't feeling important at all. He was out of his mind with worry. His only child, Rachel, was desperately ill. In the past few weeks he and his wife had begun to talk about who Rachel might marry, for she was twelve, the age when she might get betrothed. Yet now it looked as though she would never get married, and Jairus and his wife would never have grandchildren. For Rachel was dying. There was nothing anyone could do. She had been getting worse and worse, and now she seemed at the point of death. When someone told Jairus that Jesus was sailing to their town, he came running down to the shore to meet him. There was no time to lose. It looked as though Rachel might only have a few hours left.

Jairus pushed his way through the crowd until he reached Jesus. He fell at his feet and begged him to come home with him and see Rachel. 'Please,' he said. 'She's only twelve, and she's dying. Please come and lay hands on her and make her well so that she can live!'

Jesus turned at once and set off with Jairus. The crowds made it difficult for them. Jairus wanted them to run, but that was impossible. People were pressing in on Jesus from every side.

There was one person in the crowd who was just as desperate as Jairus. She was a woman called Miriam.

Miriam had been ill for twelve years. She had been married once, but only for a short time. One spring she'd started her period, and it had never completely stopped. She was bleeding all the time.

Her husband had divorced her. He had known he couldn't have sexual intercourse with her while the bleeding continued and that she'd be unable to have children. He hadn't even been able to share a bed with her, because his religion forbade it. So he'd ended the marriage.

Miriam was on her own. She didn't have any children. She didn't have anyone to look after her. No man would marry her until she got well.

She'd gone to lots of doctors, walked a long way to get to some of them. Each time it had been very embarrassing for her and expensive too. The doctors had taken everything she had. She'd started out with a little money, but now that was all gone. The doctors had done nothing to help her. She was worse than she was before. With the continual loss of blood she felt as weak as water.

When she heard that Jesus was coming to the town, she too came down to the shore. She gathered up what little energy she had left and pushed through the crowd.

She wasn't supposed to be in the crowd at all. Jewish religious law forbade it. She was allowed to go out of her house, but she was supposed to avoid touching other people if she possibly could. Jewish religious law said she would make someone unclean if she touched them, even if she just brushed against their clothes. But Miriam was desperate. Jesus was her last and only hope. She would edge her way through the crowd until she reached him, and then she would just touch the edge of his cloak. That was her plan anyway, and that would be enough. Jesus wouldn't notice, but she would. Jesus was a prophet, a holy man, a man of God. Just touching his cloak would heal her. Then she would be able to start living again.

It wasn't easy reaching Jesus. In one awful moment of despair, Miriam thought she wasn't going to manage it. But then Jesus turned and came towards her. He was with Jairus from the synagogue, the man whose daughter, Rachel, was so ill. Everyone in the town knew about Rachel.

Jesus was only a few yards away now. Miriam waited until he'd just gone past, and then she came up behind him and touched his cloak. Her whole body was flooded with a new energy. She knew at once her bleeding had stopped. She felt like a young girl again, like the person she was just before she got married.

She began to slip away, but Jesus had stopped. He knew someone had touched him. He'd felt the power going out of him. For a moment he felt as weak as water.

'Who touched my cloak?' he said. He was looking around to see who it was.

Miriam was terrified. She stopped too; she couldn't move. Jesus had found her out.

'What do you mean, who touched you?' Jesus' friends said. 'Look at these people all around you, pushing and shoving. They can't help touching you.'

But Jesus kept looking to see who it was who had drained the power from him.

Miriam knew she couldn't hide from him. Trembling, she turned, prostrated herself before him and told him everything.

Jesus listened carefully to her story. He stretched out his hand to her and helped her to her feet. 'Daughter,' he said, 'your faith has saved you and made you well. Go in peace now. Be in full health, free of your terrible affliction.'

With those words ringing in her ears, Miriam left. As soon as she was free of the crowd and had room to move, she danced and sang. She went down to the shore of the lake and splashed the water all over her. She laughed and played like a child. Life had been like death for her. Now she was alive! Now she could live life to the full.

Jairus was dancing too, frantic with impatience. What was Jesus doing stopping to talk to that woman? Jairus knew who she was. She shouldn't have been in the crowd in the first place. Rachel was on the edge of death, and Jesus had stopped to hear Miriam's life story! The delay was unbearable. What was Jesus thinking of?

Someone tapped Jairus on the shoulder. He put his mouth to Jairus' ear. 'I've just come from your house, sir,' he said quietly. 'It's bad news, I'm afraid. Your daughter's dead. You needn't trouble Jesus any further.'

Jesus overheard what the messenger said. 'Don't be afraid,' he said to Jairus. 'Just believe, as Miriam did.'

Jesus dismissed the crowd. He didn't want them at Rachel's house, peering through the windows. He told his friends to wait as well. He took just three of them with him – Peter, James and John.

When they reached the house, they found it full of weeping and wailing. The local women were mourning the death of the child, and Rachel's mother was among them.

'Why are you making all this fuss?' Jesus asked the mourners. 'The girl's not dead, she's asleep.'

The women laughed. They knew when someone was dead, and Rachel was dead. Rachel's mother didn't laugh. She just looked at Jesus through her tears, not understanding what he meant.

Jesus threw the mourners out. Then he took Rachel's father and mother, and his three friends, and went into the room where the girl was lying.

Jews weren't supposed to touch a dead body if they could avoid it. Jewish religious law said it would make them unclean for seven days. But Jesus at once took Rachel's hand. 'Get up, my little friend,' he said softly.

There was complete silence in the room. Then there was a new sound, the sound of Rachel's breathing. Slowly she raised herself. Then she jumped onto the floor, stretched herself like a cat and began to walk about.

Jesus laughed and turned to her mother and father. 'I think you'd better give Rachel something to eat,' he said. 'She'll be feeling hungry.'

Peter Gets it Right; Peter Gets it Wrong
Matthew, Mark and Luke

This story is set in the far north of Palestine, the country where Jesus lived, near a small city called Caesarea Philippi. For centuries people had thought the place was holy. A cave was there, and near it a spring, one of the sources for the river Jordan. People came to worship one of their gods at the cave. Not long before Jesus was born, King Herod had built a temple in front of the cave and had named the temple after the Roman emperor Augustus. Its walls were made of finely cut, square blocks of limestone, and were lined on the inside with beautiful marble. It was as if Herod was treating the emperor like a god. In fact, many people in the Roman empire said Augustus was the son of a god and claimed he was divine.

A few years later, Herod's son Philip had come to the place and built a city there, with more fine temples. He had named the city Caesarea, because Augustus

was known as Caesar Augustus. Herod had already
built his own Caesarea, a great port on the coast of
Palestine, so Philip called his city Caesarea Philippi,
or Philip's Caesarea, so that people wouldn't muddle
it with the port.

The tiny village of Nazareth, where Jesus had been
brought up, was very different from Caesarea Philippi.
There were no great temples in Nazareth. The houses
were made of stones picked up in the fields and placed
on top of one another, with small stones packed into
the spaces between them and then smeared with clay or
mud. The floors were of beaten earth and the roofs of
thatch. No one was rich in Nazareth, and Jesus' family
were poorer than most. Jesus was very different from
Augustus. Peter realized that, of course, but he couldn't
help dreaming that one day...

JESUS AND HIS FRIENDS were in the north of Palestine, on the
slopes of a great mountain called Mount Hermon. They were
walking along a track, talking together, and came over a ridge, when
suddenly Jesus stopped. He pointed at a spot at the foot of the
mountain. 'Look,' he said, 'there's Caesarea Philippi.'

The temples and the great public buildings of the city shone white in the morning sun. Jesus and his friends could pick out the temple to Augustus that Herod had built. 'Look at me!' the city seemed to say. 'Aren't I a grand place! And Herod was such a great king, and his son Philip is such a fine ruler! As for the emperor Augustus, he was the son of a god. Indeed, he *is* a god. Come and worship him!'

Jesus stood there in his peasant's clothes, gazing down at it all. He looked almost like a beggar, except that he didn't walk like a beggar, or have the voice or the look in the eye of a beggar.

He turned to his friends. 'Who do people say I am?' he asked quietly.

'Some say you're John the Baptist,' they replied. 'Others say you're Elijah, or one of the other prophets, come back to life.'

'What about you?' Jesus said. 'Who do *you* say I am?'

Peter stared down at the city below and at the temple of Augustus. He raised his head and looked straight at Jesus. 'You,' he said solemnly, 'are the Messiah, the Son of the living God.'

Peter was right, of course. At least, he *sounded* as though he was right.

'You mustn't tell anyone that,' Jesus replied. 'There's something very important you must understand. I know many of my fellow Jews are looking for a Messiah who will come with a great fanfare, someone who will come with great power and might, drive the Romans into the sea and sit on a great throne in Jerusalem. But great fanfares are not what I'm about, nor that kind of power, nor might, nor slaughtering Romans, nor sitting on thrones and ordering people about. That's not my way. It's not God's way either.

'I have indeed come to fight against tyranny. But I will not fight it with force. I will challenge it with suffering. As soon as we reach Jerusalem, the religious leaders will put me on trial, convict me and get me killed. I've upset them already, and I'll upset them much more before I've finished. Yet three days after my death, I will rise again.'

Peter couldn't bear to hear all this. That wasn't what he meant by Messiah at all! He took Jesus aside and began to argue with him.

'If they're out to get you, then you mustn't go to Jerusalem!' he cried. 'Stay out of trouble. Find another way.'

'Get out of my way!' Jesus exclaimed. 'You're not on God's side. You're on the side of men who just want power for themselves. Now get out of my way! You're blocking my path!'

The Light of God
Matthew, Mark and Luke

PETER WAS STILL one of Jesus' closest friends. It was just that he found it too painful to listen to him talking about being tried and condemned and killed. One day, along with James and John, he saw Jesus as he really was.

Jesus took the three of them on their own to the top of a high mountain. It was a hard climb. Why were they going all the way up there? The friends didn't know. Sometimes Jesus went up a mountain to pray. Perhaps that was it.

They got to the summit. They weren't prepared for what happened next.

Jesus was transfigured before them. His face shone like the sun, and his clothes were dazzling white.

This was Jesus as he really was – clothed in all the glory of God! It was like being on the top of Mount Sinai: the place where God had met his people after bringing them out of Egypt; where he'd appeared to them with strange, unearthly thunder and lightning, bright fire and smoke, and the long-drawn-out call of a ram's horn. It was the place where God had talked with Moses face to face, the place where he'd hidden Moses in a cleft of the rock and passed him by, dressed in all the finery of his goodness. It was the place where God had spoken from the midst of a dense mist. It was also the place where God had been so hurt by his people's disloyalty.

And there *was* Moses. The friends could see him, plain as could be. And Elijah too. Elijah had met God on Sinai as well. They were both there, sharing in this new moment of strange glory. It was like a glimpse of heaven! Moses' face once shone with the blinding light of God, so their ancient stories said. That's how Jesus' face shone now, but not, it seemed, with light borrowed from God or reflected from God. The light from Jesus' face seemed to be coming from within him.

Peter wanted the vision to last for ever. But he couldn't think what to say. 'My Lord,' he blurted out. 'If you like, we'll make three shelters for you: one for you, one for Moses and one for Elijah. Then you can all stay on this mountain, out of the cold of the night and the heat of the sun in the day.' He hardly knew what he was saying.

While he was still speaking, a dense mist, shining with the light

of the presence of God, covered the summit. From the mist came a voice, the voice of God himself.

'This is my Son,' God said, 'the one I love. He is my delight. In him I am well pleased. Listen to him!'

When they heard the voice of God, the three friends were overwhelmed. They sank to their knees, burying their faces in their hands.

Jesus went over to them and touched each one of them lightly on the shoulder.

'Get up,' he said. 'Don't be frightened.'

Peter, James and John looked about them. There was nothing to be seen except Jesus standing beside them, looking as he always did.

There was a new twinkle in Jesus' eye, but a deep sadness also. And the friends were still afraid, although Jesus had told them not to be. For, in the vision they'd just seen, hadn't Jesus' clothes seemed dazzling white, and wasn't that how martyrs were supposed to look after their deaths?

9

JESUS THE STORYTELLER AND POET

Jesus spent much of his time at the end of his short life teaching his friends and followers, and the people who came to listen to him, about the ways of God. He usually taught them not by telling them directly what to think or what to do or how to behave, but by telling them stories, or giving them sayings to remember. The stories are called parables, and the sayings are often like stories in miniature, or like short poems or lines of poetry. Jesus was a brilliant storyteller and poet.

The parables and sayings are meant to give people glimpses of a different world – the world or kingdom of God. They are also meant to help people look at themselves and the world in which they live and see things through God's eyes.

For this chapter we will be drawing mostly on the Gospels of Luke and Matthew, though we will, at times, be turning to Mark and John also. Many of the finest stories or parables are found in Luke's Gospel, and we will begin with four of them.

A Lost Sheep, a Lost Coin and a Lost Son
Luke

Often it wasn't the religious people or the good, respectable people who were so attracted to Jesus, but the people whom others ignored or despised because they were poor or destitute, or unclean by the terms of Jewish religious law, or collected taxes for the Romans. Not only did Jesus welcome such people, he ate with them. He invited them to meals, sat with them and shared his food with them. Such a thing was unheard of. Jesus was treating these people as his friends – his equals! All right, he came from a poor peasant family himself, but he claimed to be teaching the ways of God, and this was not the way to go about it. At least, that's what many of the religious leaders felt. A rich person might lay on a feast for the poor, for example, but he would never eat with them himself. Jesus' behaviour broke all the rules. The religious leaders found it deeply shocking. How could he be a good Jew and behave like that?

One day some of the religious leaders were muttering to one another about how shocked they were by many of the people who were coming to listen to Jesus. 'He actually invites them to meals,' said one of them, 'and sits in a circle with them and eats with them.'

Jesus overheard him and saw the looks of horror on their faces. So he told them these three parables.

'IMAGINE,' SAID JESUS, 'there's a shepherd looking after one hundred sheep. The flock belongs to several families from his village, and there's a boy and a girl from the village helping him. They are out in the hills of the desert and have spent the day leading the sheep to the places where they can find something to eat and water to drink. At the end of the day it's time to take the sheep back to the village. So they count them to make sure they are all there: ninety-six, ninety-seven, ninety-eight, ninety-nine… "Where's the hundredth?" the shepherd says. "There're only ninety-nine here."

'What will he do? He'll tell the boy and girl to take the ninety-nine back to the village, of course, and go in search of the one that's lost. He'll climb up the hills and down into the dry river beds. He'll look behind every rock and every bush. He'll inspect the ledges on the cliffs. All the time he'll be calling out to the lost sheep and listening for its bleating. And when he finds it, he'll be so relieved, so pleased. The sheep will be lying down helplessly and will refuse to move – lost sheep are like that. So he'll pick it up in his arms, put it on his shoulders and carry it all the way back to the sheepfold at the village, so that he can put it back with the others. It'll be very hard and hot work carrying that heavy sheep, and it'll be dark before he gets back, but he won't mind. He's found it, and that's all that matters.

'After he's put the sheep back in the pen, he'll run home on his tired legs and say to all his neighbours and friends, "That sheep I lost, I've found it again. Come on, let's have a party."'

'Imagine,' said Jesus, 'a woman who has ten silver coins. There's very little money in her village. They grow their own food and make their own cloth and lend things to one another when they need them. So those coins are very precious to her. In fact, they're the most precious things she's got. She wears them on a necklace round her throat. Of all her possessions that necklace is the most beautiful. Then one day her necklace feels wrong. She takes it off and discovers that one of the coins is missing. She can't find it anywhere.

'What will she do? She'll hunt high and low for it, of course. She'll light an oil lamp and look in all the dark corners of the house. She'll sweep the floor and listen for it tinkling against the broom. If she doesn't hear it tinkling, then she'll examine the pile of dust she's swept up, to make quite sure it's not there. She'll look in the bed, behind the clothes chest, underneath the cooking pots. And when she finds it, she'll be so relieved, so pleased. She'll go dancing all round the house, and then she'll go rushing outside to call all her women friends and neighbours together.

'"I lost one of my precious silver coins, but I've found it again," she'll cry. "Come on, let's have a party!"

'Well,' Jesus said, 'that gives you some idea how much pleasure I take in the company of these people you despise so much, and who I am proud to call my friends. And it gives you some idea also of how precious each one of them is to God. The trouble is, if you persist in thinking how good and clever you are and carry on looking down on others, you'll miss out on the party!'

'And I have another story for you,' said Jesus.

'There was a man who had two sons. One day the younger son came to him and said, "Father, when you die, your property will be divided between my brother and me, won't it? Well, I can't wait. I'd like my share now, please."

'It was a shocking thing, a terribly hurtful thing to ask. Most fathers would have been very angry. But this young man's father did as he was asked. He divided up his property then and there. It was as if he was already dead. Following the usual custom, he gave two thirds of his property to the elder son and a third to the younger son.

'Worse still was to come. The family had farmed their land for generations. For as long as anyone could remember, they'd been growing their crops in the same fields and leading out their sheep and goats to the same pastures and watering them from the same wells. Within a few days the younger son had sold the whole of his share and left home. The family and the whole village were appalled by what he'd done. He'd brought disgrace upon the village, insulted his family and humiliated his father. "Things will never be the same again," people said.

'The young man put as much distance between him and his family and his village as he could. He travelled to a distant country, where no one recognized him, where no one knew what he'd done.

'There he set out to have a good time – a very good time. He spent everything he had on having a good time. But when he'd spent the lot, things weren't so good any more. He suddenly felt a long way from home. His new friends didn't want to know him once his money was gone. He was very lonely. To make matters worse, the country he was living in was hit by a severe famine. Food became extremely hard to find and extremely expensive. He had no money to buy anything. He was starving.

'He had to look for work. He kept pestering people for jobs, and eventually someone offered to hire him to look after their pigs out in the fields. The man knew he was a Jew and that Jews were not supposed to having anything to do with pigs. It was not meant as a serious offer, just as a way of getting rid of him. But he accepted the job. He was completely desperate and very, very hungry.

'However, the pig farmer gave him nothing to eat. The pigs found food all right, wild carob pods, but he had nothing. He was still starving. He felt like sharing the pods with the pigs, but they were too bitter.

'In the end he came to his senses. Back home, he said to himself, my father's hired hands have more than enough to eat, and here I am starving to death. It's stupid! I'll go back home, that's what I'll do. And when I get there, I'll say to my father, "Father, I've done wrong. I've done wrong against God and against you. I'm not worthy to be called your son any more. I can't belong to the family after what I've done, but take me on as one of your hired hands."

'So he set off for home. It was a long journey, and he was weak from hunger. His sandals wore out, and his clothes were in tatters.

'He reached the ridge overlooking his village. Slowly, painfully, with his heart beating more from fear than the physical effort, he climbed to the top and stood gazing down on the houses and the men working in the fields.

'He started to leave the ridge and take the track towards the village. He hoped no one would recognize him, but they did. Soon he had a crowd around him. They weren't exactly pleased to see him. They remembered only too well how he'd left the village, and how he'd insulted his family and his father.

'His father was always on the alert, hoping that one day his son might come home. He heard the shouts of the crowd and looked to see what was going on. He caught sight of his son.

'He was overjoyed, but he was alarmed too. His son was in such a state! He was clothed in rags and so tired-looking, so utterly dejected. And the crowd looked as though they might knock him to the ground at any moment.

'He ran as fast as he could towards his son. He burst through the crowd, threw his arms round his son's neck, hugged him and kissed him on both cheeks.

'The son had his speech all prepared. "Father," he said, "I've done wrong. I've done wrong against God and against you. I'm not worthy to be called your son any more." He missed out the bit about being taken on as a hired hand. His father's running to meet him and then greeting him like that had taken the idea out of his head. He'd never dreamed his father would be so pleased to see him, not after what he'd done. He hadn't realized before how much his father loved him.

'His father heard what he said, but he didn't argue with him. He didn't say, "Of course I will call you my son." Actions would speak louder than words. He knew what he would do.

'"Quick!" he said to his slaves. "Fetch the very best robe, the one I use for special occasions, and put it on my son. We can't have him in these rags. And put my signet ring on his finger and shoes on his

351

poor feet. Dress him up like a king. And fetch the calf, the one we've been fattening up. Let's kill it and roast it and lay on a feast for the whole village. For this son of mine was good as dead, and now he's alive again. He was lost, but now he's found."

'And so the celebrations began.

'The older son was still out in the fields. He hadn't noticed his brother coming home. He hadn't been looking out for him, like his father. He didn't know anything of what had happened. So at the end of the day, when he approached the house and heard a band playing and the sounds of dancing, he was utterly bewildered.

'There was a small crowd of boys outside the entrance to his father's house, dancing to the music, singing and laughing. He called across to one of them. "What's going on?" he said.

'"Your brother's come home!" the boy replied. "Your father's killed the fatted calf for him, because he's come home safe."

'When he heard that, the older son was very angry. He refused to go in and join the party. He stomped about outside, stamping his anger onto the ground.

'His father had been looking out for him at the feast. When someone told him he was outside, he came out at once. "Your brother's home!" he said. "Come inside and join in the fun and have some of the roast beef. I need you to help look after our guests from the village."

'The older son exploded with anger. "Look!" he shouted to his father. "I've slaved for you all these years. I've done everything you told me. I've never gone against your wishes. And yet you've never given me so much as a goat to roast and share with my friends. Yet now, now this son of yours is back, having spent everything you gave him on wild living, no doubt, now he's back home, you kill the fatted calf for him. It's not fair!"

"'But my son," the father replied. "You're always with me. Everything I have is yours. Your brother here was as good as dead, and now he's alive. He was lost, but now he's found! How could we not celebrate? How could we stop ourselves being glad?"

'Remember this story,' Jesus said to the religious leaders, 'and you will begin to understand me. Remember the father in this story, and you will begin to understand God.'

The Good Samaritan
Luke

The parable of the Lost Son, or the Prodigal Son as it's often called, is one of the two most famous of Jesus' parables. The other one is the Good Samaritan, which is also in Luke's Gospel.

It's a story about a journey, and what happens to four different men on the road. They are all travelling through the Judean desert from Jerusalem to Jericho, a distance of about seventeen or eighteen miles. Three of them are Jews, the other is a Samaritan.

Samaritans and Jews didn't get on. They'd been enemies for years, for centuries. Many Jews despised Samaritans. Samaria lay between Judea in the south and Galilee in the north. Most Jews avoided the area if they could, and most Samaritans kept clear of the Jews. Many Jews didn't think of Samaritans as fully human. They were scum, and that was that.

The parable mentions a priest and a Levite. No

doubt they were coming from the temple in Jerusalem, where they had been helping lead the worship. Priests had the most important duties in the temple, while Levites did the more menial jobs. Twice a year each of them did a week's duty in the temple. Lots of priests and Levites lived in Jericho, so these two were probably going back home. The temple was supposed to be a holy place, the most holy place in the world for Jews, and priests and Levites had to be very careful to obey the Jewish religious laws. In fact, there were laws which applied to them, and to priests especially, which didn't apply to ordinary people.

Once again Luke puts the parable in a particular setting: a discussion between Jesus and an expert on Jewish religious law.

AN EXPERT ON THE JEWISH LAW was listening to Jesus teaching the people about the ways of God. He stood up and asked, 'Teacher, what must I do in order to be with God?'

'What do you find written in the law?' Jesus replied. 'What answer does that give to your question?'

'You shall love God with all your heart, with all your soul, with all your strength and with all your mind,' the expert answered. 'And you shall love your neighbour as yourself.'

'Absolutely right,' said Jesus. 'Do that and you will keep God company for ever.'

'But who is my neighbour?' the expert asked.

'Let me tell you a story,' said Jesus.

'One day a man was riding down from Jerusalem to Jericho. It was very hot. The desert hills were very beautiful but very bleak.

'But then he reached a particularly lonely spot in the road. There were no shepherds' tents to be seen and no other travellers in sight. Suddenly a band of robbers leaped out from behind some rocks and attacked him. He tried to put up a fight, but there were too many of them. They beat him up and stripped him of everything he had. They took his donkey and all the things he was carrying in his saddlebags. They even took his clothes. Then they escaped, leaving him bleeding and unconscious by the side of the road.

'By chance a priest was riding down the same road, just a mile or so behind. He came round a bend and saw the poor man lying there some yards ahead of him. The priest stopped his donkey. What should he do? The man had clearly been attacked by robbers. Were the robbers still around? The priest looked nervously about and strained his ears to see if he could hear anyone creeping up on him. The man lying at the side of the road wasn't moving at all. He must be dead, thought the priest. That means I shouldn't touch him. I'm a priest, and I'll become unclean if I go near him. It will mean I'll have to go to the temple and stand among all the other unclean people when they sound the gong and offer up the incense. And it will take me some time to get clean again, and it will be quite expensive too. And yet the law demands I should not leave a dead man unburied. But I can't get close enough to check that he's dead. Then again, he might not be a Jew. Oh dear, what shall I do?

'Still the man lying beside the road didn't move.

'The priest ordered his donkey forwards. Carefully he crossed to the other side of the road, kept as far away from the man as he could and then kicked his donkey into a trot and hurried on towards Jericho.

'The man who'd been attacked lay there, covered in blood. Time passed. Vultures circled overhead.

'Then a Levite came round the bend of the road. He saw the man too. He couldn't miss him. Like the priest, he stopped and looked. The same things went through his mind. He'd seen the priest riding some distance ahead of him. Clearly the priest had ridden straight past. If the priest didn't stop, he said to himself, then I shouldn't either. So he also crossed to the other side of the road and hurried past.

'More time passed. The man was still unconscious. It would be dark soon.

'But as the sun was beginning to go down behind the hills, a Samaritan came riding down the road with a string of donkeys. When he saw the man lying there, he jumped down at once, went across to him and knelt down beside him. He was still alive, thank God! He fetched a flask of olive oil and some wine from one of his saddlebags and washed the man's wounds as best he could. There was some cloth in his bags as well, expensive stuff he'd bought in the market in Jerusalem. He got it out, tore it up into strips and used the strips as bandages. Then he dressed the man in some of his spare clothes, gently lifted him up on his donkey and led it, together with his other animals, to one of the inns in Jericho.

'Right through the night the Samaritan looked after him. The man recovered consciousness, but in the morning he still wasn't well enough to leave. So the Samaritan gave the innkeeper some money and said, "Will you look after this man for me? That should be enough, but if you spend any more, I'll repay you when I come back. I don't want the poor man to be left in debt just to add to his troubles."'

When he'd finished his story, Jesus turned to the expert on the law. 'What do you think?' he asked him. 'Which of those three men was a good neighbour to the man attacked by robbers?'

'The one who showed him mercy,' the expert said.

'Then you must be like him,' Jesus replied. 'You must do as that Samaritan did. He didn't stop and try to work out the finer points of the law. He knew what he had to do, and he did it. He didn't care whether the man lying by the road was a Jew or not. He simply saw him as someone who needed his help. If you really want to be with God and follow God's ways, then be like that Samaritan.'

The Workers in the Vineyard
Matthew

In many of his parables Jesus showed that God saw things differently from human beings. In effect he was saying, 'When God is around, prepare for surprises. Prepare to think again about what is right and just and fair. Prepare to change your mind about what goodness and generosity mean. Prepare to see other people in a new light. Let God loose, and you never know what might happen.'

Our last parable, found only in Matthew's Gospel, takes us straight to the countryside of Galilee which Jesus knew so well, and to the vineyards which were a common sight there. When the grapes were at the right stage for harvesting, it was important to pick them quickly. So the people who owned the vineyards would have to hire extra men to do the work. They would sometimes hire them for a day at a time until the harvest was finished. A lot of people in Galilee didn't have land of their own and were very poor. The extra money they could make at harvest times was very important to them and their families. If someone wasn't hired, that could mean his family went hungry. So the men would gather in the marketplace of the local village at dawn, hoping that someone would hire them for the day. At harvest time the working day was twelve hours long, and the men would keep going right through the heat of midday and the afternoon.

This is how the parable goes:

'THE KINGDOM OF GOD is like this,' Jesus said.

'It was time to pick the grapes. So at six o'clock in the morning the vineyard owner went down to the village marketplace to hire some extra men. There were lots of men hanging around, hoping to be hired. Some of them were not very well. Some of them had stiff backs, or joints that didn't work properly, and some were getting on a bit. But they all tried to look as fit and strong as possible and eager for work. Indeed, they did want work. Their families depended on them.

'The vineyard owner chose a few of them and negotiated with them what they should be paid. In the end he agreed to pay them the usual amount for a day's work. He would get his manager to pay them at the end of the day, when the work was done.

'The harvesting didn't go fast enough. The vineyard owner needed more men. So at nine o'clock he went back to the marketplace, chose some more men, promised to pay them whatever was right and sent them to his vineyard. The men didn't argue about the wages; they were just pleased to have work.

'At noon, and again at three o'clock in the afternoon, the owner returned to the marketplace and picked yet more men.

'It was getting towards the end of the working day. The harvest was going well now. If they could take on a few more men, they could get it finished. So the owner went down to the marketplace yet again. It was about five o'clock; there was only one hour's work left.

'He was surprised to find some men still standing around. They must have been desperate for work.

'"Why have you been standing here idle the whole day?" he asked.

'It was a silly question, but the men didn't say so. They were too keen to get some work, even an hour, anything, just so they had something to take home to their families. "It's because nobody has hired us," they explained politely.

'"Well, I'll hire you," said the owner. "Go down straight away to my vineyard."

'An hour later, it was time for everyone to stop work. The owner went to speak to his manager.

'"Call the workers across and give them their pay," he said. "Start with the men who were hired last and work your way through to those who came first."

'So the men who'd been hired about five o'clock queued up, and each of them received a full day's pay.

'The men hired at nine, noon and three o'clock got the same.

'Finally, it was the turn of the men who'd been hired at six o'clock that morning. They'd seen what the first ones got, and they thought they'd be receiving a nice, fat bonus. They didn't. They got the usual day's wage.

'They were incensed! They looked at the money in their hands and marched across to the owner.

'"You paid this same amount to the men who started just an hour ago!" they exclaimed. 'You've made them equal to us, when we've been toiling away the whole day, right through the scorching heat. It's not fair!"

'One of them stood facing the owner. He was the self-appointed leader of the men. He waited for an answer. It had better be good.

'"Friend," the owner said, "I've done you no wrong. Did you not agree with me at the start of the day to be paid the usual day's wage? Well, that's what you've got. Take it and go on your way. I've chosen to give the men who were hired last the same as you. That is my choice. That is the way I do things."'

The Beatitudes
Matthew and Luke

Jesus lived and worked chiefly among the poor. He wanted to give them hope and show them where true hope lay. They felt they could do nothing themselves to make life easier. They were trapped in a world where they could do nothing about drought, disease or locust plague. Many were trapped into working for people who didn't care about them. Others were trapped into going down to the marketplace every day hoping for work. Many of the men knew the shame of returning home with nothing to give their wives and children. Others still were trapped in slavery. And they were all trapped in a land occupied by the Romans. As always, it was worst for the women and children.

Jesus came among these people bringing the life and the healing of God. In a few lines of poetry called the Beatitudes, or Blessings, he expressed most beautifully the extraordinary hope he was offering these people. There are two versions of the Beatitudes – one in Matthew and one in Luke. Luke's is shorter and goes like this:

'IT WILL BE WELL with you who are poor,
for the kingdom of God is yours.
It will be well with you who go hungry now,
for you will be filled.
It will be well with you who weep now,
for you will laugh.'

Here is Matthew's version:

'IT WILL BE WELL with those who depend entirely on God,
who have nobody else to turn to,
for the kingdom of heaven is theirs.
It will be well with those who mourn,
for they will be comforted.
It will be well with those who are humble,
for they will inherit the earth.
It will be well with those who hunger and thirst for justice,
for they will be filled.
It will be well with those who show mercy,
for they will receive mercy.
It will be well with those who yearn for God above all else,
for they shall indeed see God.
It will be well with those who make peace,
for they shall be called children of God.
It will be well with those who are persecuted
just because they seek what is just and right,
for theirs is the kingdom of heaven.'

Other Sayings and a Prayer

Jesus taught in parables, or sayings. The sayings are like small poems or lines of poetry. Among his sayings are these:

'THE LAST SHALL BE FIRST and the first shall be last.'

'Love your enemies. Do good to those who hate you.'

'Treat others just as you would like them to treat you.'

'Be merciful, just as God, your Father, is merciful.'

'Do not judge others, and you will not be judged.
Do not condemn, and you will not be condemned.
Forgive others, and you will be forgiven.
Give, and gifts will be given to you in good measure; like grain pressed down in your basket, shaken down, running over, gifts will be showered into your lap.'

'Why do you notice the speck of dust in someone else's eye but fail to see the great log in your own eye? How can you say, "My friend, let me take that speck of dust out of your eye," when you don't see the log in your own eye? First take the log out of your own eye, then you will be able to see clearly to take the speck out of your friend's eye!'

'You parents, if a child of yours asks for some bread, which one of you gives them a stone? Or if a child of yours asks for some fish, which one of you gives them a snake? If you then know what to give your children, how much more does your Father God in heaven know how to give what is good to those who ask him.'

'Don't look down upon anyone, just because they're small or vulnerable, or they've made a mistake. Remember, they have their guardian angels in heaven who look upon the face of God.'

Often we find Jesus' teaching set in the middle of a story. Here are two stories, taken partly from Mark, and partly from Matthew:

JESUS AND HIS FRIENDS were in Capernaum, a small fishing town at the northern end of Lake Galilee. They'd walked a long way that day.

When they were indoors, Jesus asked them, 'What were you arguing about on the way?'

His friends were too ashamed to say.

'I know what it was,' said Jesus. 'You were arguing about which one of you was the greatest, weren't you? Well, you can't have been listening to what I've been saying. Whoever wants to be first must be last of all and the servant of all.

A small child was playing quietly in the corner of the room. Jesus called her over. He put the child right at the centre of the circle of friends. The child had never been put right in the centre like that before. She was much more used to corners or quiet places where she couldn't be seen. Jesus took her in his arms. The little girl felt like the most important person in the room. She'd never been treated like this before. Her parents loved her, but she was the smallest in the family and always treated as the least important. If her parents were unfair to her or punished her, there was nothing she could do about it.

Still holding the child, Jesus said to his friends, 'Unless you change and become like children, you will not know what it means to belong to the kingdom of God. You must not try to be bigger and better than others. Instead you must be like this little child, and then you will be the greatest in the kingdom of God!'

On another occasion mothers started bringing their babies and young children to Jesus, wanting him to lay his hands on them and bless them.

Jesus' friends tried to stop them, but when Jesus saw what they were doing, he got very angry.

'What do you think you're doing?' he said. 'Let the children come to me. Don't stop them! For the kingdom of God belongs to people like them.'

So the mothers came forward, one by one, and Jesus took each of the children in his arms, laid his hands upon them and blessed them.

Here are a few of the sayings we find in John:

'I AM THE BREAD OF LIFE,' said Jesus. 'Whoever comes to me will never be hungry, and whoever believes in me will never be thirsty.'

'I am the light of the world. Whoever follows me will never walk in darkness but will hold the light of life.'

'I am the good shepherd. A good shepherd is prepared to lay down his life for the sheep. If a wolf comes to attack the flock, a hired hand, who doesn't care about the sheep, will run away. Then the wolf will scatter them and snatch one of them away. But I am the good shepherd. The sheep are mine. I know them all; they know me. It's like me and my Father, God. He knows me, and I know him. I will lay down my own life for the sheep. No one can snatch them from me.'

'I and the Father are one.'

'I am the way, the truth and the life.'

'I am the vine, you are the branches. If you stay joined on to me, you will bear much fruit.'

Finally, a prayer. For Christians it is the most famous prayer in the world, and the one they use more often than any other. Almost all Christians know it by heart. In the Gospels it appears twice, once in Matthew and once, in a shorter version, in Luke. It is the longer version Christians use in their prayers and their public worship. It is called the Lord's Prayer.

JESUS SAID, 'This is how you should pray:

'Our Father in heaven,
hallowed be your name,
your kingdom come,
your will be done,
on earth as in heaven.
Give us today our daily bread.
Forgive us our sins
as we forgive those who sin against us.
Lead us not into temptation
but deliver us from evil.'

10

JESUS IS KILLED: JESUS IS RISEN

The four Gospels of the New Testament spend all or most of their time on the last year or so of Jesus' life, and all of them devote more time to the events leading up to his death, and to those that took place after his death, than to anything else. All the Gospel writers agreed on this: Jesus' death, terrible though it was, summed up what he stood for and all that he had said and done. Jesus showed people what God was like, and he did that most clearly of all when he died, and when he met his followers again after his death.

Ever since, Christians have followed the Gospels' lead. That is why Good Friday, when they remember Jesus' death on a cross, and Easter, when they celebrate his resurrection from the dead, are so important to them. It is also why the cross is the most common Christian symbol. It is found in almost all churches — on their walls, on their roofs, in their stained glass windows, on their altars. Many Christians wear a small cross on a chain round their neck, or on the lapel of their jacket, or have a cross on a wall or a shelf at home, or hanging from the driving mirror in their car.

Each of the four Gospels tells the story of Jesus' death and resurrection in its own way, though they mostly agree on the basic pattern of events. For the story of Jesus' death and the events leading up to it, this chapter of The Book of Books *will rely mainly on Mark's account, though a few extra details will be taken from Matthew, Luke and John. For the stories about Jesus' resurrection, however, the chapter will leave Mark behind and turn instead to three stories in John.*

Riding into Jerusalem
all four Gospels

The story of the events leading up to Jesus' death begins with him coming to Jerusalem for the Jewish festival of the Passover.

Thousands and thousands of Jewish pilgrims came from all over Palestine and far beyond to Jerusalem, to celebrate the festival together in the temple. In their eyes the temple was the holiest place in all the world. They went there to meet their God, and, in a world and a land run by Romans, they went there to meet one another and celebrate being Jews. In the temple they could be proud of being Jewish.

At Passover they told once again the story of how their ancestors escaped out of Egypt, and how the pharaoh and his army were drowned in the Red Sea. God had rescued his people then. Surely, some of them thought, he will rescue us again, and this time from the Romans. Perhaps this year the Messiah will come, drive out the Romans, be crowned king, give us back our freedom and make Jerusalem the centre of the world once more.

The Romans were on their guard. Pilate, the Roman governor of Judea, who normally lived on the Mediterranean coast, had moved into the city with lots of extra soldiers. There was a Roman fortress called the Antonia which overlooked the temple, so they could keep a close eye on things. They didn't want trouble, and if people dared to start some, they'd get rid of them quickly. The priests who ran the temple didn't want trouble either. They just wanted things to go on as normal.

JESUS AND HIS FRIENDS were among those making their way to Jerusalem for the festival. Crowds of other pilgrims from Galilee were with them. The crowds included many poor people who'd listened to Jesus' teaching and found a pride they'd never had before. The people who'd been fed by Jesus near Lake Galilee were with him. Miriam, the woman who'd touched him in the crowd and been healed, was there, and Rachel too, the girl who'd been snatched away from death, with her parents. A woman called Mary from Magdala, a village on the shore of Lake Galilee was with him. She'd been terribly, terribly ill, and Jesus had healed her. Ever since then she'd kept as close to him as she could.

They were taking the road that wound up from Jericho through the hills of the Judean desert. They were only two miles from the city now.

Jesus was on foot like the rest of his followers, but he decided that he would ride into Jerusalem. He would ride into the city like a king and teach them what being a king really meant, and what sort of king God was. He needed a donkey nobody had ridden before. Nobody else was allowed to ride a king's donkey.

'You see that village up ahead,' he said to two of his friends. 'When you enter it, you'll find a donkey tied up that no one has sat on before. Untie it and bring it to me. If anyone asks you what you're doing, just tell them the master needs it, and they'll let you take it.'

The friends were a bit mystified by that, but they did as Jesus asked and found things exactly as he'd said. They brought the donkey to Jesus and threw their cloaks over its back. Jesus climbed up onto it. 'We'll take you into Jerusalem like a king, Jesus!' everyone cried.

Soon they reached the ridge of the Mount of Olives. Jerusalem lay before them. A new temple complex was being built. King Herod had started it. He wanted something better than the one that had been put up after the exile, when times were hard. His design was like his ambition – huge. People had been building it for over fifty years already, but they still weren't finished. There were great flights of steps up onto the temple platform, and colonnades that seemed to go on for ever. There was a vast courtyard where Gentiles could go as well as Jews. Around its inner walls were notices saying that if Gentiles went any further they would be put to death. Then up a few more steps was another courtyard for Jewish women. Some more steps led to the courtyard for Jewish men. No women were allowed in that. Another twelve steps higher still stood the temple itself, the house of God. Only the priests were allowed inside that. And even they weren't allowed inside the Holy of Holies. That was the holiest place of all. It was divided from the rest of the temple by a curtain. Only the High Priest, once a year, was allowed to pass through the curtain.

The pilgrims stood looking down on it all. For a moment it took their breath away. Then one of the people who'd come with Jesus from Galilee shouted, 'God bless the king!' The others cheered and took up the cry. They spread their cloaks on the road in front of Jesus, with straw and leafy branches from the fields, to make a carpet for him to ride on. 'God bless the king!' they yelled. 'God bless the king!' And so they wound their way down the hillside, past a garden called Gethsemane, towards the walls of Jerusalem.

They didn't notice that Jesus was crying. He was looking across to the city. If only, he said to himself, you knew the ways that make for peace.

So they entered Jerusalem. The pilgrims from Galilee and

Samaria got swallowed up in the huge crowds. The shouts of 'God bless the king!' were lost in the general hubbub. Nothing remarkable or strange happened, just a lot of pushing and shoving in the narrow streets, while the Roman soldiers kept watch over the temple courtyards from their fortress. It all seemed a dreadful anticlimax. Would nothing happen?

Jesus and his friends eventually managed to get up onto the temple platform and into the first courtyard. Jesus looked around him and carefully observed everything that was going on. He would be back soon. But it was getting late, and he and his close friends had to find lodging for the night. It was far too expensive to stay inside the city. So they went back up the Mount of Olives and over the ridge to the village of Bethany. It was just two miles away, and Jesus had friends there. They could stay there during the festival.

Mayhem in the Temple
all four Gospels

THE DAY AFTER JESUS had ridden into Jerusalem and gone to the temple he was back, and this time he was ready for action. He'd seen enough. He'd seen how people were treated in the temple. Priests were more important there, it seemed, than other people. The rich were more important than poor people. Men were more important than women. Adults were more important than children. People who lived in Jerusalem were more important than peasants from Galilee, with their country accents and their country dialect. And sick people, or disabled people, were not thought holy enough to be allowed to get close to God.

All this drove Jesus into a rage. These people – the sick, the disabled, the peasants from the villages of Galilee who had such a hard time of it, the women, the poor – these were the very people he lived with, the people who came to him for help, the people he taught, the people he loved! And they were the very ones who loved him! And as for the children, had he not set a child right in the centre of his circle of friends and told them they must all become like children?

The temple was meant to be the place where everyone could get close to God, whoever they were. It was meant to be a place where anyone in the world could find God's love and generosity, especially those who needed it most. But it wasn't like that at all. Those who needed God most were kept at a distance.

The temple was supposed to be a place where the poor found God's passion for justice and went away with their pockets bulging with good things. But the previous day Jesus had watched the peasants from Galilee changing their money into the special coins they had to use in the temple. He'd seen them using that money to pay for doves they could ill afford to offer as sacrifices.

He'd seen enough. It was time for action! So now, on his second day in the city, he marched into the temple precincts and began driving out those who were buying and selling. He overturned the tables of those changing the money, he upset the seats of the dove-sellers, and he stopped the priests and the Levites carrying their sacred vessels from one part of the temple to another.

'God said,' he shouted, '"My house shall be a house of prayer for all nations, for everyone in the world!" You people who run this place, you've turned it into a den of thieves! The poor come, and you make them poorer still. People come here, who've been put down all their lives, to find some dignity and honour, and you send them away with less than they had before.'

The poor people, the abused people, the people who usually had no say in anything, cheered loudly when they heard Jesus say that. The blind and the lame came flocking round him so that he could heal them, and the children started shouting, 'God bless the king! God bless the king!'

The chief priests, and some other Jewish leaders known as scribes, heard the commotion and came to see what was going on. It was intolerable! This Jesus was out to stop the whole workings of the temple. If people couldn't change their money or buy their doves, and if the priests and Levites couldn't carry the sacred vessels to where they were needed, the worship of God would cease completely. The temple would be finished! A person could be flogged and put to death just for prophesying the destruction of the temple. This Galilean was not just prophesying its destruction, he was acting to bring it about.

And those blind and lame people, what were they doing there? People like that weren't allowed in the temple. And the children shouting 'God bless the king!' What were they thinking of? Children were supposed to keep quiet when adults were around. And listen to what they were shouting too. 'God bless the king!' They'd cause a riot, if they weren't careful. And then the Roman soldiers would come running from the Antonia and turn the temple precincts into a battleground.

The man had to be stopped. There was no question about that. But how? That was the problem. The people round him were hanging on his every word. They clearly adored him. If the temple police came and arrested him straight away, that would definitely cause a riot.

So they let Jesus alone for the time being. They would bide their time.

But Jesus couldn't leave the temple alone. Soon he was back again, standing with his close friends watching the women put their offerings into the large trumpet-shaped chests in the Court of the Women. Rich women were there from Jerusalem and other cities, dressed in fine robes and throwing lots of money into them – silver, even gold. Then a widow who was extremely poor shyly approached one of the chests and put two tiny copper coins into it.

'See that old woman over there,' said Jesus indignantly. 'She's given more than all those other women put together. They've got plenty of money left – they won't go short. But that widow has put in everything she had. She's got nothing to live on at all now. What will she do? I'll tell you: beg on the streets or starve to death! That's what this place has brought her to. She came here with almost nothing. She should have gone away with her pockets full to bursting. Remember what Moses saw on Mount Sinai, when God passed him by? He saw all God's goodness, grain and wine, flocks and herds, dancing in the streets – life like a watered garden! That's what this poor widow should have found here. But now she's gone away with *nothing*! It's all back to front and upside down.'

Jesus is Anointed Messiah
all four Gospels

Centuries before Jesus was born, when David's son Solomon became king in Jerusalem, they led him down to a spring called Gihon, beneath the walls of Jerusalem. A priest anointed his head with holy oil. The people shouted 'Long live the king!' They put a crown on his head and set him on a throne. They sang a special coronation psalm, about God declaring to the new king, 'You are my son.' Then, so they believed, the Spirit of God descended upon him to give him the power and the wisdom to reign.

Now Jesus had already been down to the Jordan river, when he was baptized by John. He'd heard God say to him, 'You are my Son.' God's spirit had come upon him too. More recently on the way down the Mount of Olives the people had shouted, 'God bless the king!' and the children had shouted those same words in the temple court. But no one had anointed him. No one had put a crown on his head. No one had set him on a fine throne.

Jesus was anointed, but not by the High Priest, nor in the temple, nor with any grand ceremony. It was the most extraordinary anointing of a king ever performed!

JESUS WAS IN BETHANY, in the house of a leper called Simon, eating a meal with him and some friends. As a Jew Jesus wasn't supposed to eat meals with lepers or even enter their houses. Lepers were said to be unclean. Their houses and all the things they touched were supposed to be unclean. But Jesus didn't bother with such things. He never let religious rules and regulations stop him getting close to people. People like Simon were the ones who needed him most. People like Simon were the ones whose company he enjoyed the most too.

They were in the middle of their meal, when suddenly a woman burst in, carrying a long-necked alabaster jar containing a very expensive, highly scented ointment, called spikenard. Most of the men in the room were shocked. It was unheard of for a woman, a complete stranger, to interrupt a group of men eating together. What on earth did she think she was doing? But they didn't have time to ask her that, because next she did something quite astonishing. She broke off the thin neck of the jar and poured the ointment all over Jesus' head. Its sweet, heady scent filled the room.

They all looked at the woman open-mouthed – all, that is, except Jesus. He knew exactly what she'd done.

For a spell there was complete silence. Then someone blurted out, 'What a waste!' 'Worth a whole year's wages,' said another. 'It could've been sold and the money given to the poor,' said a third. 'You shameless idiot!' they all said to the woman.

'Let her alone!' Jesus cried. 'Let her alone. She knows what she has done. It is an act of love, a fine thing, a fine and generous thing.

'You will always have the poor with you,' he continued. 'There will be plenty of opportunities for you to be kind to them. But you will not always have me.' He paused and looked at the woman. 'Don't you see?' he said to the others. 'She has anointed me. I am now the Anointed One, the Messiah, the Christ! This woman has played the part of the High Priest. Simon, this house of yours has become the very house of God.

'But this woman knows very well what kind of king I will be, and what kind of crown and throne they will give me. She has anointed me for burial also, you see. You know how women anoint dead bodies for burial. Well, this woman, whose name I don't even know, but who loves me with such a generous love, knows full well that I am as good as dead. And so she has come to prepare me for heaven. I think the scent of her ointment will have reached there already.'

He turned to the woman. 'You will always be remembered for this,' he said. 'Wherever people tell my story, they will speak of your great love, your generosity and your wisdom.'

Betrayal
Matthew, Mark and Luke

The chief priests and scribes were determined to stop Jesus. But how? That was the problem. They didn't expect to get any help from Jesus' followers, of course. But that's precisely what they were given, and from one of his closest friends too, one of the men who'd been with him up in Galilee all the time he was teaching and healing the people there, someone called Judas Iscariot.

JUDAS SLIPPED AWAY from Bethany when he thought no one was looking, went into Jerusalem, found his way to the chief priests and told them he would hand Jesus over to them.

'I can tell you exactly what he's been saying about the temple,' he said. 'And I know his movements. Tonight I'll lead you to him. I know where he and his friends will be. It'll be an out of the way place. No crowds. No fuss. No risk of a riot. I'll go up to him and give him a kiss of greeting. Then you'll know which one he is, and you can arrest him.'

'Excellent! Excellent!' the priests cried. 'This is just the chance we've been looking for! We're very grateful to you, Judas. Don't worry, you're doing the right thing, and you'll be nicely rewarded for your trouble.'

Judas left and hurried back to Bethany to join the others.

The Last Supper
all four Gospels

As part of the Passover celebrations, Jesus and a group of his friends were going to have a special meal together. They would commemorate the time when the Israelites escaped from Egypt, crossed the Red Sea and entered the desert to meet God on Sinai. At least, that's what the friends thought the meal would be about. Jesus had other ideas. In fact, the friends were in for quite a few surprises that evening.

'WE NEED TO FIND SOMEWHERE for our Passover meal and get everything ready,' his friends said to Jesus. 'Where do you want us to go?'

Jesus chose two of them and gave them their instructions. 'Go into Jerusalem,' he said, 'and a man will meet you. He'll be carrying a water jar on his head. Usually the women do that, as you know, and the men who sell water in the street use leather bottles, so you'll pick him out quite easily. He'll lead you to a house he knows. When you get there, say to the owner, "The teacher asks, 'Where is the room where I may eat the Passover with my friends?'" He'll show you a large upstairs room, with everything we need already there. Then you'll be able to get the meal ready for us.'

The two friends went off, and they found things exactly as he'd said. When evening came, Jesus arrived at the house with the rest of his friends.

While they were eating, they noticed Jesus was very quiet. He seemed preoccupied, thinking of something else.

Suddenly he said, 'One of you in this room is going to betray me.'

The friends were shocked. 'Not me!' 'Not me!' 'Not me!' they cried.

'It's one of you who is eating with me at this very moment,' Jesus said.

'Teacher,' said Judas. 'Surely you don't mean me?'

Jesus looked across at him.

A little later in the meal Jesus took a loaf of bread, said a prayer of blessing over it, broke it, handed the pieces to his friends and said, 'Take, eat; this is my body, which is given for you. Do this in remembrance of me.' Then he took a cup of wine, said a prayer of thanks and handed it round. 'This is my blood,' he said, 'poured out for many for the forgiveness of sins.' He paused, and then added,

'My body and blood will mark a new beginning, a new friendship with God, a new finding of forgiveness. I tell you, I will not drink wine again until I drink it at a great feast with God, once everyone allows God to reign and all things at last are well.'

The friends didn't know what to make of these strange, wonderful words. They were not what they expected in a Passover meal at all. But they would never forget them.

The same evening they had another surprise. Jesus got up, laid aside his outer robe, tied a towel round his waist, poured water into a pitcher and began to wash the dust off their feet and dry them with the towel.

He came to Peter. 'Master, are *you* going to wash *my* feet?' Peter asked.

'You will understand one day,' Jesus answered.

'But you can't!' Peter cried. 'I mean, it's work for a slave to do. Even slaves, if they're Jewish, can't be told to do it. But you're not a slave. You're our Master, our Lord, our Teacher! We could wash your feet to show how much you mean to us, but you can't wash ours. You've got it all back to front.'

'I understand all that,' said Jesus, 'but if I don't wash your feet, how can I show you how much I love you? And how can you be my friend, Peter, if you won't let me near you?'

'In that case, wash my hands and face as well!' Peter exclaimed.

Jesus laughed. 'Your feet are enough,' he said. He straightened up and looked round at the rest of his friends. 'Do you understand what I have done?' he asked. 'You call me Teacher, Master, Lord, and yet I have washed your feet. I have acted as your disciple, your slave. With me things *are* back to front, you see, the same as they are with God. You must all follow my example. You know how kings often lord it over their subjects. They look down on people and keep them under their thumb or their boot, while making sure everyone says how kind and generous they are. You must not be like them. The oldest among you must be like the youngest; your leader must be like your servant. Just look at me, with this wet towel round my waist. Do I look like a king?

'Yet I will be your teacher once more and give you something you must remember. It is very simple: love one another. As I have loved you, so you also must love one another.'

Arrest
all four Gospels

THE PASSOVER MEAL was over. Judas had already slipped out. Jesus and his friends sang a psalm together, a special psalm for the Passover, and then went out through the city walls and down into the Kidron Valley the other side.

They were beginning to climb the slopes of the Mount of Olives towards the garden of Gethsemane, when Jesus said to his friends, 'You will all desert me.'

'I won't!' protested Peter. 'Even if everyone else does, I won't!'

'Peter,' Jesus replied, 'this very night, before the cock crows twice, you will deny me three times.'

'Even if I have to die with you, I swear I will not deny you!' said Peter.

The others all said the same.

So they came to Gethsemane. It was dark. There was no moonlight. No stars shining either.

'Sit here,' Jesus said, 'while I pray. Peter, James and John, you come with me.'

The four of them went further into the garden, among the twisted olive trees. As soon as they were hidden from the others, Jesus became very agitated. 'My heart is ready to break with fear,' he said. 'Stay here and keep awake.'

He went on a bit further on his own. He fell to the ground and prayed to God. 'Abba, my Father,' he said, 'you can do anything.

I don't want to go through with this. Do something to get me out of it!' He was shaking violently. He buried his forehead in the dust. 'Yet not what I want, but what you want,' he said.

He got to his feet, still shaking, and went back to Peter, James and John. They were fast asleep. 'Peter,' he said, 'couldn't you keep awake just one hour? Wake up, stay awake and pray. Pray that you will not be tested in this way yourselves.'

He returned to the same spot as before. He prayed the same words. He waited for God to speak to him. Silence. Only the wind gently ruffling the leaves of the trees.

Once again he came back to the three friends. He desperately needed their comfort, their strength, their support. But they were asleep again. He stood there looking down at them. They woke up with a start and didn't know what to say.

He turned and went a third time to pray, to find God's company, to bring God close. But when he listened for God, he still only heard the wind in the trees. For the third time he came back to his friends. For the third time he found them sleeping.

'Still asleep?' he said quietly. 'Still taking it easy?' He turned his head and listened. There was a new sound. They were coming to get him. He could see the flickering lights of torches through the trees.

'Get up!' he shouted to his friends. 'They're here!'

The friends were still stumbling to their feet, when Judas arrived, leading a band of soldiers from the temple guard, armed with swords and wooden clubs. Judas marched straight up to Jesus. 'Teacher!' he cried, and kissed him.

The soldiers arrested Jesus immediately.

Jesus looked at the weapons they were holding. 'So you think I'm a dangerous bandit, do you?' he said. 'Why didn't you arrest me when I was in the temple?'

His friends were terrified. They could get arrested themselves if they stayed with Jesus, or, even worse, they could get killed. So they deserted him and ran off as fast as they could. All except Peter. He ran out of the garden, but then hid behind some trees to watch what happened.

Jesus was left on his own with Judas and the soldiers. The flames of the torches cast strange shadows among the trees. The moon and the stars were still hidden behind thick cloud.

The soldiers started to march Jesus away.

The Unfair Trial
all four Gospels

THE SOLDIERS LED JESUS BACK into the city, through the gate in the walls, along the narrow, winding streets. It was very late and the streets were deserted. The sound of their feet echoed against the walls of the houses.

They took him to the house of the High Priest, where the chief priests, scribes and elders were already gathered. They were expecting him. This was the Sanhedrin, the highest Jewish court in the land.

Peter had been following the soldiers at a distance. After they'd disappeared indoors, he crept into the courtyard of the house. He couldn't go any further. He would have to wait. It was a cold night, but fortunately there was a fire burning in a brazier. He crouched down close to it and spread his hands to the flames. There was no one else about.

In a large room upstairs the Sanhedrin put Jesus on trial. They were breaking their own rules by meeting like this at night, but that didn't matter to them. Justice didn't matter either. They just wanted to get rid of Jesus. The man was too much of a risk. He had challenged the whole operation of the temple. That couldn't be tolerated.

They realized that Pilate, the Roman Governor, would want Jesus dead as much as they did, though for a different reason. His soldiers would have heard people hailing Jesus as a king. Surely he would see Jesus as a direct threat to his authority and the authority of the emperor in Rome. They would hand Jesus over to Pilate in the morning.

They would need to get the crowds on their side as well. That shouldn't be too difficult, they thought, at least as far as the people who lived in Jerusalem were concerned. Most of them depended on the temple for their livelihood, and Jesus was threatening to bring the temple to an end. As for the others, including the peasants from places like Galilee, Pilate would think of something.

The trial was rigged. The priests had bribed some people to give evidence against Jesus, but some people said one thing, some another. Their evidence didn't agree.

The High Priest became impatient. Time was getting on, and they needed a proper case to put to Pilate, or they'd look stupid. Jesus wasn't helping matters either, as far as the High Priest was concerned. He hadn't said a word. They'd been giving him a chance to answer the charges, but he'd kept silent the whole time, with his eyes fixed on the floor.

'Have you nothing to say?' the High Priest asked. 'What about all these things they're saying against you?'

Jesus said nothing.

The High Priest lost his temper. 'Look at you!' he shouted. 'You're the Messiah, the Son of God, are you?' He laughed.

Jesus raised his head and looked across at him. 'I am,' he said quietly. 'And when I die, you will see the Son of God seated at God's right hand, coming with the clouds of heaven to defeat the forces of tyranny and put an end to the misery you cause. You think you have me in your power, but look more deeply. And when I die, look into the depths of God, and you will find me there!'

'That is blasphemy!' cried the High Priest. He tore his clothes, to mark the end of the trial and to show that the prisoner was a blasphemer. He looked round at the other members of the Sanhedrin. 'We don't need any more witnesses,' he said. 'You've heard his blasphemy from his own lips. What sentence do you pass?'

There was only one sentence they could pass. Anyone convicted of blasphemy had to be put to death. 'The man deserves to die!' they cried.

They gathered round Jesus. Some of them spat in his face. One person fastened a blindfold round his head, and they started to hit him. 'Come on, prophet!' they yelled, 'Let's have some prophecy!' Then the temple guards took over and gave him a beating.

Peter's Denial
all four Gospels

WHILE ALL THIS WAS GOING ON, Peter was down below in the courtyard, still warming himself near the fire. It was nearly dawn. A few people were up already and going about their duties.

One of the High Priest's servant-girls came past and noticed Peter crouching there. The flames from the fire lit up his face. She stopped for a moment. What's that man doing there? she said to herself. She stared at him a bit harder. Wait a minute! I think I recognize him! I was up in the temple the other day, when that

Jesus caused all the trouble. This man was with him, I'm sure of it.

'You were with Jesus, weren't you?' she said out loud. 'That man from Nazareth, who's been causing all the trouble.'

'I don't know what you're talking about,' said Peter.

He got up and went into the passage leading from the courtyard into the street. It was darker there, a better place to hide perhaps. In the next street a cock crowed.

Time passed. There were quite a few people around now. The same servant-girl came past the end of the passage. She saw Peter hiding there. 'Hey!' she called out. 'This man's one of Jesus' friends. I recognize him.' Everyone stopped and stared at him.

'I am *not*,' Peter cried. His heart was thumping.

They all gathered round him. 'Yes you are!' they exclaimed. 'We can tell from your accent! You're from Galilee. You *must* be one of his friends!'

Peter was very frightened now. 'I solemnly swear, by God, the Lord of heaven and earth, I do not know the man you're talking about!'

At that moment the cock crowed for the second time.

Peter remembered what Jesus had said as they were on their way to Gethsemane: 'This very night, before the cock crows twice, you will deny me three times.'

He broke down and wept.

Pilate
all four Gospels

THE MORNING HAD ARRIVED. It was time to send Jesus to Pilate. So the priests tied Jesus' hands together and led him through the streets to the palace where Pilate was staying during the festival.

Pilate was delighted that they'd managed to arrest Jesus without causing any disturbance in the city. He knew why they'd been so keen to get their hands on the man, but he didn't worry about any of that. All he was interested in was the report he'd received from his own troops, that the Galilean was going round calling himself a king, and that he had a large crowd of followers who believed he was. Apparently, some children had been shouting, 'God bless the king!' inside the precincts of the temple. Clearly he had to get rid of the man, or he'd have a major riot on his hands, and the emperor back in Rome wouldn't be pleased at all. The emperor didn't like riots.

Jesus was led into his presence. Pilate looked him up and down. His hands were tied, and his face was bruised and swollen with the beating he'd had from the temple guards. He could see people had been spitting on him.

'So,' he said, with a sneer in his voice, '*you* are this king I've been hearing about, are you?'

'So you say,' said Jesus.

The chief priests leaped in at once with their accusations. Pilate expected Jesus to defend himself. But he didn't. He seemed to know the game they were playing and was having nothing to do with it.

'Have you nothing to say?' Pilate asked angrily. 'Look at all the charges they're bringing against you!'

Jesus remained silent. Pilate was astonished. In his experience Jewish troublemakers usually had a great deal to say for themselves. But this man clearly wasn't frightened.

'Well, we'll have to see what the crowd thinks, won't we?' he said.

They were in an upstairs room, overlooking a large courtyard at the front of the palace. The courtyard was seething with people. Pilate looked down on them all. He had nothing but contempt for

them. And yet he was still afraid of them. If some of them were supporters of this strange, silent Galilean, then they could turn very nasty when he condemned him to death. It was a tricky situation.

Fortunately, he had an idea. There was a man under guard in the palace, called Barabbas. He was a leader of the Dagger Men. The Dagger Men, in the eyes of the Romans, were notorious Jewish terrorists. Barabbas and his gang had caused a riot and had stabbed several Roman soldiers to death. Pilate was waiting to have them crucified after the festival, once the pilgrims had gone home. But perhaps he could let Barabbas off after all. Barabbas was a broken man. The Roman torturers had done their work well. He wouldn't cause any more trouble, and the rest of his gang would be executed anyway. Pilate knew he wouldn't be taking any real risk if he released him. But the crowd wouldn't know that, of course. They'd like it if Barabbas was set free. He often released one of his prisoners at Passover, to keep the crowds happy. They'd come to expect it. This time he could give them a choice: Barabbas or Jesus. They could choose the one they liked best, only he and the priests would see to it they got Barabbas. Yes, Pilate thought to himself, this could work out very nicely. He gave orders for Barabbas to be fetched from the dungeons. Then he went over to the priests and explained his plan. The priests left the room and went outside to mingle with the crowd.

There was a large platform out in the courtyard, and in the middle of it a grand seat like a throne. Some soldiers escorted Pilate to the platform, and he sat down. More soldiers came behind him, leading Jesus and Barabbas.

'As you see,' Pilate called out, pointing to Jesus, 'I've got your precious king. Would you like me to set him free for you?'

'No, Barabbas!' the crowd shouted.

Those priests have done a good job, thought Pilate. 'Then what shall I do with this king?' he said to the crowd.

'Crucify him!' they yelled.

'Why,' said Pilate, pretending to be horrified, 'what's he done wrong?'

The crowd yelled all the louder, 'Crucify him! Crucify him!'

My word, said Pilate to himself. Those priests are clever! Crucifixion's a Roman punishment. Getting Jews to call for a Jew to be crucified! Whoever heard of such a thing? The priests have got them completely hysterical.

'Very well,' he said to the crowd, 'I'll do as you say.' He turned to the soldiers. 'Let Barabbas go. As for this Jesus, give him a good flogging and then crucify him.'

He got down from the platform and went inside the palace to get on with his work. It had all gone remarkably smoothly, he thought.

Jesus is Crowned King
all four Gospels

THE SOLDIERS TOOK the flogging very seriously. They knew just how far to go. Too many strokes of the whip and you could kill a man. Then you'd have no one to crucify. You had to get it just right: nearly knock the life out of him, but not quite.

When they'd finished, they took Jesus indoors, to the part of the palace where the rest of the soldiers were gathered.

'Look what we've got!' they called out. 'We've got the king of the Jews, we have!'

The others gathered round. 'He doesn't look like much of a king, does he?' one of them said.

'We'll have to dress him up,' said another. 'Come here, Your Majesty. We can do better than king of the Jews. We'll make you look like the emperor himself!'

'The emperor wears purple, so let's put this lovely purple cloak on you,' they cried.

'And the emperor wears a laurel wreath too. Oh, what a pity, Your Majesty, we don't have any laurel. But we do have this nice crown of thorns. You'll have to have this instead. Let's put it on for you. This is your coronation, Your Majesty!'

They jammed the crown of thorns onto Jesus' head and knelt in front of him. 'Hail, king of the Jews!' they shouted.

They struck him about the head with a cane and spat in his face. The room was filled with their laughter.

Finally they'd had enough. They took the cloak off him, dressed him again in his peasant clothes and led him out to crucify him. An officer called a centurion was in charge of the execution party.

Crucifixion
all four Gospels

THE SOLDIERS HUNG a tablet round Jesus' neck. It had the words, 'The king of the Jews' on it. Pilate wanted everyone to see what happened to people who dared challenge Roman power.

Jesus had to carry his own cross – or at least its horizontal beam – to the place of execution. It was heavy and difficult to manoeuvre through the narrow streets. He'd had too much of a beating. The torture had left him very weak, and his legs were like jelly. He collapsed on the ground, the beam of the cross falling on top of him.

'Get up!' the centurion shouted, and kicked him hard. It was no good. The strength wasn't in him. A Jew called Simon, from the city of Cyrene on the north African coast, happened to be passing by.

'Hey, you!' the centurion called. 'Come and carry this man's cross! We've a job of work to do, and we want to get it done before next week.'

So the little procession wound its way once more through the streets of Jerusalem, some of the soldiers in front, some at the rear, with Jesus in the middle and Simon lugging the cross along behind.

They came to a place outside the city walls called Golgotha, or the Place of the Skull. Some women offered Jesus some drugged wine to dull the pain, but he wouldn't take it.

Then the soldiers stripped him naked and crucified him. They fixed a two metre piece of wood upright in the ground, nailed Jesus's wrists to the beam that Simon had been carrying, hauled him up with ropes, tied and nailed the two parts of the cross together and nailed Jesus' feet to the vertical piece. Finally, they fixed the tablet with 'The king of the Jews' on it just above his head.

So now, at last, the king-making ceremonies were complete. Jesus was set on a cross for all to see. The cross was his throne.

'Father God, forgive them,' Jesus said, panting hard for breath. 'They don't know what they're doing.'

The soldiers divided his clothes among them, casting lots to see which piece each of them should have.

Two bandits were crucified with Jesus, one on his left, one on his right.

It was a noisy place. People had come to see the execution, and they started yelling abuse at Jesus. Even the chief priests and some of the scribes were there. 'He saved others,' they said, 'but he can't save himself!'

'Come on, Messiah!' they all shouted. 'Get down from the cross, and we'll all believe you then!'

One of the bandits joined in the mockery. 'You can save us at the same time!' he shouted.

'You're a fine one to talk!' the other bandit cried. 'This is your last chance to do something right. We know why we're here, but this man has done nothing wrong. And he *is* a king, I know it.' He looked across at Jesus. 'Jesus,' he said, 'remember me when you come into your kingdom.'

'I tell you, my friend,' Jesus replied, 'this very day you will be with me in paradise.'

Three hours passed. It was noon. It was meant to be the brightest part of the day, but suddenly the sun disappeared, and a thick darkness fell over the whole land. It was as if the sun had turned to ashes, as if the whole of creation was in mourning.

The darkness lasted for three more hours. The desolation was complete. Most of Jesus' friends had deserted him. Even God had abandoned him. At least, that's what it seemed like. Those mock trials before the temple authorities and Pilate, the brutality of the temple guards and the Roman soldiers, the fearful pain, the continual fighting for breath, and now this strange, terrifying darkness, all seemed to have shut God out. He was nowhere to be seen, nowhere to be heard. Words of an ancient psalm filled Jesus' mind. He raised his head and yelled them into the dark: 'My God, my God! Why have you abandoned me? Why? Why? Why?' Then, with one last great gasp, he died.

At that very moment, in the temple inside the city, the great curtain separating the innermost room, the Holy of Holies, from the rest of the sanctuary split from top to bottom. Jesus' death had brought God out into the open. They couldn't keep him hidden away any more! They couldn't pretend that only High Priests were good enough to enter his presence. Just when Jesus felt most abandoned by him, God came out to walk the streets of the city, as once he had walked the paths of the Garden of Eden. In that darkness, beneath Jesus' cross, it had seemed almost as if God himself had died. In truth, Jesus' death had set God free.

The centurion at the foot of the cross sensed the meaning of it all. He looked up at Jesus. 'This man was God's Son!' he cried.

Now the execution was complete, the few friends of Jesus in the crowd crept closer. Three women were there who'd followed him in Galilee and who'd travelled to Jerusalem with him. Among them was Mary of Magdala.

There was also one member of the Jewish Sanhedrin who hadn't agreed with what they'd done to Jesus. His name was Joseph, and he came from a town called Arimathea. He'd kept quiet long enough. He plucked up his courage and went to Pilate to ask if he could have Jesus' body for burial. The Romans usually left the bodies of crucified men hanging there. Joseph couldn't bear to think of Jesus' body just left to rot, or picked over by vultures.

Pilate had had enough of Jesus. 'Do with him what you like,' he said.

So Joseph ran off, bought a new linen shroud in the market and went as quickly as he could with some of his friends to Golgotha. They took Jesus' body down, wrapped it in the sheet and carried it to a tomb which had been cut out of the rock, the kind they could walk into if they bent their heads down. Joseph had meant to be buried there himself one day, but no matter. They laid Jesus' body inside, and rolled a huge stone across the entrance. Then they hurried away.

Jesus' devoted follower, Mary of Magdala, had followed the little burial procession, keeping her distance so she wouldn't be noticed. She had seen that Joseph and his friends hadn't had time to give Jesus a proper burial. They hadn't washed his body, nor anointed it with sweet-smelling oils. The next day was the sabbath, and Mary wouldn't be able to do anything then. But as soon as dawn broke on the day after that, she would come back to the tomb and set things to rights. How she would move the stone, she didn't know. She would deal with that problem when she came to it. She walked away, wondering when the tears would come and she would be able to let out her grief.

'Mary'
John

❧

MARY GOT UP VERY EARLY on the Sunday morning and went off to the tomb. She hadn't been able to wait for the dawn. It was still dark, but there was enough light to show her, when she got to the tomb, that something very strange had happened. The stone was rolled back from the entrance, and someone had removed Jesus' body!

She knew the house where Peter was hiding with Jesus' other friends. She ran there as fast as she could.

'They've taken Jesus out of the tomb!' she cried. 'I don't know where they've put him! Who would do such a thing?'

The tomb was in a garden. Mary told them exactly where it was, and Peter and one of the others went running off to see what had happened. Mary followed them as quickly as she could.

Peter's companion got there first. Mary was right. The stone which must have sealed the entrance had been moved aside. The sun had just risen above the horizon, and its first rays shone into the tomb, turning its stone to gold. He looked inside. The tomb was empty, except for the linen shroud Joseph had used, lying on the ledge where the body had been placed. Only the body wasn't there! No smell of death either!

At that moment Peter came running up and went straight inside. He also saw the shroud and a cloth which Joseph must have tied round Jesus' head. But Jesus wasn't there.

His companion bent his head and came in. He didn't fully understand, but he knew something very good had happened in that place. The tomb wasn't empty at all. It was full of the life of God!

The two men went home bewildered, not knowing what to make of it. Yet Mary didn't leave. She had reached the tomb again, and she didn't know what to do, but she knew she couldn't leave. She hadn't deserted Jesus when he was crucified, and she wouldn't desert him now. She stood outside the tomb, weeping.

Suddenly she caught the scent and the rustle of heaven. She bent down to look inside the tomb. There were two angels sitting on the ledge as bold as brass, as if they belonged there! What was heaven doing in this garden? It wasn't the time for heaven. It was the time for tears, and plenty of them.

'Why are you crying?' the angels asked.

'Why do you think?' Mary answered. 'They've taken away my Lord, my Friend, my Teacher, and I don't know where they've laid him.'

She straightened herself. A lot of use they were, she said to herself. Call themselves angels!

She turned round. A figure was standing there. It was Jesus.

'Why are you crying?' the figure said. 'Who are you looking for?'

Mary thought he must be the gardener. 'Oh sir!' she cried, 'If you've taken him away, tell me where you've laid him, and I'll go and fetch him.'

'Mary,' the figure said.

Now she recognized the voice. It was Jesus! 'Teacher!' she cried.

She took a step forward. 'You can't hold on to me, Mary,' said Jesus quietly. 'I am free now. But go to the rest of my friends and tell them what you have seen and heard. And tell them I will be with God soon.'

Then he was gone, and the angels with him. Mary went running off to tell the others. She burst in upon them and exclaimed, 'I have seen the Lord! I have *seen* him!'

Thomas Gets it Right… in the End
John

THAT VERY EVENING, when the friends were all together, wondering what might happen next, and still afraid that the Roman soldiers or temple guards might come looking for them, Jesus appeared among them.

'Peace be with you!' he said. 'I bring you the peace of God, God's well-being, life in all its fullness, life like a watered garden.'

Mary of Magdala understood, but the others couldn't believe their eyes or their ears. The last time most of them had seen Jesus, he was being dragged off by the temple guard from Gethsemane.

But then Jesus showed them the marks of crucifixion, and they knew for certain who it was.

They were overjoyed. They'd thought everything was lost. They'd thought that tyranny had won. They'd thought the Dark Forces had got him at last, and that death was holding him tight.

But death can't hold the life of God. They knew that now.

They could see and hear it was true.

'Peace be with you!' Jesus said again. 'Just as God, our Father, sent me, so I send you. You must continue the work I have begun.'

Then he breathed upon them and said, 'Receive the Holy Spirit, the Spirit of God. Go and take God's forgiveness into the world!'

Once upon a time, in the Garden of Eden, God had got down on his hands and knees and had breathed life into the first human child. So now, the risen Jesus, fresh from his victory over the Dark Forces of tyranny and death, breathed new life into his friends – life that would mean they could live life in all its fullness and bring life and blessing to others.

But there was one of Jesus' close friends who was missing: a man called Thomas. He had gone to Golgotha, wanting to see the place where Jesus had died.

When he came back, the others told him the news with great excitement. 'We have seen the Lord!' they cried.

'Jesus was crucified,' Thomas replied bitterly. 'He'll be marked for eternity by that cruel death. I won't believe what you say unless I see for myself its scars upon him.'

Thomas was right, of course. Jesus couldn't have returned to life as if nothing had happened. If he was risen from the dead, then he would take the marks of crucifixion into the heart of God, and heaven and earth would be changed by them.

Another week passed. Thomas was still sunk in grief. Every day he went to Golgotha. The pain of losing Jesus was unbearable, almost like the pain of crucifixion.

Then Jesus came to them once more, and this time Thomas was there.

'Peace be with you!' Jesus said. He looked at Thomas. 'See, Thomas,' he said to him, 'look at these marks upon me, the marks of nails and thorns, the marks of their brutality. Reach out and touch!'

But how can you touch the very life of God? Thomas didn't try. He simply answered, 'My Lord and my God!'

Peter Goes Fishing
John

JESUS' FRIENDS LEFT JERUSALEM and returned to Galilee. One day seven of them were sitting on the shore of Lake Galilee, looking out across the water. Peter was there, and Thomas, and James and John. They remembered the time when they'd been out in a boat and nearly drowned in a terrifying storm. A wave as big as a cliff had been about to smash them to pieces, but Jesus had woken up, made the wave disappear and turned the lake into a flat calm. They hadn't been able to work it out then. They understood now.

'Let's go fishing!' Peter said suddenly.

'What a good idea,' they said. 'Just like old times!'

In fact, the old times were gone. With Jesus risen from the dead, these were strange, new times. It was as if the world was brand-new – fresh from the hand of God.

They spent the whole night fishing. They caught nothing. As the sky above the eastern hills began to turn red, they started to head back for the shore. It was very strange. Just like the day, thought Peter, James and John, when Jesus had first called them to follow him.

As the boat approached the shore, they could see a figure standing there. He seemed to be waiting for them.

'Have you caught anything?' the figure shouted.

'Not a thing,' they called back.

'Throw the net over the right side of the boat and see what you get,' the strange figure said.

Peter, James and John looked at one another. Their memories of that earlier day's fishing became even clearer.

They cast the net over the right side of the boat, and immediately it got so full of fish, they could scarcely haul it in! The figure on the beach laughed.

'I know who that is!' one of the friends cried. 'I'd recognize that laugh anywhere. It's Jesus, our friend, our Lord.'

Peter couldn't wait to meet him. He jumped into the water and swam to the shore, while the others brought in the boat.

A charcoal fire was burning on the beach. 'Fish for breakfast, I think!' Jesus said, and laughed again. It was like the laughter of God.

Peter helped his friends bring the catch ashore. There was bread as well. Jesus took the bread and some of the fish and gave it to them.

They remembered the time when Jesus had fed all those poor, starving people by the lakeside. It was a meal of bread and fish then as well. The friends hadn't really understood at the time what it all meant. They understood now.

When the meal was over, Jesus turned to Peter.

'Peter,' said Jesus, 'do you love me more than anyone else?'

'Yes, Lord,' replied Peter, 'you know I love you.'

'Then look after my people for me,' said Jesus.

He said a second time, 'Peter, do you love me?'

'Yes, Lord. You know I love you.'

'Then take care of my people.'

A third time he said, 'Peter, do you love me?'

'Lord,' Peter said, 'you have the wisdom of God. You know all there is to know. You know I love you.'

'Feed my people,' Jesus said. 'Take away their hunger.' He paused. Then, very quietly, he said the same words he had said to Peter when he'd first met him: 'Come with me.'

Three times Peter had denied Jesus. Three times, by the house of the High Priest, he had said he didn't even know who Jesus was. He had let him down just when he needed him most. He hadn't been there to see him die or give him any comfort in those last, terrible hours. Peter had thought he would never forgive himself for that, nor be forgiven. He thought he would bear its shame for the rest of his life.

But now Jesus had forgiven him and shown him he could forgive himself too. Jesus had not accused him, blamed him, judged him nor condemned him. He had just asked him whether he loved him. Three times he'd given him the chance to say so. Those three denials were answered now. Peter had thought he would never be able to say to Jesus how much he really loved him. But now he had. One by one those denials of his had been swallowed up by love and by the forgiveness of God.

Now that he was forgiven, he could indeed go with Jesus. He could follow him to the ends of the world and continue the work he had begun.

11

FROM JERUSALEM TO ROME: THE CHURCH BEGINS

Luke didn't end his story with the resurrection of Jesus. After he'd finished his Gospel, he wrote a second volume, called Acts, or the Acts of the Apostles. Acts picks up the story where his Gospel leaves off and tells what happened to Jesus' followers, and how more and more people came to follow him, not just in Palestine, but in other parts of the Mediterranean world. Acts is therefore the story of the beginnings of the Christian church.

Luke tells that story mostly by speaking of what two particular followers of Jesus did, and what happened to them. The first of those is Peter, who had been one of Jesus' closest friends in Galilee. The second is Paul, a strict Jew, who had never met Jesus during his lifetime, and who, indeed, was a determined opponent of the church in its earliest days and put some of its members in prison. Luke tells how Paul became a follower of Jesus and helped the church to spread outside Palestine.

In concentrating so much on Peter and Paul, Luke has left many people's stories untold. He mentions Mary, Jesus' mother, once very near the beginning of Acts, but then tells us nothing more about her.

What became of her? Did she die soon afterwards? Or was she a great leader of the church in Jerusalem or in Galilee? We don't know. Mary of Magdala is also an important figure in the Gospels, including Luke's. She saw Jesus' crucifixion, and she was one of the first to meet him after he was risen from the dead. Was she also important in the early church? Quite possibly. But we don't know. There's nothing about her in Acts at all.

Nobody can tell the whole story, of course. It's not fair to criticize Luke for only telling part of it, but we must remember that a lot else happened which is not in Acts, and in particular, we must realize that women almost certainly played a much bigger part in the early life of the church than Luke lets on.

The Full Truth

When John the Baptist baptized Jesus, the Spirit of God came to him and gave him the power to defeat the dark forces of evil and establish God's love and forgiveness on the earth. After his resurrection from the dead, Jesus promised his followers that God's Spirit would come upon them also to give them the strength to carry on his work.

That day came soon, but first his friends had the most extraordinary experience.

JESUS' FRIENDS WERE GATHERED on the Mount of Olives overlooking Jerusalem. Jesus appeared among them, stretched his hands over them and spoke these ancient words of blessing:

'The Lord God bless you and keep you.
The Lord God make his face to shine upon you
and be gracious to you.
The Lord God lift up his face towards you
and give you peace.'

As he was speaking, a dense mist enveloped him. It was the same as
that strange mist which once had hidden the summit of Mount
Sinai when God met Moses and gave him the Ten Words. Much
more recently it had fallen on another mountain when Jesus was
transfigured before Peter, James and John, and they had seen him as
he really was. It had shone then with the light of the presence of
God, for it was God's covering, God's cloak, God's very mystery.
Now it shone even more brightly. It shone with the brightness of
heaven and sparkled with the love of God. It surrounded Jesus, and
he disappeared from their sight, as if he had become part of the
brightness and mystery of God.

At last the friends knew the full truth about Jesus.

Wind and Fire

FIFTY DAYS AFTER PASSOVER there was another Jewish
festival: Pentecost. Once again Jerusalem was full of Jewish pilgrims
from all over Palestine and from many countries beyond its borders.

Jesus' friends were all together in one room. Mary, Jesus' mother,
was among them. All of a sudden there came a sound like that of a
rushing wind, and flickering tongues of fire appeared and touched
each one of them. The sound was like the sound of the Spirit of God

blowing like a wind over the dark heap of water at the creation of the world, and the tongues of fire were like the flames that danced for Moses at the burning bush.

The friends were caught up, cradled and sent whirling by the Spirit of God. Now they would have the courage, the wisdom and the energy to carry on the work of Jesus.

Filled with enthusiasm they rushed out to meet the crowds of pilgrims thronging the city. The words came pouring out of them, almost as if they weren't speaking them themselves, almost as if angels had crept inside their heads. The Jews who heard them were amazed. They came from so many different places, with so many different languages. And yet they could all understand everything! It was as if each group of them heard the friends speaking in their own native language!

The people remembered the ancient story of the city of Babel, of how God made its proud builders speak different languages. Things in that story got so bad that fights broke out, and they had to stop building. They became scattered over the face of the earth, and the city fell into ruins. But this was Babel upside down and back to front! They'd come to Jerusalem with a host of different languages, but now they could understand everything. Instead of fights, perhaps there could now be peace, and unity and well-being in place of scattering and ruin.

Some people, however, thought the friends of Jesus were drunk. 'They've been drinking too much wine for the festival!' they said.

Peter spoke up for the friends. 'No we haven't,' he replied. 'After all, it's only nine o'clock in the morning. No, this is what some of our prophets were looking forward to. They said the days would come when God would pour out his Spirit on everyone, upon men and women, old and young, slaves and free. Then we would see visions and dream dreams, they said. Well, my people, those days have arrived! We have seen those visions! We are dreaming those dreams!

'It's all because of Jesus of Nazareth. Jesus set people free. He calmed the wild sea when it was driven to a frenzy by the Dark Forces. He sent a man's madness marching into the water. He filled the hungry, gave a blind man his sight and snatched a girl from death. And yet you turned against him, you and your leaders at the temple. You handed him over to the Romans, and they crucified him.

'You thought that was the end of him. It wasn't the end at all, but the beginning. God has set him free from death! He is part of the brightness and the mystery of God! Your leaders treated him like dirt, but I tell you he shines like the gold of heaven. The Romans treated him like a criminal, yet he showed us all what it really means to be a king.'

Peter's words cut through to the heart of the people.

'What can we do to make amends?' they asked.

'Bring your sorrow and your guilt to God,' Peter replied. 'And come to us to be baptized. Then you will find the forgiveness of God, as we have, and you also will receive God's Spirit.

'John the Baptist baptized people in the river Jordan. Jesus himself was baptized by John. That's when the Spirit of God flew to him like a bird. Well, you don't have to go down to the Jordan. We will baptize you here in Jerusalem, and the Spirit which flew to Jesus will fly to you!'

About three thousand Jews were baptized that day.

Stephen is Killed

The early followers of Jesus in Jerusalem didn't all speak the same language. Babel may have been turned upside down and back to front, but the Christians who'd been brought up in Palestine still spoke Aramaic, while those who'd come to Jerusalem from other countries spoke Greek. They all worshipped in the temple, but when it came to their special times of prayer and the meals they ate together, they met in separate houses.

Lots of very poor people joined the church in those days. Everybody pooled together what they had so that nobody suffered or went hungry. At least, that was the idea. Sometimes people would sell some of their possessions, or even houses and land, and put the money into the common fund, so the poor could be helped. One wealthy man called Barnabas, who was a Levite and helped run the worship in the temple, sold a field and presented the money to the twelve leaders of the church for them to buy food for those who needed it. The twelve were all men like Peter, James, John and Thomas, who'd been friends of Jesus since the Galilee days.

Unfortunately, the followers of Jesus who spoke Greek didn't get a fair share. They complained that when the daily food rations were handed out, their poor widows weren't given as much food as the widows who spoke Aramaic. They were very poor women, who didn't have anyone else to look after them. The matter was a serious one.

'All right,' said the twelve, 'it's true we're all Aramaic speakers. We were born and bred in Palestine. You Greek speakers need your own leaders, who can make sure that everything's fair between us.'

So they chose seven people. One of them was a young man called Stephen.

STEPHEN WAS A MARVELLOUS SPEAKER. Out in the streets he always drew a crowd and spoke about Jesus with great courage and conviction. However, he seriously upset some of the people in the city, especially when he got onto the subject of the temple. The people he upset most were Greek speakers like himself who'd deliberately settled in Jerusalem so they could be close to the temple. When he started saying how much Jesus had criticized the temple, and then declared that it should never have been built in the first place, they got extremely angry. They tried arguing against him, but that was no use. So they got as many people as they could on their side, arrested him and took him off to the Sanhedrin. The Sanhedrin was the highest Jewish court in the land. The same court had put Jesus on trial, convicted him of blasphemy and handed him on to Pilate to be crucified.

The members of the Sanhedrin looked at Stephen. His face shone like the face of an angel. Yet the charges against him were very serious. 'They tell us,' they said, 'that you are saying dreadful things about this most holy place of ours. Have you anything to say?'

'Yes I have,' replied Stephen eagerly. 'I've got a lot to say! I'm a Jew just as much as you are. But I think you'll agree our history is full of disappointments. God's been trying so hard with us ever since the beginning, but we've always been difficult and caused him much grief. Look how we turned our backs on him and Moses at Sinai! Together God and Moses had released our ancestors from slavery in Egypt, and there was Moses on the summit of Mount Sinai, gathering together all God's precious teaching to bring it down to our ancestors. Then what did they do? They turned to Moses' brother Aaron and said, "We're fed up with Moses and this God of his. Make us a proper god, one made with hands." So they made that golden calf. You all know the story.

'And things didn't get any better when our people started living in Palestine, did they? No, they still worshipped gods which had been made with hands, gods that weren't really gods at all, and were certainly nothing like our God, who made the whole of heaven and earth.

'And to make matters much worse, King Solomon built a temple here in Jerusalem. Out in the desert, when our ancestors were living there, God had a tent. It was just a tent, but that was good enough for God. He could pack it up and go where he liked. But Solomon wanted to keep him shut up in Jerusalem, so he built him a temple. That was made with hands as well, like the golden calf and all those other gods.

'So you see, we've always been making life difficult for God. When he sent prophets to put us on the right track, what did we do? We persecuted them, sometimes even killed them! And when, finally, he sent his own Son, Jesus, you got him killed as well! Is there no end to your opposition to God?'

That put the Sanhedrin and all those who'd arrested Stephen in an uproar.

'Look!' Stephen shouted, 'I can see into heaven! I can see God in all his fine glory, and Jesus standing at his right hand!'

The crowd and the members of the Sanhedrin put their hands over their ears. They couldn't bear to hear any more of this. They dragged Stephen out of the room and through the streets of the city until they reached a place outside the city walls. Then they started hurling stones at him. He was guilty of blasphemy, they said, and deserved to be stoned to death.

Stephen was brought to his knees by the stones. Kneeling on the ground he cried with all the strength he had left, 'Lord, forgive them!'

With those words he died.

Paul Meets the Risen Jesus

When Stephen was stoned to death, people took off their coats so they could aim the stones better and throw them harder. They laid them at the feet of a young Jew called Paul.

Paul was enraged by what Stephen had been saying. He was a Greek-speaking Jew as well, and just as attached to the temple as the others. He was glad to see Stephen killed. He hadn't realized how dangerous these followers of Jesus were before. But now he did. He became their most fanatical opponent. He started going from house to house, arresting them and throwing them into prison, men and women alike.

Paul wasn't the only one, however. Many of Jesus' followers had to escape to other parts of Judea, or to Samaria, or even beyond, to places like Damascus, a city in Syria. That's how the church first spread beyond Jerusalem. The twelve stayed behind in Jerusalem, but they had to go into hiding.

ONE DAY PAUL SET OUT for Damascus. He was planning to go around the synagogues of the Jews living there, search out any men or women who were followers of Jesus and bring them back to Jerusalem to face trial before the High Priest. He had official letters from the High Priest in his pocket, giving him the authority to make the arrests.

He was approaching the city, when a blinding light suddenly filled the sky. It wasn't lightning. It wasn't the sun. It was the light of God, and it brought Paul to his knees. Then he heard a voice coming straight from heaven.

'Paul, Paul,' said the voice, 'why are you persecuting me?'

'Who are you?' Paul asked.

'I am Jesus,' the voice said. 'I am the one you are persecuting. When you go in search of my friends, you go in search of me. When you arrest them, you arrest me. When you throw them into prison, you imprison me, and when you threaten them with trial in Jerusalem, you threaten me.

'But Paul, my friend, I have work for you to do. Get off your knees, carry on to Damascus, and I will send you someone to tell you what that work is.'

Paul got up from the ground. The light of God had blinded him, and he couldn't see a thing. There were others travelling with him. They'd heard the voice but had seen nothing, and they didn't know what to make of it. One of them took Paul by the hand and guided him to Damascus, to a house in Straight Street. For three days and nights he ate no food and drank nothing. He was fasting, waiting to be told what Jesus had in mind for him.

Paul and Ananias

ONE OF THE FOLLOWERS of Jesus in Damascus was a man called Ananias. Three days after Paul had reached the city, Jesus appeared to Ananias in a vision.

'Ananias,' Jesus called.

'Here I am,' he replied.

'There's something I want you to do,' said Jesus. 'I want you to go to Straight Street and see a man called Paul. I want you to lay your hands upon him and give him my blessing, so that he can see again. He's expecting you.'

'Surely not!' Ananias cried. 'I've heard all about that Paul, Lord! He's been going up and down the streets of Jerusalem, throwing your followers into prison, Lord, and now he's come all the way to Damascus to arrest all your friends here. He's got letters from the High Priest. You're asking me to go to him and say, "Hello Paul, how nice to see you. I'm a follower of Jesus, and I've come to be arrested, just to make your job a bit easier." You can't ask me to do that!'

'Of course I'm not asking you to do that, my friend,' Jesus answered. 'I met Paul on the way here. I've got some important work for him to do. I want him to travel far and wide for me and tell my story to the Gentiles, and to the Jews scattered over the empire who've never heard of me.'

Ananias was a brave man. He still wasn't sure what he would find when he got to Straight Street, but he went all the same.

Paul was sitting in the corner of the room, looking at the floor, unable to see anything. He was already feeling weak from lack of food and drink. Ananias approached him cautiously. At least Paul didn't look in a fit state to arrest him, or anyone else, for that matter.

Ananias coughed gently. 'Paul,' he said, 'the Lord Jesus who met you on your way to Damascus has sent me here. He's asked me to lay my hands on you so that you may see again and be filled with the Spirit of God.'

Paul turned his head in the direction where the voice had come from. He saw nothing, not even a vague shape. But then he felt Ananias's hands upon his head, and suddenly he could see clearly once more. He could see *everything* now. He could see how wrong he'd been to persecute Jesus and his followers. He could see that Jesus was the very Son of God.

He got up and threw his arms round Ananias's neck and embraced him. Ananias thought he was going to squeeze the life out of him, he hugged him so hard!

'Now you're a follower of Jesus, I must baptize you,' Ananias said.

So Paul was baptized, and after that he took some food and drink. It was the best meal he'd ever had.

Escape in a Basket

AFTER ANANIAS HAD BAPTIZED HIM in Damascus, Paul said to him, 'Take me to the synagogues. I've got something to tell them.'

'I must introduce you to the other followers of Jesus first,' said Ananias. 'I think they're in for a bit of a surprise.'

They weren't the only ones. When Ananias introduced him to the other Jews in the synagogues, they could hardly believe it. They'd heard all about Paul and what he'd been doing in Jerusalem and why he'd come to Damascus. And here he was telling them that Jesus was the Son of God. It was unbelievable!

Some of them believed it, though.

And some got very angry. 'He's supposed to be arresting those followers of Jesus,' they said to each other, 'not joining them! He's the worst of the lot! You can't stop him talking! If we don't do something, he'll cause real trouble.'

So they hatched a plot to kill him. Fortunately, Paul got to hear of it. By then he had many supporters and friends in the city, not just Ananias, but clearly it had become too dangerous for him to stay. The trouble was, his enemies were watching the gates of the city day and night. How would he get out?

'In a basket,' said one of his friends.

'Pardon?' said Paul.

'In a basket,' she repeated. 'Tonight, after it's dark, we'll put you in a basket and lower you down over the walls.'

'You must be joking!' Paul cried.

But they weren't. And that's how Paul escaped from Damascus.

When eventually he arrived back in Jerusalem, he wanted to join the twelve, but they were very frightened of him. They didn't believe what some people were saying. Surely, he was the last person on earth who would become a follower of Jesus. No, it must be a trick, they thought. He would arrest them and hand them over to the temple authorities.

But Barnabas, the Levite who'd sold the field, met Paul, heard his story and introduced him to the twelve. Barnabas told them how Jesus had stopped Paul in his tracks on the way to Damascus, and how he'd been preaching in the synagogues there.

So Paul joined their company and began preaching openly about Jesus on the streets of the city. But the Greek speakers who'd stoned Stephen to death started plotting to kill him too. So his friends took him down to a port on the Mediterranean coast, called Caesarea, and put him on a boat for Tarsus, a city in a region called Cilicia, on the mainland north of Cyprus. Tarsus was where Paul had been brought up.

Peter and a Soldier Called Cornelius

PETER ALSO TRAVELLED DOWN to the Mediterranean coast, and eventually found himself in the Jewish town of Joppa. Thirty-five miles north of Joppa was Caesarea. In Caesarea there lived a centurion called Cornelius. He was from Italy, but he'd retired from the army and settled in the town. He and his family got to know many of the Jews there. They became very fond of them and were attracted by their religion and its worship. They joined them for prayer, or to listen to their Scriptures. They kept their festivals and believed in their God. They didn't quite become Jews, nor did they observe all the Jewish laws and customs. But they were very generous and gave a lot of money to the leaders of the synagogue for them to hand on to the poor.

One day at three o'clock in the afternoon, one of the Jewish times of prayer, Cornelius was in his house praying. He had a most extraordinary vision. He saw an angel, clear as could be. His room had become a patch of heaven!

The angel called his name, 'Cornelius.'

He stared at the angel, quite overcome. 'What is it, Lord?' he asked.

'God knows you very well, my friend,' said the angel. 'He hears your prayer and knows all about your generosity. Now, there's something he wants you to do. Down in Joppa there's a man called Peter. He's staying with someone called Simon – a tanner, who lives by the sea. Send some people to fetch him here.'

That was all. No explanation. Nothing about this Peter, except where he was staying. Cornelius had never heard of him. What did it all mean? Well, there was only one way to find out. He sent two of his slaves, and a soldier friend of his who also worshipped the Jewish God, down to Joppa.

At noon the next day, when Cornelius's little party had nearly reached Joppa, Peter went up the steps onto the flat roof of Simon's house. He turned in the direction of Jerusalem and began to pray. The sun was hot, and he started to feel sleepy. The next thing he knew he was asleep. Then a strange feeling of hunger came over him, and he dreamed he saw a sheet being lowered down from heaven with all sorts of animals and birds and reptiles inside it. There were pigs snuffling about on it and camels, hares, geckos, crocodiles, lizards, eagles, buzzards, kites, ravens, owls and vultures – all the things which Jews were strictly forbidden to eat.

Peter was disgusted by the sight, but in the middle of the strange dream he heard a voice. 'Up, Peter!' the voice said. 'Kill and eat!'

'Certainly not!' Peter cried. 'How can I? I'm a Jew! God has forbidden us to eat any of these creatures. They're unclean. If we eat

them, we aren't Jews any more. You can't stop me being a Jew!'

The voice came again, 'What God has made clean, you must not call unclean.'

Three times all this happened. Then the sheet disappeared, and Peter woke up with a start.

What did it mean? Peter was dumbfounded. It went against everything he'd been taught, right from the time when he was small. The Jews were a holy people. They could have plenty to do with Gentiles. They could do business with them or welcome them to their synagogues. But they still had to keep themselves separate, particularly at mealtimes. They were forbidden to eat some of the things Gentiles ate. There were stories about times in the past when Jews were being persecuted and forced to abandon their religion. Some of them refused to eat Gentile food and were put to death as a result. Peter knew those stories well. His mother had told them to him when he was a boy. They were heroes and heroines of his, those people who'd refused to eat the unclean food.

He heard voices down in the street. Three men were standing at the gate to the house.

'Is this the house where Simon, the tanner, lives?' they were asking. 'And is there someone here called Peter?'

Peter was wide awake now, but he heard another voice inside him. 'Go with those men, Peter,' the voice said. 'I have sent them myself. You've nothing to worry about.'

Peter knew that voice. It was the voice of the Spirit of God.

So he went down from the roof and approached the three men. 'I'm Peter,' he said. 'I'm the one you're looking for. What do you want?'

'We're from someone called Cornelius,' they replied. 'He's a centurion up in Caesarea. He's a good man and worships in the synagogue there. All the Jews love him. He had a vision of an angel, and the angel said we were to fetch you to come with us to Caesarea so we could all hear what you have to say.'

It still didn't make sense, but something was going on, that was certain. The vision of the sheet, and now Cornelius's vision of an angel. God was definitely up to something!

'You'd better come in,' Peter said to the men. 'Stay the night here, and tomorrow I'll come with you.'

The next day Peter and some other followers of Jesus from Joppa set out to travel with the three men up the coast to Caesarea. Eventually they came to Cornelius's house.

Cornelius was expecting them. He'd called together some of his relatives and close friends. When Peter arrived at the gate of the house, Cornelius ran to meet him and fell at his feet.

'No, please,' said Peter. 'Get off your knees, my friend. I'm a human being, like you.'

Cornelius led Peter inside his house, and Peter was surprised to find quite a crowd of people there. They were all Gentiles, like Cornelius himself.

Peter looked at them all, and suddenly he realized what his vision of the sheet meant. 'What God has made clean, you must not call unclean.' That's what the mysterious voice had said. The same words had been repeated three times. 'What God has made clean, you must not call unclean.' The voice wasn't really talking about animals and birds but about people – people like all the men and women and children gathered in that house in Caesarea, in that room, waiting for him to speak. The time for the Jews to keep themselves separate from Gentiles was over. The time for him, Peter, the Jew, to keep himself apart was over as well.

'You know,' he said, 'how we Jews keep ourselves separate from you Gentiles. For centuries we've thought it was necessary to do that in order to be the people of God. I've believed that since I was a boy. But I was wrong. God has shown me that. Now what is it you want me to say to you?'

Cornelius repeated the story of his vision of the angel, which Peter had already heard in Joppa. 'You've been kind enough to come all this way,' Cornelius concluded, 'and we're all here to listen to what God tells you to say.'

'God told our ancestor Abraham to be a blessing to all the people he met,' Peter began. 'He said that all the families of the earth would find God's blessing through him. I understand what that means now. It means... it means the Jewish people must be wide open to everyone who is a friend of God and keeps him company and works with him to bring his blessings to the world. That means people like you, all of you in this room. Yes, I've some fine things to tell you! If you're going to belong to the people of God, you must hear all about Jesus of Nazareth.'

So Peter told them everything he had to tell: all about Jesus being baptized by John; the days in Galilee; Photina; the madman among the tombs; Miriam and Rachel; Jonathan and all the rest; then about how the Romans and the temple authorities wanted to get rid of him and how he'd been crucified. 'But death couldn't hold him,' Peter said, 'God set him free! We saw him. We ate breakfast with him on the shore of Lake Galilee. It sounds extraordinary, and it is. But it's true! And here I am, in your house, telling you all about it. That's extraordinary too.'

Just as Peter was finishing, Cornelius and his whole family and friends were overwhelmed by the Spirit of God. It was just like that Pentecost in Jerusalem all over again, when first the Spirit had come upon Jesus' friends.

423

'Well,' Peter said to his friends from Joppa, 'what are you waiting for? You'd better baptize them in the name of Jesus Christ.'

After that Peter stayed several days with Cornelius and his family. The church would never be the same again.

Paul and Barnabas Get Mistaken for Gods

In this story Luke tells how Paul and his companion
Barnabas heal a man who has never walked before.
Luke doesn't give that man's name, but we have called
him Philon.

BARNABAS WAS THE FOLLOWER of Jesus who'd first introduced Paul to the twelve in Jerusalem. Some time after Paul had been sent to Tarsus, the church in Jerusalem asked Barnabas to go to Antioch, a large city in Syria. From there he travelled to Tarsus to look for Paul, and when he found him he took him back to Antioch. They stayed there together for a whole year, teaching a great many people about Jesus. It was in Antioch that the followers of Jesus first became known as Christians.

One day the Christians in Antioch were worshipping together when the Spirit of God said to them, 'I have work for Paul and Barnabas to do beyond Antioch. You must send them on their way.'

So Paul and Barnabas travelled together to many places, taking the story of Jesus with them wherever they went. They often used roads which the Romans had built, and one day they came to a place on one of those roads, called Lystra. It was a small remote town, several hundreds of miles from Antioch. There had been a village on the site for over two thousand years, but it was never famous. The people still had their own language, or dialect, and they worshipped the old Greek gods, like Zeus. There was a small temple to Zeus just outside the town.

Paul was preaching about Jesus as usual, trying to make himself understood in simple Greek. He wasn't finding it very easy.

Then he noticed a man listening to him. He was sitting on the ground at the side of the crowd. His name was Philon. Everyone in Lystra knew old Philon. He'd been disabled since he was born and had never walked in his life. So he'd never had a job, but used to sit there all day, begging. It was hard work just keeping himself alive. He wasn't actually very old at all, but he looked it.

Philon had never heard anyone like Paul before. There was something about Paul, and Barnabas too, that fired a strange hope deep inside him. He'd never imagined he would ever be able to walk, but now he began to wonder whether these two Jewish visitors could get him up on his useless feet and make his legs move.

Paul noticed the look in Philon's eyes. He stopped talking and looked across at him. 'Friend,' he called, 'stand up! Stand up on your feet!'

The crowd laughed. 'Old Philon's never stood up in his life,' they said. 'You're a poor old cripple, aren't you, Philon…? Hey, Philon, what are you doing? You'll fall over! Hey, Philon, you can walk. You can walk!'

Philon *was* walking.

The people of the town had never seen anything like it. Nothing ever happened in Lystra. People got born, they got married, they had children, they worked till they dropped, they died. That was about it. But this was something amazing, something mysterious, something utterly wonderful. This was straight out of heaven. Philon thought so too.

'The gods have come down to earth in human form!' someone shouted.

'Yes,' said another, looking at Barnabas, 'that one must be Zeus!'

'And this one,' said a third, pointing at Paul, 'must be Hermes, the messenger of the gods, because he does all the talking.'

Two young boys ran off to the temple of Zeus. 'You'd better come quickly!' one said to the old priest. 'Zeus is here! He's in the town now! You know old Philon? He can walk!'

'And Hermes is with him!' cried the other. 'They're both here, in our town, in Lystra! Come on!'

The priest was very excited. 'We must make some garlands for them,' he said, 'and sacrifice some oxen. This is a great day, the greatest day in the history of this temple!'

It wasn't long before a little procession approached the town gates. At the front walked the priest of the temple in all his robes, and then came his assistants and the two boys. The priest was carrying garlands, while his assistants were leading two oxen.

'What are you doing?' cried Paul and Barnabas. 'We're human beings, just like you. We're not gods. We worship the God who made the heaven and the earth and the sea, the birds, the animals and plants, and all the fish. We worship the God who gives you the rain. It is his energy that bursts the seeds you sow and makes them grow. He fills your stomachs with food and your hearts with joy. He sets you dancing in the streets, even if you haven't walked all your life and have had to sit against the wall, begging. This is the God we bring you!'

They only just managed to stop the people sacrificing the oxen to them.

But then some other people arrived in the town who were bitter enemies of theirs. Paul had once set off from Jerusalem to Damascus in order to arrest the members of the church there. These people were as angry about the followers of Jesus as he'd been then, as fanatical as he'd been before he met Jesus on the Damascus road. They were prepared to go a long way to stop Paul and Barnabas.

They accused them, and especially Paul, of all sorts of things and managed to win over the people. They told them Paul was guilty of blasphemy, and that he was attacking their most precious beliefs. So one moment the people were worshipping Paul and Barnabas as gods, the next they were hurling stones at Paul to kill him.

When they thought he was dead, they dragged him outside the town and left him for the wild animals and the vultures. They seemed to have forgotten all about Philon.

But Paul was not dead, and not everyone in Lystra forgot Philon. Barnabas and Paul moved on, but soon they came back for a time, and a small community of Christians grew up there. Philon was one of the leaders, of course.

A Riot in Ephesus

Paul spent three years based in a city on the Mediterranean coast, called Ephesus. Ephesus was not like Lystra. Lystra was a small, out-of-the-way place, and most people had never heard of it. But Ephesus was one of the most famous cities in the Roman empire. Most famous of all was its temple dedicated to the Greek goddess Artemis. It was one of the seven wonders of the world. Pilgrims came to it from many countries. The Ephesians regarded Artemis as the guardian of the city, the one who kept them safe and ensured their well-being.

She was good for business as well. The pilgrims who came to the city always wanted to take something home with them when they left. Some silversmiths in the city made little silver shrines for people to buy. The shrines would remind them of their pilgrimage and also help them to pray to Artemis when they got home. The shrines were very popular, and a lot of people in Ephesus were kept in work making them. It was a good trade all round. Until Paul came along.

PAUL STARTED TELLING the story of Jesus in a synagogue in the city of Ephesus. For three months he was there. Some of the Jews in the synagogue became Christians, some didn't. In the end, the ones who'd become Christians agreed to form a new synagogue, a Christian synagogue, and that is what they did.

But Paul wanted to reach the Gentiles too, the people who weren't Jews and didn't go to the synagogues. Among his followers in the city were some wealthy men and women, and they put up the money for him to hire the lecture hall of Tyrannus and speak there every day. He made a great impact upon the people who came to hear him, and a great many of them began to turn their backs on Artemis and the other Greek gods.

The silversmiths didn't like that. Trade was beginning to suffer. They weren't selling as many of their shrines as usual. If they didn't do something fast, some of them would be put out of business, and a good many men would find themselves unemployed.

A man named Demetrius had one of the biggest shrine businesses in the city. He called all the other silversmiths and their workers together for a meeting.

'This Jew called Paul,' he said to them, 'keeps telling people that gods made with hands are not proper gods at all. A lot of people are beginning to believe him.'

'I'll say,' said another. 'More than beginning. Some people hang on his every word.'

'My trade's half what it was,' said a third man. 'I've had to lay off half my men already. Skilled workers they were. How are they going to support their families now?'

'It's not just our trade,' said Demetrius. 'It's our great temple as well. One of the wonders of the world, it is. If this Paul goes on like this, it'll become nothing but a ruin! It costs a lot of money to keep it going, and if the pilgrims stop coming, it will mean the end of it. It's as simple as that. And what about Artemis herself? She's a great goddess, *our* goddess, and Paul's treating her like dirt!'

A large crowd had gathered while Demetrius was speaking. His words whipped them up into a fury. 'Great is Artemis of the Ephesians!' they shouted. 'Great is Artemis of the Ephesians!' People came from all sides to see what the noise was about, and soon the whole city was in an uproar.

'Let's go to the theatre,' Demetrius shouted, 'and have this out, once and for all!'

So everyone started rushing off towards the theatre. It was in the open air, shaped like half of a huge bowl. The seats were stone benches running right round the semicircle. It could hold twenty-four thousand people. Soon it was full.

Some people dragged two of Paul's Christian companions there, Gaius and Aristarchus, and Paul wanted to go himself to rescue them and speak to the crowd. But his friends told him it wouldn't be safe.

'But they've got Gaius and Aristarchus!' he cried. 'They might kill them!'

'They'll kill you if you go there,' his friends said, 'and what good will that do Gaius and Aristarchus?'

Just then two men came running up to Paul. 'We've come from the Asiarchs,' they said, 'the ones who are friends of yours. They said to tell you to stay away from the theatre. It's far too dangerous.'

The Asiarchs were some of the most respected people not just in Ephesus, but in the whole region. 'You can't ignore their advice, even if you ignore ours,' his friends said to Paul.

They still had difficulty persuading him, but in the end they succeeded. Paul didn't go to the theatre.

Inside it there was pandemonium. Some were shouting one thing, some another. Most of the people didn't know why they were there or what was going on. They'd been caught in the swirl of the crowd as it was rushing along, and by the general excitement.

Things were getting ugly and could turn violent any moment. The crowd included a number of Jews. Although they weren't members of the church, they wanted to defend Paul, and Gaius and Aristarchus too. They didn't want violence, and they agreed with a lot of what Paul and the others had been saying anyway.

They pushed a Jew called Alexander to the front. He was a powerful speaker. Perhaps he could make people see sense. He motioned for silence and began to speak. But when he explained that Paul was preaching the same God as the Jews, and people realized he was a Jew himself, they shouted him down.

'Great is Artemis of the Ephesians!' they shouted. 'Great is Artemis of the Ephesians!' They were all shouting the same thing now. It sounded like a war cry. They kept it up for two whole hours. It was a terrifying sound.

Eventually the town clerk managed to quieten them down. 'Citizens of Ephesus!' he cried. 'What are you so worried about? Our temple to Artemis is world-famous, and the statue of the goddess inside it too. That statue, as you know, is not made with hands, because it fell straight from heaven. That's what we all believe. What have we got to worry about, then? These Jews, Gaius and Aristarchus, Alexander and Paul, haven't robbed the temple. They haven't spoken any blasphemy against Artemis. If Demetrius and his companions have a complaint to make, they should do things properly and take it to the courts. Ours is a great city, and you people are threatening to bring shame upon its head by your behaviour. We'll be lucky if we're not charged with rioting by the Roman authorities. Go home now, and go quietly. We all know how great Artemis of the Ephesians is. You don't have to go on shouting it.'

Fortunately, that worked. The crowd broke up. People left the theatre and went back to their homes or their work, and Gaius and Aristarchus, and Alexander too, were all safe.

But it was time for Paul to leave. There was no more he could do in the city, not while feelings ran so high. He bade farewell to the members of the Ephesian church and sailed for Macedonia.

A Riot in Jerusalem

CHRISTIAN COMMUNITIES BEGAN to spring up all round the eastern part of the Mediterranean, thanks to the work of Paul and his companions. Paul did more than anyone else to spread the story of Jesus outside Palestine and to bring Gentiles into the church.

After much travel round the churches he'd founded, Paul returned to Jerusalem. He knew he would be in danger there, but he was determined to go all the same. 'If necessary,' he said, 'I'm prepared to die. Whatever happens, I must be loyal to Jesus to the end.'

He was right: it was dangerous. For a start, some members of the Jerusalem church were still very suspicious of him. Many of the Jewish Christians there still thought it was important for all Gentile converts to behave like strict Jews and obey Jewish food laws. They'd heard that Paul didn't make them keep to those rules. They couldn't understand him and thought he was doing great harm. They suspected he'd stopped being a Jew.

As it turned out, they weren't the ones who brought things to a head, but some non-Christian Jews from Ephesus. Most of the Jews in Ephesus had been friendly towards Paul, including the ones who hadn't joined the church or the Christian synagogue there. But a few of them thought he was a dangerous troublemaker. He'd caused a riot in their city, they said, and if he wasn't careful, he'd force the Roman authorities to intervene, and then all the Jews would suffer along with the Christians.

Some of these Jews were visiting Jerusalem on a pilgrimage. They were on their way into the temple one day when one of them said, 'Hey, look! There's that Paul over there! And he's got

Trophimus with him!' Trophimus was a Gentile from Ephesus.

'He must have taken him into the temple,' said another.

'Yes,' said a third, 'into the court reserved for Jewish men, no doubt. He wouldn't have left him on his own, would he? No, he would have taken him into the court with him. That means he has defiled the holy place. This is extremely serious.'

Paul and Trophimus had disappeared, but the next day the same men saw Paul in the temple again, in the inner court. They seized hold of him and shouted to their fellow Jews, 'This man's been bringing Gentiles right into our court! He's made this holy place unclean!'

That did it. There was an immediate riot. Paul was dragged out of the temple, and they would have killed him on the spot if the Roman soldiers hadn't intervened.

The tribune, the senior Roman officer in charge, took Paul, bound him in chains and tried to find out what was going on. But the mob kept shouting, 'String him up! Get rid of him!' The soldiers had to carry Paul up the steps to the barracks to get him away from them.

'We had an Egyptian here recently who was serious trouble,' said the tribune. 'We dealt with his followers, but he escaped. You're not him, are you? Because if you are, you should start saying your prayers now.'

'No,' said Paul. 'I'm a Jew from Tarsus. I'm not here to make trouble. Will you let me speak to the crowd?'

'You'll have a job,' the tribune replied. 'But you can have a go if you want.'

Paul managed eventually to quieten the crowd down and addressed them from the top of the steps, outside the door to the barracks.

They listened to him for a bit, but then their anger exploded once more. The Roman officer took him inside the barracks and shut the doors.

'Right,' he said to one of his centurions, 'take this troublemaker and flog the truth out of him. I want to get to the bottom of this.'

The soldiers led him away to another room in the barracks, where the instruments of torture were kept. They tied Paul to a bench and were just about to start hitting him with a whip when he said to the centurion, 'Is it legal for you to flog a Roman citizen who hasn't been tried, or found guilty of any crime?'

When he heard that, the centurion ran off to the tribune. He burst in and cried, 'The man's a Roman citizen!'

The tribune came at once. 'Are you sure?' he asked Paul.

'Of course I am.'

'I'm a citizen too,' said the tribune. 'I had to pay a lot of money to get my citizenship.'

'I was born a citizen,' Paul replied.

'I do apologize, sir,' the tribune said. 'We'll have to sort this out another way. Centurion! Untie him, please.'

The Threat of an Ambush

THE TRIBUNE DIDN'T UNDERSTAND what charges were being brought against Paul. So the next day he ordered the Sanhedrin to meet, took Paul down and stood him in front of them. The Sanhedrin was the Jewish court which had tried Jesus before he was crucified, and which had been so enraged by Stephen.

Some of the members of the Sanhedrin thought Paul had done

nothing wrong, but an argument broke out, and that soon became violent. The tribune was afraid Paul would get torn to pieces, so the soldiers took him back to the barracks. They'd got nowhere.

Then things got worse still. The next morning over forty Jews went to the High Priest with a plan. They were fanatical enemies of Paul and believed he was threatening the very future of Judaism.

'We've taken an oath,' they said to the High Priest. 'We won't eat or drink anything until we've killed Paul. Ask the tribune to bring him down to your house. Tell him you want to make a proper investigation of his case. The tribune will agree to that. He wants to get things sorted out as soon as possible. He'll be grateful for your offer. Then we'll ambush him on the way and kill him.'

Now a young nephew of Paul was living in Jerusalem. He got to hear about the ambush, managed to get inside the barracks and told his uncle all about it. Paul called one of the centurions. 'Take this young man to the tribune,' he said. 'He's got something to tell him.'

The centurion took him to the tribune's room. 'A young man to see you, sir,' he said. 'The prisoner Paul asked me to bring him to you. He's got something to tell you, sir.'

'What is it?' the tribune asked.

'There's a plot to ambush and kill my uncle, sir,' Paul's nephew explained. 'The High Priest will ask you to bring him down to his house tomorrow. Don't take any notice of him, sir. There'll be over forty men lying in wait for him. They've taken an oath not to eat or drink until they've killed him.'

'Well done, lad,' the tribune said to him. 'Now don't tell anyone you've been here or spoken to me. Do you understand?'

'Yes sir,' he replied.

After Paul's nephew had left, the tribune turned to two of his centurions. 'We'll have to get this Paul out of Jerusalem and quickly,' he said. 'Get some troops together. I want you to take Paul down to Caesarea tonight, to the governor. I'll write him a letter to take with you, explaining what's been going on.'

Paul Asks to See the Emperor

WHEN PAUL REACHED CAESAREA, Felix, the Roman governor, read the tribune's letter and promised to hear his case as soon as his accusers arrived. 'Go back to Jerusalem,' he said to the centurions, 'and inform the High Priest that I've got Paul here. Ask him to come down and tell us what all this is about.'

So the High Priest arrived in Caesarea, with some of the elders from the temple, and a man called Tertullus, who put the case against Paul.

'Your Excellency,' said Tertullus. 'This man's been causing trouble among Jews all over the world. He's the ringleader of a dangerous sect. We caught him trying to defile the holy temple, so we arrested him, your Excellency.'

'I was not trying to do anything of the sort,' said Paul. 'I'm a good Jew, sir, a devout Jew. I'm not a troublemaker. It's all about Jesus and his resurrection. That's what the argument is really about.'

Felix realized Paul wasn't guilty. But he kept him in prison all the same, to keep the High Priest and his supporters happy. He also hoped Paul or his friends would give him a handsome bribe. But no bribe came, so he kept him in custody in Caesarea. Paul was there for two years, till Felix was recalled to Rome and a new governor arrived, and he had to be tried all over again.

The new governor's name was Festus. When eventually he had Paul and his accusers up before him, Festus found it difficult to follow all the arguments. He thought it would be much better if Paul could be tried before him in Jerusalem. He could get better advice there, and there would be a good chance the whole thing could be settled quickly. He turned to Paul and said, 'Would you be willing to go to Jerusalem and be tried before me there?'

'I'm not trying to escape death,' Paul replied. 'If I'm guilty of a serious crime, I'm willing to pay the penalty for it. But I won't get a fair trial in Jerusalem. I appeal to the emperor.'

'In that case, to the emperor you will go,' Festus answered.

Some days later the Jewish king Agrippa and his sister Bernice arrived in Caesarea to welcome Festus to Palestine. Festus told Agrippa about Paul, and Agrippa asked if he could see him and hear what he had to say.

So Paul told Agrippa his whole story. 'So you see, Your Majesty,' he concluded, 'in taking the story of Jesus to the Gentiles, I'm only being true to my faith as a Jew. God told Abraham to be a blessing to all he met. And one of the prophets said that we Jews should be "a light to the nations". That's all I'm doing. Trying to take God's blessing and forgiveness and light to as many people as I can.'

After Paul had finished, Agrippa left the room with Festus. Festus said to him, 'The man's done nothing wrong, has he?'

'Certainly not,' Agrippa agreed. 'If he hadn't appealed to the emperor, we could have set him free. As it is, we will have to send him on to Rome.'

Shipwreck

PAUL AND SOME OTHER PRISONERS, guarded by a Roman centurion and his soldiers, set sail for Italy. The wind was against them, and they made very slow progress. It was getting late in the year, a risky time to be out in a boat in the middle of the Mediterranean.

They'd reached a place called Fair Havens on the southern coast of the island of Crete. When they left Crete, they would be out in the open sea.

Paul said to the centurion and the soldiers, 'Sirs, it's too dangerous to go on. I've travelled a great deal, and I know what storms can spring up at this time of year. If we leave this port, we'll lose the ship and its cargo, and many of us will drown.'

The centurion listened to what Paul said, but he wanted to hear what the captain and the owner of the ship thought, and he wanted to get the opinions of the crewmen and other experienced travellers.

'The trouble is,' said the captain, 'Fair Havens is not a suitable place to spend the winter, till we can sail again in the spring. Sometimes the winter storms blow right into the harbour here, and the boat could get wrecked. I think we should sail west along the coast to Phoenix. There's a much safer harbour there.'

'What do the rest of you think?' asked the centurion.

'We agree with the captain,' they said.

So they waited for a moderate south wind, which would blow them in the right direction, and set sail. But they hadn't left Fair Havens far behind, when the wind turned and became very violent. There was nothing they could do. They had to run with the storm.

They managed to hoist up the lifeboat and get ropes underneath the hull of the ship to stop it breaking apart. They lowered the sea anchor to prevent themselves being driven onto rocks. Yet still the storm blew, the wind as strong as ever. It blew all night, and the next day they began to throw the ship's cargo overboard. The day after that they threw the ship's tackle into the sea to make it lighter still. But it was no use. They were helpless in the face of the storm and drifted on day after day, night after night, taken wherever the wind and waves wanted to take them. There was no sight of land now, and everyone except Paul gave up any hope of reaching safety. But one night Paul had a vision.

He stood up in the middle of them all, braced himself against the pitching and rolling of the boat and shouted above the roar of the wind and waves, 'My friends, you should have listened to my advice back in Fair Havens. But do not despair. An angel of God appeared to me in a vision last night. "Do not be afraid, Paul," the angel said to me. "You will reach Rome and put your case to the emperor, just as you wish to do. And God will save everyone on this ship. The ship itself will be lost, but no one will drown." So take courage, all of you. God will see us through. He's brought me out of many a

tight spot in the past, and I know he will do so again. We will have to run aground on some island.'

It was the middle of the fourteenth night since they had left Fair Havens, and the sailors suspected they were approaching land. They thought they could just hear waves breaking on a shore, and the sea under the boat sounded different somehow. The water was getting shallower. They let down four anchors from the stern, to stop the boat going onto the rocks and prayed for the daylight to come.

It was still pitch dark, but they could hear they were getting nearer and nearer the shore. They were afraid the boat would get smashed to pieces on the rocks, and they started lowering the lifeboat.

Paul saw what they were doing and went straight to the centurion. 'The sailors are going to abandon ship,' he said. 'If they go, there's no hope for the rest of us.'

The centurion turned to some of his soldiers. 'Quick!' he said. 'Stop the sailors getting away! Cut the ropes of the lifeboat and set it adrift.'

They hadn't eaten anything for days. There hadn't been any time for meals, they'd been too busy trying to save the ship from being turned over by the storm. They were weak and exhausted.

Just before dawn Paul said to them all. 'You all need to eat something to get your strength up. You'll need it to survive. Don't worry, none of you will lose even a hair from your heads.' He paused. 'Well,' he continued, 'I'm going to have some bread anyway.'

He took a loaf, gave thanks to God, broke a piece off and started to eat. The others watched him and then began to eat too.

After the meal, they threw the rest of the cargo into the sea. If they were to run aground, they needed the ship to be as light as possible.

Morning came. They didn't recognize the island, but they spotted a beach beneath some cliffs.

'Let's make for the beach,' the centurion said.

They cast off the anchors, put up the sail and turned the ship towards the land. But they didn't see the sandbar just underneath the water. The ship drove into it and stuck fast. The waves crashed into the ship's stern and started smashing it to pieces.

'We'll have to kill the prisoners, sir,' the soldiers shouted to the centurion. 'We can't let them jump overboard and escape.'

'Don't you dare kill any of them,' the centurion replied. 'I want that man Paul to be kept safe.' Raising his voice above the crash of the waves and the cracking of the timbers of the ship, he yelled, 'Abandon ship, everyone! If you can swim, then swim for your lives! If you can't, then hold onto something and get to the shore that way.'

So they jumped into the sea and swam for the shore, or held onto planks that had broken away from the ship. Miraculously, none of them were drowned. There were two hundred and seventy-six people on board, and they all reached land safely, as Paul and the angel had said they would.

Paul Reaches Rome

THE ISLAND THEY HAD REACHED was Malta. They had to stay there for the winter, but three months later, when the weather had improved and it was safe to sail again, they took another boat, first to Sicily and then up the coast of Italy to a port called Puteoli. There were already a number of Christians there, and they greeted

Paul as soon as he arrived. The centurion allowed him to stay with them for seven days.

When the seven days were up, Paul set off, still under guard, on the last stage of his journey. It would take them five days to reach Rome.

The Christians in the city heard he was coming, and when he was still over forty miles away, some of them arrived to welcome him. Ten miles further on yet more of them came. So Paul entered Rome a prisoner, but surrounded by friends.

Inside the city he was allowed to live in his own lodgings, with just one soldier guarding him. He was free to speak to anyone who came to see him.

There were a great many Jews in Rome. None of the accusations against Paul had reached their ears, and when he told them all about the riot in the temple, and what happened after that, they readily accepted his account. 'But we do want to hear more about Jesus,' they said. 'We know he has some followers in many places, including this city, and we know many Jews elsewhere are deeply upset by them. Tell us more. We want to know what the truth is.'

So Paul talked to a great many of them for hours and hours. Some were convinced by what he said; some weren't. Some became Christians; others didn't.

He was in Rome under guard in his lodgings for two whole years. Whenever people came to him, whether they were Jews or Gentiles, he gave them a warm welcome and would willingly tell them all about Jesus, the whole story from beginning to end. Nobody tried to stop him.

And so Christianity had reached Rome. It had all begun in Bethlehem and in Nazareth, the tiny Jewish village hidden away in the hills of Galilee. The Romans had tried to stamp it out. They had put Jesus to death on a cross. Yet God had set him free, and now here was Paul, one of the greatest of Jesus' followers, preaching about him in the capital city of the Roman empire!

The church had come a long way in a very short time. In the years and centuries ahead it would spread throughout the entire world.

12

LETTERS TO CHURCHES AND
A FINAL VISION

We don't just know about Paul from Luke and the stories he tells in the Acts of the Apostles. We also know about Paul from Paul himself, for he wrote letters to some of the Christian communities, and some of those letters have survived. When they first arrived, they would have been read out loud to everyone there, and they were obviously regarded as great treasures, to be preserved very carefully and handed on from one generation to the next.

These letters are the earliest documents in the New Testament. They were written before any of the Gospels, and before the book of Acts.

Most of the churches Paul wrote to were ones he'd founded, and he was writing to keep in touch with them, give them encouragement and deal with problems which had arisen, or with questions they'd raised. He wrote one of the letters, to the church in Rome, before he'd even visited Rome, and it's not entirely clear to us now why he sent it. He was hoping to visit Rome at the time, and perhaps he was introducing himself and his teaching to the Christians there before he arrived. Perhaps he'd heard of divisions between Jewish and Gentile Christians there and was trying to bring them together. Perhaps both.

These letters, except perhaps that letter to the church in Rome, are like one half of a conversation, a bit like overhearing someone talking on the telephone. We can hear what Paul is saying, but we can't hear the Christians at the other end. We don't know exactly what they've been saying to him to make him talk the way he does. We have to try to work it out from what he says, and sometimes that's very hard.

Nevertheless, there are some marvellous passages in his letters which are not too difficult to understand. This final chapter of The Book of Books *will include a few of them, and then will finish with two passages from the last book in the Bible, Revelation.*

Quarrelling Christians

The first passage from Paul's letters comes from near the beginning of one he wrote to the church in Corinth in Greece. He refers to a man called Apollos. Paul founded the church at Corinth, and Apollos was a companion who'd spent some time with the new Christians there, teaching them more about Jesus and what being a follower of his meant. He'd obviously made a big impact upon them. Peter, the old friend of Jesus, was also very popular there, though we don't know whether he'd actually visited them. Even if he hadn't, they would have known stories about him, and the kind of things he'd been doing and teaching since Jesus' death and resurrection.

Paul wrote the letter while he was at Ephesus, and Apollos was with him at the time. Three men from the

Corinthian church had arrived in Ephesus and were also with him, and some slaves, relatives or friends of a woman called Chloe had also brought him news about the church there. So Paul knew a lot of what was going on. He wasn't pleased with everything he heard.

'SOME OF CHLOE'S PEOPLE have told me there are quarrels among you. Some of you say, "I support Paul." Others of you say, "I support Apollos." or, "I support Peter" or, "I support Jesus Christ."

'What are you thinking of? Are there four churches? Has Christ been split into four? You mustn't follow me or Apollos or Peter. You must follow Christ. But it's no good some of you saying, "Oh, but we do! It's just everybody else who doesn't!"

'I want there to be no divisions among you. I want you to be united, with the same mind and the same purpose, working with each other and not against each other. I don't want any of you going around thinking you're terribly clever and wise either, and saying the only people who are right are the ones who agree with you.

'Remember, the cross of Christ is at the centre of it all. I know it doesn't make sense. I know it seems like weakness or folly. I know many of our Jewish brothers and sisters want miracles instead, or a Messiah who will come in triumph, trailing all the pomp and power of a great king. And I know many of the Gentiles want someone wise and clever, someone highly educated, with fine words and arguments. Then we come along and preach about a man from a peasant village no one has ever heard of, who died a criminal's death on a cross! I know the crucified Jesus *looks* weak – completely powerless in fact. But I tell you, look at him, and you will see the power of God. I know the crucified Jesus looks foolish to some. But I tell you, look at him, and you will see the wisdom of God. For God's foolishness is wiser than human wisdom, and God's weakness is stronger than human strength. Jesus turns everything upside down.

'Look at you, my friends. Not many of you are clever by human standards, not many of you are powerful people or respectable people. A lot of you are slaves or poor, the kind of people who get looked down upon or treated like dirt. Yet look at you now. Friends of God! You put the clever people and the high and mighty people to shame. Everything is upside down and back to front with God, and he's chosen you to make that plain.

'So if you want to boast, don't boast about yourselves or about me or Apollos or Peter. Boast about God and what he's done.

'After all, my friends, look at me! When I came to Corinth, I didn't use lots of clever words and difficult arguments. I didn't impress you with my fine speaking. I was nervous. I came in fear and trembling. I brought with me the Spirit and the power of God, nothing else. But they were enough. So you see, your faith doesn't rest on my wisdom. It rests on God.

'What is Apollos? What am I? Just servants of God, that's all. We're like gardeners, working in God's garden. I came to Corinth and planted the seed. Apollos followed me and did the watering. But we didn't make the plants grow. God did that. You are God's work. We helped a bit, but it's God you should thank.

'You know the great temples in Corinth? You've heard of the temple in Jerusalem? Well, *you* are God's real temple! You are where his Spirit dwells. You are a holy place. Just think of that!'

Paul's Hardships

Two letters from Paul to the church in Corinth survive. In between writing them he visited Corinth again. Yet the second letter shows that things there had got even worse. Some other Jewish Christians had arrived in the city and had turned the church against him. He decided he would have to defend himself. His defence is very revealing. It shows just how much he'd had to endure since he'd started to follow Jesus and take the news of his love to the towns and cities of the eastern Mediterranean.

'REMEMBER,' PAUL WROTE to the Corinthians, 'I'm a Jew too. Those other Jewish Christians have been telling you I'm not being true to the faith of my ancestors. That's rubbish. I'm an Israelite, a descendant of Abraham, just as much as they are. And like them I'm proud to be a servant of Christ. Think how much I've been through because of following Jesus. I've been thrown into prison over and over again. I've been flogged countless times for preaching about Jesus. Often I've nearly lost my life. Five times my fellow Jews have given me thirty-nine strokes of the lash. Three times I've been beaten with rods by the Roman authorities. Once I was stoned. Three times I've been shipwrecked. For a whole day and night I was adrift on the open sea. I've made more journeys than I can count. I've risked my life wading across rivers. I've been in danger from robbers and bandits, in danger from my fellow Jews, in danger from Gentiles, in danger in cities, in danger out in the middle of nowhere, in danger on the sea, in danger from false Christians. I've been worn-out with work. I've had countless sleepless nights. I've gone without food and drink. I've been cold and naked, almost frozen to death.

'And then, to add to all that, I have my care and concern for all the churches pressing down on me every day. If any of their members are struggling, I struggle with them. If any of them are tripped up by someone else and made to fall flat on their faces, I burn with their shame.

'The God and Father of our Lord Jesus knows all this is true.

'Oh, one thing I forgot. When I was in Damascus, the governor there wanted to arrest me and was keeping watch on the city gates. But I was let down in a basket from a window of a house built into the wall, and so I escaped his clutches.'

'You are the Body of Christ'

The next section takes us back to the First Letter to the Corinthians.

'ALL OF YOU HAVE GIFTS. The trouble is, some of you think your gifts are more important than other people's. Some of you think that if people don't have the same gifts as you, they are not proper followers of Christ.

'But we can't all have the same gifts. And anyway, the same Spirit of God is behind them all and in them all. We see the Spirit of God, the creative, mysterious energy of God, at work in all your gifts. In your gifts, God comes out of hiding. And those gifts are not given to you so you can boast about them and think you are better than others. They are there for the benefit of the whole church, the whole community.

'Let me make myself clear. The Christian community is like a body. The body has lots of different parts, doesn't it? The foot can't say, "I'm not part of the body because I'm not a hand." The ear can't say, "I'm not an eye, so I don't belong to the body." That would be really silly. But if the whole body was an eye or an ear, that would be really silly too. How would we smell anything? The eye can't say to the hand, "I don't need you." The head can't say to the feet, "I don't need you." That would be really, really silly. One part of the body can't say to another, "I'm more important than you." All the parts of the body are equally important. They have to look after one another, because if one part suffers, they all suffer. If you poke something in your eye, your body hurts. If you stub your toe, your body hurts. If you cut your hand, your body hurts. It feels as though your whole body hurts. But if a crown is put on your head, or a fine cloak on your shoulders, your whole body walks tall and feels proud.

'Now, you Christians at Corinth all make up a body, and not just any old body. You are the body of *Christ*. You come from different families, different backgrounds. Some of you are slaves, some are free; some of you are men, some are women, some are children; some of you are small, some of you are big. But you all belong to Christ. You are all Christ's friends. You are all caught up in Christ and carried along by him. Christ lives in you, and you live in him. Christ is your home, your safe place, your room. Christ is where you live and grow.

'You are the body of Christ. Through you Christ still walks this earth.'

Love is the Greatest of All

Sometimes Paul writes in a poetic style. This passage from his First Letter to the Corinthians is perhaps the most famous one he ever composed.

'I MAY SPEAK fine words,
I may speak the language of angels,
but if I have no love,
I am like a noisy gong or a clanging cymbal.

'I may understand all mysteries,
have all the knowledge in the world;
I may have faith enough

to move mountains,
but if I have no love,
I am nothing.

'I may give away everything I own,
I may surrender myself, my very life,
but if I have no love,
I gain nothing.

'Love is patient;
love is kind;
love envies no one;
love does not boast;
it is not full of itself
or rude.
It does not seek to have its own way,
or just look after itself.
It is not quick to take offence;
it keeps no score of wrongs.
It does not gloat over other people's wrongdoing;
its delight is in the truth.

'Love bears all things,
believes all things,
hopes all things,
endures all things.

'Love never falls,
never fails,
never ends.

Prophecies will cease,
for all will be revealed.
Knowledge will come to an end,
for all will be known.
Now we know but a little
and prophesy in the dark.
But the little will be swallowed up in the whole,
and darkness will be banished by the light.

'When I was small,
I spoke like a child,
I thought like a child,
I worked things out like a child.
But when I grew up,
I left behind the ways of a child.

'Now, when we search for God,
we see but blurred reflections in a mirror.
In the end we will see him face to face.
Now I know him only in part.
Then I will know him as he knows me.

'Three things endure:
faith, hope and love,
these three.
And the greatest of these is love.'

Life After Death

This passage also is from the First Letter to the Corinthians.

'CHRIST WAS RAISED from the dead. So we will be raised from the dead also. But someone will ask, "How are dead people raised? What kind of body do they have?" I'll tell you. Except I can't tell you, because it's beyond my imagining.

'You know when you put a seed in the ground. It's a tiny thing, isn't it? If you didn't know, when you look at a seed in your hand, you'd never guess that a plant could grow from it, a stalk of wheat, perhaps, or a flower, or a great tree. You could never guess a poppy from its tiny seed, or an oak tree from looking at an acorn.

'When we die, we're rather like a seed. A real seed splits apart in the soil, and a fresh plant grows from it. After we die we emerge, as Jesus did after his death, as a new creature. And yet we will still be ourselves. You don't get poppies from acorns, or oak trees from poppy seeds.

'We are poor, weak things, and we all die. But you should see us when God has raised us from the dead! We will have an honour, a dignity, a power and a glory we never dreamed of, and death will have no more hold over us.'

A Beautiful Hymn

Another church Paul founded was at Philippi, an important city in Macedonia. Once while he was being held in prison, he wrote a letter to the church there, in which he quoted a beautiful hymn. It must be one of the earliest Christian hymns to have been written. In the following passage we first hear Paul addressing the Philippian Christians, then we hear the hymn itself.

'I AM SO FOND OF YOU ALL, and you have given me so much. Now make my joy complete by all having the same mind, and by showing the same love for each other. Don't try to put yourselves above other people. Be humble and think of others as better than you are. Don't follow your own interests all the time, but pursue each other's interests.

'Just think of Christ. Just think like Christ…

'For he was in the form of God,
but he did not think to seize equality with God
or keep tight hold of it.
Instead he emptied himself
of all honour and glory.
He made himself nothing,
taking the form of a slave,
coming to birth in human form.

'Sharing the human lot,
he humbled himself still further.

For like a slave,
treated like a criminal,
he went as far as death
and died a slave's death,
the death of the worst of criminals,
death on a cross!

'And that is why God has exalted him!
That is why God has given him the name above all names,
so that at the name of Jesus every knee should bow,
in heaven, on earth and under the earth,
and every tongue should cry,
"Jesus Christ is Lord!"
to the glory of God the Father.'

A Final Collection

Finally, a few verses and passages from a letter Paul
wrote to a group of churches in Galatia, a region in
what we now call Turkey, and from the letter he wrote
to the Christians at Rome.

First, from the Letter to the Galatians:

'THERE IS NO LONGER Jew or Gentile, slave or free, male or
female. For you are all one in Christ Jesus.'

'My friends, you have been called to be free. But don't use your
freedom to do whatever you like. Use it for each other. Through

love, act as slaves to each other. For the whole of God's teaching to the people of Israel can be summed up in this: "Love your neighbour as yourself.'"

'This is what the Spirit of God produces in people: love, joy, peace, patience, kindness, generosity, loyalty, gentleness and self-control.'

And three passages from the Letter to the Romans:

'WHILE WE WERE still helpless, Christ died for us. He died for us although we'd turned our backs on God. It's rare for someone to be willing to die to save a good person. But we weren't good people when Christ died for us. So you see just how much God loves us. We were enemies of God, and yet God still came in search of us, still made friends with us, through the death of his Son. So you see just how safe with God we are now.'

'All who are led by the Spirit of God are sons and daughters of God. For God has not made you his slaves, to cower before him and fear his rod. He's adopted you as his own children. That's why, when we pray to God, we cry, "Abba! Father!" That cry comes from the Spirit of God deep within us and reminds us that we are indeed children of God. And if we are his children, then we must be his heirs. We are heirs to everything God has, fellow heirs with Christ!'

'If God is on our side, who can be against us? He gave his own Son! Surely then, he will give us everything else, all the gifts he has to give. Nobody can bring any charge against us, for God himself pronounces us innocent. Nobody can condemn us, for Christ pleads our case. What can separate us from the love of Christ? Can hardship do it, or distress, or persecution, or hunger, or exposure, or danger, or sword? I know what the words of the old psalm mean, "For your sake we are being done to death all day long; we are treated like sheep for slaughter." They fit my own experience. And yet still we have won the battle. With Christ loving us so much, we have emerged as more than conquerors! I am convinced there is nothing in death or in life, in the realm of spirits and supernatural powers, in the world as it is or the world as it will be, nothing at all in all creation that can separate us from the love of God in Christ Jesus our Lord!'

Visions of Heaven

The last book in the Bible is called Revelation. It gives us a vision of the final overthrow of the Dark Forces, of the reign of God and of heaven. The Bible begins with a mass of water, heaving in the dark, and then a garden. It ends with that heap of water gone and a city in place of the garden. And yet there is a clear echo of that garden in the vision of the heavenly city, and just as the Bible also begins with God, here in Revelation it ends with God.

We began with God and we end with God. And of course, we've been keeping God company all the way along. The Bible is God's book. It is about God; it is bright with God. God is greater than the Bible by far. The Bible most certainly is not God, though some treat it as if it were. And yet for so many centuries so many people have kept stumbling upon God in its pages and, overwhelmed by God's friendship and love, have found the strength and the wisdom to work with him.

The Bible is all about keeping God company.

Now for some closing passages from Revelation:

'THEN I SAW A NEW HEAVEN and a new earth, for the first heaven and the first earth had passed away.

'There was no more sea, no more black water threatening to engulf God's creation, no Dark Forces trying to drown God himself.

'I saw the new Jerusalem, the holy city, coming from heaven dressed in all her finery, adorned like a bride arriving for her

husband. Her bridegroom was God, and all heaven and earth were
at the wedding.

> 'Then I heard a loud voice, saying,
> "See, God has pitched his tent here,
> the Tent of Meeting,
> where all is in perfect order,
> where all is very good, very beautiful,
> like the world when first it was made.
> See, God has made his home with children,
> with men and women.
> He will dwell with them,
> and they will be his people.
> God himself will be with them,
> and he will wipe every tear from their eyes.
> Death will be no more,
> and there will be no more grief,
> no more crying,
> no more pain.
> For the first things have passed away."'

'Then an angel showed me the river of the water of life. It sparkled bright as crystal and flowed from the throne of God down the middle of the broad, straight street of the city. On either side of this river was growing the Tree of Life. Every month it produces a new crop of fruit, and all can pick and eat. And the leaves of the tree are for the healing of the nations.

'There will be nothing unholy in that city. All will be holy, for all will be filled with God. All in the city will worship him. They will see his face, they will see him as he is, and they will bear his name upon their foreheads.

'There will be no more night, no darkness, no fear of the dark, no hurried lighting of lamps, no terror, no dark deeds. And there will be no need of a sun to shine by day, for the city will be filled with the light of the glory of God.

'And God's friends will reign with him in splendour for ever and ever.'

BIBLE REFERENCES

Chapter 1: In the Beginning

God Makes the World: Genesis 1:1 – 2:3

God Plants a Garden: Genesis 2:4b – 3:24

Things Get Nasty: Genesis 4:1–16

The Great Flood: Genesis 6:5 – 9:17

Babel Babble: Genesis 11:1–9

Chapter 2: God's New Family

Abraham and the Great Promise: Genesis 12:1–7

Sarah's Cunning Plan: Genesis 16:1–6

Hagar and the God Who Sees: Genesis 16:7–14

Sarah Overhears the Promise: Genesis 18:1–15; 21:1–3

Hagar and the God Who Saves: Genesis 21:8–21

Abraham and Isaac: Genesis 22:1–18

A Tricky Twin and a Bowl of Stew: Genesis 25:19–34

Jacob Steals a Blessing: Genesis 27:1–40

The Gate of Heaven: Genesis 27:41–46; 28:10–22

Face to Face with God: Genesis 32:3–31

Face to Face with Esau: Genesis 33:1–17

Jacob and His Sons: Genesis 35:16–19; 37:1–35

Joseph the Slave: Genesis 37:36; 39:1–20

Joseph the Prisoner: Genesis 40

Joseph in the Palace: Genesis 41

Joseph and the Famine: Genesis 42:1–25

A Strange Discovery: Genesis 42:26 – 43:13

Benjamin: Genesis 43:15 – 45:15

The Reunion: Genesis 45:25–28; 46:28–34

Chapter 3: Moses and the Mountain of God

The Brave Midwives and the Pharaoh: Exodus 1

Moses' Brave Mother and Sister: Exodus 2:1–10

Moses Meets God in the Desert: Exodus 2:11 – 4:16

God and the Pharaoh: Exodus 5:1 – 12:32

God Splits the Sea: Exodus 14

The Mountain of God: Exodus 19:1 – 20:17: Deuteronomy 5:6–21

More Teaching from God's Mountain: Exodus 23:4–5; Leviticus
19:9–10; Deuteronomy 22:8; 16:9–15; Exodus 23:9; Leviticus
19:18; Deuteronomy 6:5

The Golden Calf: Exodus 32:1–30 with reference to Exodus
24:9–11; Exodus 25–31; 16:1 – 17:7

Making a New Start: Exodus 32:31 – 33:23; 34

The Death of Moses: Deuteronomy 34:1–7

Chapter 4: Living in God's Land

The Fall of Jericho: Joshua 6:1–25

Eluma, a Woman Despised: Judges 13

Hannah, a Woman Without a Child: 1 Samuel 1:1 – 2:21

'Samuel! Samuel!': 1 Samuel 3:1–18

King Saul: 1 Samuel 3:19 – 4:1; 8:4–20; 9:1 – 10:1a

David the Shepherd Boy: 1 Samuel 16:1–13

David and Goliath: 1 Samuel 17:1–51

David on the Run: 1 Samuel 19:9–10; 24:1–22; 26:1–25 with reference to 2 Samuel 7:8–16

David and Bathsheba: 2 Samuel 7:8–16; 11:1–27

David and Nathan: 2 Samuel 12:1–24

Elijah and the Contest on Carmel: 1 Kings 18:2–46

Elijah on the Run: 1 Kings 19:1–18

Elijah, Ahab and the Vineyard: 1 Kings 21:1–24

Chapter 5: The People of God under Threat

'Let Justice Roll Down Like Water': Amos 1–2; 5:10–12, 24; 6:1–7; 8:4–6; 5:18–23; 7:10–17

Hosea and the Love of God: Hosea 11:1–9

Jerusalem will Never be Taken!: Psalms 17:8; 46:1–5, 7, 11; 48:12–14

Jeremiah Speaks the Truth: Jeremiah 2:1–13; 19; 21:8–11; 22:1–5; 38:1–13

Jerusalem Falls: 2 Kings 24:8 – 25:21; Jeremiah 38:14–28; 43:1–7

Sad Songs of Lament: Psalm 74; Lamentations 1:1–6; 1:11b–14, 16, 18; 2:9, 20; 3:21–22; 5:14–15

Dreaming of Home: Isaiah 40:1–11; 54:1–10

A Valley Full of Bones and a New Garden of Eden: Ezekiel 37:1–14; 43:1–5; 47:1–12; 48:35

Rebuilding Jerusalem: Nehemiah 1–2; 4:1–23; 6:15–16

Daniel: God in the Flames: Daniel 3

Daniel in the Lions' Den: Daniel 6

Chapter 6: Fine Stories, Fine Poems

Ruth, Naomi and Boaz: Love Wins the Day: Ruth 1–4

Jonah, a Big Fish, a Great City and the Forgiveness of God: Jonah 1–4

The Book of Job: Shaking a Fist at Heaven: Job 1–2; 3:1–19; 16:9–17; 5:8–18; 8:1–4; 11:1–19; 19:2; 22:1–11; 12:7–25; 9:22–24; 29–31; 9:14–20; 38–39; 40:2 – 42:9

Songs of Light: Psalms 23 and 121

Chapter 7: The New Beginning: Jesus is Born

Disgrace Turned Quite All to Grace: Matthew 1:18–25

Gifts Fit for a King: Matthew 2

Mary Meets an Angel: Luke 1:26–38

Mary's Song: Luke 1:39–63

Jesus is Born: Luke 2:1–20

Jesus' Real Home: Luke 2:21–22; 41–51

Chapter 8: Who Was Jesus?

John Baptizes Jesus: Mark 1:1–11 (Matthew 3; Luke 3 1–22)

A Reading in the Synagogue: Luke 4:16–30; Numbers 6:24–26

Peter, James and John: Luke 5:1–11 (Matthew 4: 18–22; Mark 1: 16–20)

Photina: the Woman at the Well: John 4:1–42

Commander of the Dark Forces: Mark 4:35–41 (Matthew 8:23–27; Luke 8:22–25)

A Madman Among the Tombs: Mark 5:1–20 (Matthew 8:28–34;

Luke 8:26–39)

The Hungry are Filled: Matthew 14:13–21 (Mark 6:30–44; Luke
9:11–17; John 6:5–13)

A Man Sees for the First Time: John 9

A Woman and a Girl are Brought Back to Life: Mark 5:21–43
(Matthew 9:18–26; Luke 8:40–56)

Peter Gets it Right; Peter Gets it Wrong: Mark 8:27–33 (Matthew
16:13–23; Luke 9:18–22)

The Light of God: Mark 9:2–8 (Matthew 17:1–8; Luke 9:28–36)

Chapter 9: Jesus the Storyteller and Poet

A Lost Sheep, a Lost Coin and a Lost Son: Luke 15

The Good Samaritan: Luke 10:25–37

The Workers in the Vineyard: Matthew 20:1–15

The Beatitudes: Luke 6:20–21; Matthew 5:3–10

Other Sayings and a Prayer: Matthew 20:16 (Mark 10:31; Luke
13:30); Luke 6:27; Matthew 7:12; Luke 6:36; Matthew 7:1–11;
18:10; Mark 9:33–37 and Matthew 18:1–4; Mark 10:13–16
(Matthew 19:13–15); John 6:35; 8:12; 10:11–15, 30; 14:6; 15:5
Matthew 6:9–13 (Luke 11:2–4)

Chapter 10: Jesus is Killed: Jesus is Risen

Riding into Jerusalem: Mark 11:1–11 (Matthew 21:1–9; Luke
19:29–42; John 12:12–15)

Mayhem in the Temple: Mark 11:15–19; 12:41–44 (Matthew
21:12–16; Luke 19:45–48; 21:1–4; John 2:13–16)

Jesus is Anointed Messiah: Mark 14:3–9 (Matthew 26:6–13; Luke 7:36–50; John 12:1–8)

Betrayal: Mark 14:10–11 (Matthew 26:14–16; Luke 22:3–6)

The Last Supper: Mark 14:12–25 (Matthew 26:17–29; Luke 22:7–23); John 13:2–16, 34

Arrest: Mark 14:26–50 (Matthew 26:30–56; Luke 22:31–53; John 13:36–38; 18:1–11)

The Unfair Trial: Mark 14:53–65 (Matthew 26:57–68; Luke 22:54–55, 63–71; John 18:12–24)

Peter's Denial: Mark 14:66–72 (Matthew 26:69–75; Luke 22:56–62; John 18:16–18, 25–27)

Pilate: Mark 15:1–15 (Matthew 27:1–2, 11–26; Luke 23:1–5, 13–25; John 18:28 – 19:1)

Jesus is Crowned King: Mark 15:16–20 (Matthew 27:27–31; Luke 23:11; John 19:2–3)

Crucifixion: Mark 15:21–47 (Matthew 27:32–61; Luke 23:26–56; John 19:17–42)

'Mary': John 20:1–18

Thomas Gets it Right... in the End: John 20:19–28

Peter Goes Fishing: John 21:1–19

Chapter 11: From Jerusalem to Rome: The Church Begins

The Full Truth: Acts 1:6–11 and Luke 24:50–53; Numbers 6:24–26

Wind and Fire: Acts 1:12–14; 2:1–41

Stephen is Killed: Acts 6:1 – 7:60

Paul Meets the Risen Jesus: Acts 8:1–4; 9:1–9

Paul and Ananias: Acts 9:10–19a

Escape in a Basket: Acts 9:19b–30

Peter and a Soldier Called Cornelius: Acts 10

Paul and Barnabas Get Mistaken for Gods: Acts 14:8–21

A Riot in Ephesus: Acts 19:1–10; 19:21 – 20:1

A Riot in Jerusalem: Acts 21:13–14; 21:17 – 22:29

The Threat of an Ambush: Acts 22:30 – 23:25

Paul Asks to See the Emperor: Acts 23:33 – 26:32

Shipwreck: Acts 27

Paul Reaches Rome: Acts 28:11–31

Chapter 12: Letters to Churches and a Final Vision

Quarrelling Christians: 1 Corinthians 1:10–13; 1:18 – 2:5; 3:5–16

Paul's Hardships: 2 Corinthians 11:16–33

'You are the Body of Christ': 1 Corinthians 12

Love is the Greatest of All: 1 Corinthians 13

Life After Death: 1 Corinthians 15:20, 35–43

A Beautiful Hymn: Philippians 2:1–11

A Final Collection: Galatians 3:28; 5:13–14, 22–23; Romans 5:6–8, 10; 8:14–17, 31–39

Visions of Heaven: Revelation 21:1–4; 22:1–5